Dreaming in French

The Paris Years of

Jacqueline Bouvier Kennedy,

Susan Sontag, and

Angela Davis

Dreaming
in French

Alice Kaplan

The University of Chicago Press : Chicago and London

ALICE KAPLAN is the author of *The Collaborator: The Trial and Execution of Robert Brasillach*, *The Interpreter*, and *French Lessons: A Memoir*, all available from the University of Chicago Press. She holds the John M. Musser chair in French literature at Yale. She lives in Guilford, Connecticut, and in Paris.

The University of Chicago Press, Chicago 60637
The University of Chicago Press, Ltd., London
© 2012 by Alice Kaplan
All rights reserved. Published 2012.
Printed in the United States of America

21 20 19 18 17 16 15 14 13 12   2 3 4 5

ISBN-13: 978-0-226-42438-5 (cloth)
ISBN-10: 0-226-42438-3 (cloth)

Library of Congress Cataloging-in-Publication Data

Kaplan, Alice Yaeger.
    Dreaming in French : the Paris years of Jacqueline Bouvier Kennedy, Susan Sontag, and Angela Davis / Alice Kaplan.
        p. cm.
    Includes bibliographical references and index.
    ISBN-13: 978-0-226-42438-5 (cloth : alk. paper)
        ISBN-10: 0-226-42438-3 (cloth : alk. paper) 1. Onassis, Jacqueline Kennedy, 1929–1994—Homes and haunts—France—Paris. 2. Sontag, Susan, 1933–2004—Homes and haunts—France—Paris. 3. Davis, Angela Y. (Angela Yvonne), 1944—Homes and haunts—France—Paris. 4. Women—United States—Biography. 5. Students, Foreign—France—Paris—Biography. 6. Women—United States—Intellectual life. 7. United States—Civilization—French influences. I. Title.
HQ1412.K37 2012
944'.361083609252—dc23
[B]
                                                                            2011026598

Illustrations on title page: (*left*) Jacqueline Bouvier's student ID photograph (1949), courtesy Claude du Granrut; (*center*) a detail from a photograph of Susan Sontag in Sevilla (1958), courtesy Harriet Sohmers Zwerling; (*right*) a detail from a photograph of Angela Davis following her acquittal (1972), © Michelle Vignes, courtesy Standford University Libraries.

♾ This paper meets the requirements of ANSI/NISO Z39.48-1992 (Permanence of Paper).

For Florence, Sylvie, and François
And for *L'équipe*

Contents

Illustrations

Illustrations

Introduction

On August 23, 1949, the *De Grasse* set sail from New York Harbor. Regular ocean crossings for civilians had just resumed the previous year on liberty ships refurbished for tourists, and the departure of a group of young women from Smith College—the third set of juniors bound for Paris since the end of the war—made the news. They were feted by the French consul in New York, with a luncheon and photo shoot with society columnist Hedda Hopper. On board ship they got special attention. The last night of the voyage, the captain asked them to sing Edith Piaf's "La vie en rose," the hit song they all knew by heart, whose simple words lulled them with dreams of a happiness that was unattainable in any other language. One of the girls in their group was asked to sing a verse of her own. Perhaps it was because her name was French, or because she looked glamorous. Though she was from Vassar, not Smith, she had been accepted into Smith College's rigorous Junior Year in Paris. The other students knew about her triumphant Newport début and about the New York gossip columnist who had named her "Queen Deb of the Year," but where they were going, it didn't matter.[1]

1. Jacqueline Bouvier and fellow Smith juniors on board SS *De Grasse* (1949).
Left to right: Elizabeth Curtis, Mary Snyder, Jacqueline Bouvier, Mary Ann Freedman, and
Hester Williams. Photograph © Bettmann / CORBIS.

. . .

Jacqueline Bouvier's 1949 trip to Paris was a flagship voyage, the harbinger
of a golden age of study abroad that began in the aftermath of the Second
World War and continued for three decades, sending thousands of American students into French homes and French universities. She was the first of
three exemplary women whose lives were transformed by a year in France,
and who, in turn, transformed the United States. What Jackie Kennedy,
Susan Sontag, and Angela Davis owed to their time abroad and how their
American fame reverberated back to France are the questions at the heart of
this book, a triptych of three young women's cultural, academic, and social
lives in Paris, and a study of influence in several directions. They differ from
the best-known expatriates of the last century—Djuna Barnes, Gertrude
Stein, Josephine Baker—because they lived in France as students, their careers uncharted. They each crossed the threshold of the Sorbonne between

1945 and 1964, during the period the French call the country's "thirty glorious years," *les trente glorieuses.*[2] Glorious for some, violent and reactionary for others, this long quest for modernization and affluence stretched from the postwar recovery in 1945 to 1975.

Two of them were French majors in college, and the third had imbued herself with French literary and cinematic culture on her own terms. Each woman had a unique beauty and a perception of the world that was unmistakably hers, and each made Paris her own.

Jacqueline Bouvier went abroad on the Smith College Junior Year in Paris in 1949–50, became First Lady of the United States, and later, a successful book editor. Susan Sontag went to Paris by way of Oxford, on a fellowship from the American Association of University Women in 1957–58. She was a prolific essayist and novelist, a controversial New York intellectual who spent her summers in Paris. Angela Davis arrived in Paris for the Hamilton College Junior Year in France in 1963–64. A philosopher and an activist, she survived imprisonment and a murder trial, and became a university professor with an endowed chair. If you reduce them to identity labels, they are the soul of diversity: a Catholic debutante, a Jewish intellectual, an African American revolutionary, from the East Coast, the West Coast, and the South. They have often been reduced to their images: a sheath dress and a double strand of pearls, a mane of black hair with a white streak, an afro and a raised fist. They have been part of the national conversation, the subject of fascination, the object of wildly divergent interpretations.

The France where each of them lived as a temporary resident with a *carte de séjour* changed from 1949, when Jacqueline Bouvier arrived, to 1964, when Angela Davis left. Jacqueline Bouvier's France was drained by the German occupation and scarred by the camps. It was a damaged place, rebuilding its economy with American funds from the Marshall Plan. While Susan Sontag was in Paris in 1957–58, France shattered over the question of Algerian independence, the Fourth Republic crumbled, and Charles de Gaulle returned to power. Angela Davis, in 1963, lived in the aftermath of the loss of Algeria. The France she knew was a Gaullist France, a France without empire where the dark monuments of Jacqueline Bouvier's and Susan Sontag's Paris began to be scraped clean.

All three women dreamed about France long before they ever crossed the ocean. Paris, and the French language, existed in their imaginations, even in their parents' imaginations, so that they went abroad accompanied by the ghosts of ancestors and the echoes of public conversations. Jacqueline Bouvier arrived with her upper-class connections; Susan Sontag, the self-invented European, with her opinions; Angela Davis, with her sense of justice and her fearlessness. They were in their twenties, reaching that existential threshold where you start to see what you can do with what you've been given. France was the place where they could become themselves, or protect themselves from what they didn't want to become, as products of their families, their societies.

Their Parisian years offer a glimpse of Jacqueline Bouvier, Susan Sontag, and Angela Davis before they became public figures. Were they always extraordinary young women of whom the greatest things were expected, or has fame distorted the stories of their youth? It is touching to imagine them before their images were frozen in the public mind, before they learned to pose or avoid photographers, when they still had the luxury of being students, though not exactly ordinary students. Jacqueline Bouvier had her discerning eye for all things beautiful, Susan Sontag her diaries full of lists and observations and endless movies seen, books read, Angela Davis her analytic tools, her understanding of politics and language. They couldn't know what the future held.

I have listened to them speak French, in radio and television archives, looking for clues. There are no recordings from their student years, but many from the years of their prominence. Jacqueline Kennedy, interviewed as First Lady on French television, spoke in a slow, singsong whisper, plaintively—a schoolgirl French, with each syllable carefully chosen. When she didn't know the grammar, she knew just how to disguise what she hadn't mastered with a winning grace. Susan Sontag, a public intellectual who frequently appeared on cultural broadcasts, stumbled in her first French interviews, then learned to speak fluently, with an absolute confidence and a total disregard for native intonation and accent because her own sense of language was so firmly intact. (She drove her French translators crazy because she was convinced she knew the language better than they did.) Angela Davis returned to Paris on a book tour more than ten years after her junior year abroad. Interpreters sat with her in interviews, but she ended up giving them the words. Her grammar and vocabulary were advanced, and she had an artful control of her intonation, placing the emphasis exactly where she wanted. When she was arguing, her voice grew higher, faster, more urgent.

4 :

They were, in French, as we all are in a foreign language, translations of their American selves.

The men came too. Norman Mailer, Chester Himes, William Styron, Saul Bellow, Richard Wright, Arthur Miller, S. J. Perelman, James Baldwin, Art Buchwald, James Jones, Irwin Shaw, and George Plimpton came to France on GI bills, on Guggenheims, on Fulbrights; they explored their demons, went native or not, got rich or stuck it out in maids' rooms and cheap hotels. They produced an oeuvre, an expatriate literature of the postwar era that is gritty, irreverent, macho, frequently alcoholic, and as far as is imaginable from the experience of women abroad. The odyssey of American men in Paris, from Hemingway to Richard Wright, is canonical, as familiar to us as a ride on a *bateau mouche*. For the women students of the same generation, no matter what their ultimate destinies, the traces of their experience are harder to convey. They resonate sometimes with the grand houses and marriage plots of Edith Wharton, sometimes with the everyday language play of Gertrude Stein's *Tender Buttons*. Like Patricia Franchini, the study abroad student in Godard's *Breathless* who betrays her gangster lover, they want to know what "*dégueulasse*" means.[3] These young women are determined not so much to "embrace irresponsibility"—James Baldwin's idea about the expatriate student—as to embrace a new language and master a highly coded way of life.[4] Jacqueline Kennedy Onassis called the young women abroad "the slight expatriates . . . swaddled in sweaters and woolen stockings, doing homework in graph-paper cahiers."[5] You can define them in those postwar years by what they were not: they weren't veterans studying on the GI bill, men who were world weary, restless, made older than their years by military experience. The women spending their junior year in Paris were often not yet twenty-one when they left their sheltered colleges. During their time abroad they may have looked demure and regimented, but the experience was life altering to them. Their oeuvre consists of their diaries, their letters home, their snapshots, their word lists, fading in countless attics. Their stories have not had a place in the great American tradition of expatriate literature.

In 1947, a few months before Jacqueline Bouvier entered Vassar College as a freshman, the French philosopher Simone de Beauvoir visited twenty American campuses as an official *missionaire* of the cultural services of the French Embassy. She was as excited about discovering the United States as any American college student discovering France. Her stops included the women's colleges Smith, Wellesley, Mills, and Vassar, institutions with active French departments and large numbers of students schooled in the language who were eager to learn about Paris. Beauvoir, during those months in the United States, listened to the many young Americans who were listening to her. She practiced and honed her propensity for cultural generalization about women, young people, and intellectual life in general, and later she transferred many of those generalizations to her sociological study *The Second Sex*, which founded contemporary feminist thought.

She had the ambition, which became Susan Sontag's and later Angela Davis's ambition, to construct theories about culture and to grasp, through the strength of her thinking and by means of philosophical tools, the truth of a given situation.

Reviewing the diary Beauvoir published about her trip, the American writer Mary McCarthy made fun of the French writer's knee-jerk leftism, her exaggerated sense of the wealth of Vassar girls, and her naive ideas about American capitalism.[6] McCarthy ridiculed Beauvoir's idea that the shops on New York's Fifth Avenue were "reserved for the capitalist international," that "there was no friendship between the sexes; conformity reigned." She complained that Beauvoir thought Vassar was for aristocrats, whereas she, McCarthy, had gone there on scholarship.

Beauvoir was untouched by the criticisms; her diary was a record of one consciousness, her own: "This is what I saw and how I saw it. I have not tried to say more."[7]

The American women traveling in the opposite direction would have observations just as trenchant, analyses just as pressing as Beauvoir's. Living on Paris time, six hours later than their friends back on campus and their families at home, they would experience, over a period of many months, an isolation from much that was familiar, and a particular form of solitude. With that solitude came the greatest luxuries: the time to read, the opportunity to wander, and the chance to think new thoughts.

ONE

Jacqueline Bouvier

1949–1950

Imaginary Aristocrats

In one way at least, she was like so many other American girls: her relationship to France began as a fantasy. In her case, the fantasy was a family story, passed down in a book. She learned, as a very young girl, from a story written by her grandfather, that she was descended from French royalty.

The story was both false and prophetic. It was false because her family origins were common. It was prophetic because when Jacqueline Bouvier went to France for her junior year in 1949, she quickly gained entry into the social circles of the leading families of Paris—captains of industry, counts and countesses, duchesses and marquis. When she returned ten years later as First Lady, she was as close as an American woman could get to being a queen, and her aristocratic friends came to her court at the Elysée Palace and the Château at Versailles.

That is the quick version of a story with many twists and turns, from fantasy to reality, with its connection to the intense hopes and dreams of a generation of postwar women on both sides of the Atlantic. Not only did

Jacqueline Bouvier Kennedy make good on her grandfather's fantasies; she in turn created fantasies of France among hundreds of thousands of American women. French women, too, claimed her as one of their own.

In fact there was very little about Jacqueline Bouvier that was genuinely French. She had both a first name and a last name that resonated with Frenchness, and she pronounced her first name with a French intonation—Jacque*leen*. But she was only one-eighth French, through her father, whose great-grandparents, Michel Bouvier and Louise Vernou, had met in the 1820s through the circle of French immigrants in Philadelphia.[1] Jacqueline's mother, Janet Lee, who affected ties to the Southern aristocracy, claimed she was descended from the Maryland Lees, even though her ancestors were New York Irish immigrants, just as Jacqueline's paternal grandfather had claimed to be descended from French royalty even though his ancestors were Provençal shopkeepers.[2] Both sides of the family dissembled in order to climb the social ladder, whether it be in the Hamptons and Manhattan with the Bouviers or in Newport and McLean, Virginia, where she lived from the age of thirteen with her mother and her patrician stepfather, Hugh Auchincloss. The Bouviers and the Lees alike operated within the great American tradition of immigrant ambition, which held that in making yourself anew, you had the right to embellish the past.

In medieval times, common people in France went without last names as long as they were without land. They were known by their labor: shepherds were "Bergers"; bakers were "Boulangers"; carpenters "Charpentiers"; and each of those occupations has become a common French last name. "Bouvier," equally commonplace in French, comes from the job of the men who herded cattle (*boeufs*)—the cowboys. The cowboys became villagers: around the time of the French Revolution, Jacqueline Bouvier's people were shopkeepers in Pont-Saint-Esprit in le Gard (southern France)—modest commoners who would have rolled their *r*'s and eaten earthy stews of garlic and olive oil and fish from the Rhône, which flowed through the town.

The first Bouvier to emigrate to the United States was one of those commoners, a carpenter who had been conscripted into Napoleon's army. After the defeat at Waterloo and the restoration of the monarchy, he was on the wrong side of the state. Throughout the summer of 1815 and especially in the south of France, armed royalists roamed the countryside in search of Napoleon's troops, massacring generals and foot soldiers alike. Amid this "white terror," Michel Bouvier fled to America with others of his kind and began a lucrative career as a cabinetmaker in Philadelphia for Napoleon's exiled brother Joseph. Michel Bouvier's progeny progressed rapidly, until Jacqueline's great-grandfather earned a place on the sought-after social register of the Philadelphia elite, a distinction unheard of for a Catholic in those days.[3]

In 1927, when Major Bouvier, Jacqueline's grandfather, a wealthy New York attorney, wanted to put in writing an account of his family's social success, he published, at his own expense, a book called *Our Forebears*, describing the Bouviers as "an ancient house of Fontaine near Grenoble" and the Vernous (the ancestors of Michel Bouvier's wife, Louise) as "one of the most illustrious and ancient families of the province of Poitou."[4] The center of Bouvier's genealogical invention is an annotated registry of coats of arms. This heraldry cited the name of any Bouvier or Vernou in France whose name had a "de" added to it. Special mention was made of Bouviers who had earned titles by serving as secretaries to members of parliament. The major's prose is peppered with mentions of royal decrees, marriages of notables to nobles, and descriptions in untranslated French of Bouvier and Vernou coats of arms. He claims for his ancestors both revolutionary zeal as French supporters of the American Revolution and unsullied loyalty to the French aristocracy they embodied—having it both ways.

About Michel Bouvier, the defeated soldier who fled France in fear for his life, Jacqueline's grandfather says only that he arrived in Philadelphia from Pont-Saint-Esprit in 1817. Yet Michel Bouvier's was the real American story. He used his status as a veteran of Napoleon's army to cultivate Joseph Bonaparte. Bouvier helped Bonaparte build his estate, then rebuild it after a fire. He married up in social class, speculated in land rich with coal, and settled his large family in a brownstone mansion on the smartest street in Philadelphia. He had gone from immigrant carpenter to cabinetmaker to businessman and real estate tycoon in less than forty years. When he took his family back to visit Pont-Saint-Esprit in 1853, the rough-and-tumble foot soldier of old whose daughters had attended the fanciest schools, he was more than qualified to tell tales of American streets paved with gold.[5]

Jacqueline Bouvier's journey to Paris was thus a reverse migration—at least a temporary one. It's hard to know whether she still believed the family legend, but she was certainly curious about the French Bouviers. Her host sister, Claude, remembers that Jackie investigated her French roots during her year in France—she may have visited the place mentioned in *Our*

Forebears on her way to grander estates in Beauvallon, outside Saint-Tropez, where she was entertained by the truly noble du Luart and de Lubersac families in the summer of 1950.[6]

Her ancestral home, Pont-Saint-Esprit, was so obscure compared to glamorous Saint-Tropez that it is worth noting, if only as a stroke of coincidence, that it came into ghoulish prominence a year after Jacqueline Bouvier returned from Paris. In 1951, a mold in the local bread poisoned a number of townspeople. In a frenzy, some victims threw themselves out of windows and ran through the streets screaming. Others simply dropped dead. One of Jacqueline's distant cousins still living in Pont-Saint-Esprit, a lawyer named Marcel Divol, who was a Bouvier on his mother's side, fought the long legal battle on behalf of the victims against the town baker and flour supplier.[7] It was a tale of tragedy in a simple Provençal community looking much as it had in the days of Napoleon—bleached stucco houses, open-air fountains, dusty squares with chickens and dogs underfoot. Nothing there would have resonated for Michel Bouvier's twentieth-century descendants, who had grown up on a steady diet of aristocratic lore and imagined their forebears living in castles surrounded by moats.[8]

During the Kennedy-Nixon campaign of 1960, Jacqueline Kennedy's French roots were much discussed, and her grandfather's genealogical pamphlet made the rounds of the newsrooms. French journalists looking for a story at Pont-Saint-Esprit on the eve of the election, with nothing but the aristocratic rumors as source material, found a family named Bouvier living in squalor on a farm on the outskirts of the town and delighted at the contrast with the soon-to-be resident of the White House. Within a year of the Kennedy presidency, Jacqueline Kennedy was receiving so many letters each week from French people claiming to be her cousins that her staff gave up responding to them. On the eve of her state visit to France in 1961, an impoverished farm dweller in Pont-Saint-Esprit named Danielle Bouvier set out in an automobile for Paris: two journalists had promised her an audience with the First Lady. Danielle's car crashed en route, killing her.[9] Like the mysterious poisoning of 1951, her tragic death would be seen, in future decades, as a sign of the "Bouvier-Kennedy curse." Yet a regional French archivist investigating the Danielle–Jacqueline Bouvier connection soon revealed that neither Danielle nor any of the poor Bouviers in Pont-Saint-Esprit were related by blood to the American Bouviers: most of the real Bouvier descendants were now living in Marseille, Nîmes, and Valence.

If Jackie Bouvier had ever believed in her grandfather's myth—and no child in any branch of the family was without his or her copy of *Our Forebears*, specially inscribed by the major—it must have been like believing in the tooth fairy. By the time she got to France as a college student and saw the modest streets of Pont-Saint-Esprit, she was probably disappointed, and certainly disabused of the legend.

French Attributes

The family's French connection meant the world to Jacqueline's grandfather Vernou Bouvier, who encouraged in his progeny an allegiance to all things French, and to a certain idea of themselves as noble in a grand tradition. The family chauffeur was French; French was spoken at lunch once a week at her grandfather's estate and continued to be the language for meals at her mother's house as well.[10]

Jacqueline Bouvier delighted in peppering her English with French phrases, something she learned to do better and better as she continued her French studies in a series of private schools. As her own French aura strengthened, however, the French side of her family was floundering. Her handsome father, nicknamed Black Jack Bouvier, a Wall Street broker in the family tradition, had squandered an already reduced family fortune in a series of womanizing and alcoholic misadventures. After Jacqueline's parents divorced, when she was eleven, her mother married the more solid financier Hugh Auchincloss. Divorce was a social and a religious scandal, and Jacqueline suffered. An outsider from the white Anglo-Saxon Protestant society her mother married into, she was also estranged from Catholic rites and rituals now largely forsaken.[11]

We can only speculate about the effect of the divorce on the young girl's psyche and about the intensified place of France in her imaginary life. In her father's absence from her new home, and in her knowledge of his financial mishaps, Jacqueline Bouvier's French identity was something she could hang onto, something that set her apart both from her Irish mother and from a rather colorless stepfather, who remained a host rather than a parent. Now that the Bouvier family fortune was lost, all that seemed left of the old opulence was Jacqueline's horse, which had, of course, a French name, "Danseuse." Her father boarded it for her at a stable near Central Park and his Seventy-Fourth Street apartment, hoping this would ensure regular visits

: 11

from her. Since his own father's mansion had been sold for taxes, he couldn't offer her the grandiose settings of the Auchincloss's Newport or Virginian estates.[12] Danseuse was a source of great complicity between father and daughter. During Jacqueline's year abroad, riding became a passport into the social life of the French upper classes, in the Bois de Boulogne and later through the ritual hunt—the *chasse à courre*—at the Château de Courances.

In a sense there is nothing unusual about Jacqueline Bouvier's attachment to French. Spoken or written or read, the language has always held pride of place among the American elite, encouraged in schools as much as in shops and restaurants. In her case it may have appeared to be an affectation, but it corresponded to a real need to maintain her identity in the face of pressure to conform—a shield against her stepfather and mother.

Much later, when she became a Kennedy woman, Jacqueline's Frenchness distinguished her from a family whose every ritual, every home, and every habit of speech was defined by the Irish-American clan. Jack Kennedy, too, had had his own stints in Paris, working at the American embassy through a connection from his father, ambassador to the United Kingdom, but French phonetics had never made a dent on his accent.[13] "Pahk yah cah in Havahd yahd"—which is the line people use to make fun of Boston accents—consists in stripping words of their r's, and of course nothing can be more French than an r pronounced deep in the throat, with relish. When you listen to recordings of Kennedy speaking haltingly with a French journalist about the Algerian war or about de Gaulle, he sounds like so many well-educated men of his generation, schooled in French through exercises in grammar and translation, as if they'd never have to speak it.

It is difficult to know how many of the French attributes given to her in dozens of books and articles are as fictional as her grandfather's biography, as if her own need to identify with France was taken up by everyone around her and embroidered with their own threads. One of her biographers reports that young Jacqueline Bouvier wrote essays about the French Enlightenment and the French Resistance in World War II for her school newspaper at Miss Porter's. Actually, like any regular high school senior, she wrote about spring fever and contributed cartoons about a frizzy-haired, gangly student named "Frenzied Frieda."[14] She is identified with the great salonnières—with the French women who, in the seventeenth, eighteenth, and nineteenth centuries, organized Parisian social life in their parlors and through their literary correspondence. Students at Miss Porter's remember her fondness for Madame Récamier, the nineteenth-century salon hostess painted by David.[15] The memory may be apocryphal, though it points to a problem for her generation: the lack of role models for women who aspired to beauty and wit at the same time, who wanted a life that was both sensual and intellectual.

The many French books in her personal library, sold at auction after her death, from Stendhal to the Abbé Prévost and George Sand, tell a story of her attachment to French culture that was fostered by friends and admirers as much as by her own literary taste. David Pinkney, the dean of American historians of France in the 1960s, sent her his book on Haussmann's rebuilding of Paris during the reign of Napoleon III with this inscription: "To JBK: Don't confuse me with Baron Haussmann and I shan't confuse you with Eugénie." The allusion was to Napoleon III's wife, who was beautiful but frivolous, and to Napoleon's engineer and designer Haussmann, a homely but terribly effective civil servant.[16] Perhaps the surprising thing about Pinkney's gift wasn't just that Jacqueline Kennedy had received a scholarly book from an academic historian, but that he could count on her to understand the rarefied joke in his inscription. This isn't just an issue of a superior cultural literacy. What strikes us today is that Jacqueline Kennedy was focused on a time and a place so far from her own. She was a French time traveler, a voracious reader and a person who lived in her head, through her dreams and her imagination. In every account of her life, from the kiss-and-tell accounts of her husband's infidelities to glamorized hagiographies, this quality shines through. People who didn't like her remembered her as aloof and snobbish, while the friends who loved her admired her solitude and reserve. She had a counterlife. And she nurtured her counterlife with images and words and histories that came from France and that sustained her from the time she began to read her grandfather's fantasies of the family, through the lonely pressures of her existence in the White House, to the very last months of her life when, as an editor at Doubleday, she helped two British historians shape their history of France at the Liberation—the France she had known at age twenty.

Orientation

Jacqueline had taken a luxurious European tour with two girlfriends the previous summer—her first post-Liberation crossing. In Paris they went to museum after museum, and she had tried out her French with the guide at Versailles.[17] Now she was returning to France to live. The 1949–50 semester abroad was her own liberation from many years of girls' schools—Miss Chapin's in Manhattan, Miss Porter's in Farmington, Connecticut; Vassar College in Poughkeepsie, New York, where after two years she had grown restless and bored with the place that had so enchanted a forty-year-old Simone de Beauvoir on her tour of American campuses in the spring of 1947—a few months before Jacqueline Bouvier's freshman year. In her diary of that American trip, Beauvoir gives us a down-to-the-hemline picture of the college environment that Jackie Bouvier would reject, and she does so from the perspective of an intellectual woman who had come of age in the Paris that Jackie was about to discover. Vassar, Beauvoir wrote in her American diary, was both "aristocratic" and delightfully relaxed.[18] In the college library— more like a living room than the enormous Bibliothèque Sainte-Geneviève, with its rows of tables and straight-backed chairs, where Beauvoir had studied for her philosophy exams—the French writer was fascinated by the sight of girls reading, "so comfortable and free . . . curled up in deep armchairs or sitting cross-legged on the floor, scattered through little rooms by themselves or gathered together in large halls . . . How I envy them." Jacqueline Bouvier, by the age of nineteen, had had her share of chintz upholstery and reading rooms, of campuses filled with girls in rolled-up jeans and oversized shirts, and of weekend trips to New York on the train down the Hudson. She had thrived in Helen Sandison's famous Shakespeare seminar, and in a class on the history of religion. But simply reading about places was stale; she wanted to see them for herself.

Vassar had no study-abroad program, so Bouvier had applied to the program run by Smith and was accepted, one of a group of thirty-five. Smith had been sending women for a year of study in Paris since 1925, always accompanied by a member of its French faculty. After a wartime hiatus, the program had resumed in earnest in 1947–48. Unlike the other programs in Paris—the University of Delaware's, for example, which focused on foreign relations—the Smith College Junior Year in Paris was designed specifically for French majors, with the idea of preparing young women for a career in teaching. For that reason, and to defend itself against the perception that France was a place for adventure and frolic, Smith's program operated according to the highest academic standards and with an understanding that French, and only French, would be spoken, in and out of class. Part of the tradition of the Smith program and other programs like it was to send students for an intense preparation or linguistic *stage* in the provinces in late August and September before bringing them to Paris for the start of the French academic year—quite late by American standards. The Smith group went to the southeastern city of Grenoble, reviewing their grammar at the foot of the Alps.

Although most of Jacqueline Kennedy Onassis's papers are inaccessible to scholars, one of her first letters home from Grenoble has been published in *As We Remember Her.* The letter is a precious source because of the way it is written, because of what it says—even for its silences.

She is recounting two field trips with the Smith group—first to Aix and Arles, in Provence, then a shorter trip to the prehistoric caves at Sassenage, closer to Grenoble.

> I just can't tell you what it is like to come down from the mountains of Grenoble to this flat, blazing plain where seven-eighths of all you see is hot blue sky—and there are rows of poplars at the edge of every field to protect the crops from the mistral and spiky short palm trees with blazing red flowers growing at their feet. The people here speak with the lovely twang of the "accent du Midi." They are always happy as they live in the sun and love to laugh. It was heartbreaking to only get such a short glimpse of it all—I want to go back and soak it all up. The part I want to see is La Camargue—a land in the Rhône delta which is flooded by the sea every year and they have a ceremony where they all wade in on horses and bless it—La Bénédiction de la Mer— gypsies live there and bands of little Arab horses and they raise wild bulls.
>
> Last Sunday we all went to Sassenage. . . . We visited the grottoes . . . and danced in a lovely little restaurant under rustling trees by a brook with a waterfall—the magic broken only by two "pièces de résistance" of the restaurant—"Bongo, Bongo, Bongo" and "Chattanooga Choo-choo." We missed the last tram and had to walk back to Grenoble (all the way back)— about five miles![19]

The letters young women write home from Europe are like any correspondence, varying wildly according to the addressee. Parents get one kind of information, sisters another, best friends still another. There's nothing really intimate about this letter, and at the same time it tells a great deal about Jacqueline Bouvier. You can listen to it with your eyes closed and see the poplar-lined fields in Arles as surely as if you were looking at a painting—the hot blue sky and blazing red flowers are Van Gogh's colors. Its twenty-year-old author already has an artist's eye, a writer's pen. Her voice is here, the wide-eyed enthusiasm, the mix of wonderment and fun, the voracious curiosity. She has a wealthy girl's naïveté, coupled with idealism, about the lives of French farmers and country dwellers—her ancestors, after all, whom she imagines carefree and happy in the sunshine. Of course there are horses, the fantasy of the famous Arab horses and the bulls in the Camargue and her longing to see them up close. Then there is the turn in her story from breathless enthusiasm to sophisticated quip, which everyone from her closest friends to Norman Mailer has described as fundamental to her wit. Her observations always came with a sly wink at something that was silly, or incongruous, and that delighted her. She was full of mischief. And in describing the one piece that didn't fit, the American pop melodies in the middle of the French countryside, she was also writing the history of an Americanization of Europe that had spread with the arrival of the GIs in 1944 and made its way from Saint-Germain-des-Prés to the tiniest villages.

It's worth noting too, because it's surprising, that there is no best friend mentioned in the letter, no descriptions of any of the girls in her group. Who said what to whom, who was dancing longest, who got sick from the food are the kinds of things you might expect to find in a girl's letter home from France. Nor does a single French person make an appearance—no flirtatious waiters or *patronnes* in flowered housedresses. Instead there are flowers and sky and horses and "people," people in the collective sense, smiling, dancing, and enjoying, American and French. There's the sense of a stage set, with Jacqueline in the role of observer, not quite the hostess yet, but already measuring the pleasures that can be had from a day in the country. What mattered to her in that magical year was the gaze outside herself and her world onto a larger landscape. Even before she became Jacqueline Kennedy, she was a keen observer of beauty.

From the Grenoble orientation, her classmate Marjorie Flory still remembers a cold château with a single toilet for twelve people, and a single teacher whose name is lost to time but whose personality isn't. He was their French grammar and phonetics teacher, pompous and supercilious, who bragged to them about the dictionary he was writing. He asked them to read aloud from risqué passages of *Madame Bovary* while he picked at their accents and intonation, though he had a marked Provençal accent of his own, the *accent du Midi* that Jacqueline Bouvier refers to in her letter home. When called upon, Jacqueline, a perfect mimic, read the sentences from *Madame Bovary* out loud, duplicating his rolling r's and singsong intonation. He had no idea why the American girls in his class burst out laughing—he thought he was amusing himself at their expense, and couldn't understand that they were poking fun at him.[20]

That was school. Orientation also meant the women's first independent train trips, their discovery of Europe. Martha Rusk, one of Jackie's closest friends on the program, remembers their return from a trip to Spain:

> When we came back, we traveled third class on the overnight train. Jackie had a traveling outfit: a flared red cotton skirt, a simple white blouse. We would take turns changing places so we wouldn't get cricks in our necks. As I was switching places with her in the middle of the night, Jackie handed me a hat pin. "Take it, you'll need it," she said, and I couldn't understand what she was talking about. It was to stab the guy I was about to sit next to, when he tried to grope me.[21]

Jackie was an expert in protecting her friends against unwanted advances. And if you needed someone to negotiate tickets at a train station or get help with baggage, she was the person you wanted on your trip. Spanish, French, and later German: she could understand, and make herself understood, in all three languages.

Avenue Mozart

By the time the young women relocated to Paris for the start of fall classes, it was nearly October. Because there was a shortage of families willing to take boarders, some of the girls lived in Reid Hall, the old porcelain factory in the heart of Montparnasse that had served as a dorm and classroom space for Americans in Paris since before World War I. Others, like Jacqueline, were lucky enough to stay with French families, and for them the connection to the postwar era would be far more intense.

Five full years had passed since the Liberation, but the Paris that greeted Jacqueline and her fellow students was still heavy with the memory of war. We think of Paris as a city of glimmering white stone buildings, but until the 1960s those buildings were black with soot. Jacqueline Bouvier lived in a dark dark place. (It was Malraux, who guided her through the Louvre in 1961, who would order the cleaning of the buildings. When he first articulated the plan, one of his colleagues quipped: wouldn't it be cheaper to blacken the Sacré-Coeur?)[22] Coal for heating was scarce in 1949, and so were food supplies; Jacqueline had her own ration card for sugar and coffee, a relaxed version of the food rationing that had been going on since the Nazi occupation but a restriction nonetheless.[23]

Of all the culture shocks for the Smith group in those postwar years, the most intense was the most necessary aspect of everyday life: the toilets, even grimmer in the city than in Grenoble.[24] Little had changed in the realm of water closets in a century. In an ordinary apartment building, there was often a single WC on each floor, at the landing of the staircase. The large apartment where Jacqueline Bouvier stayed with her aristocratic hosts had four bedrooms but a single bathroom. Smith girls remember one bath a week at their family lodging—which meant going to one of the many public baths scattered throughout the city if you wanted more. The nicest rooms, like Jacqueline Bouvier's, had their own sinks and sometimes their own bidets, an invention that guaranteed superior intimate hygiene. French cafés and restaurants, however, had the worst facilities possible for the women: standup Turkish toilets, which consisted of two elevated pads for the feet over a porcelain base with a hole in it. "Toilets: ugh!" Mary Ann Hoberman remembered. "Those holes in the floor over which you had to squat—these existed even in quite nice restaurants. And toilet paper was often nonexistent or consisted of cut-up newspapers."[25] Squatting over these devices was treacherous in skirts and even more so if you wore thick white bobby socks (part of the Smith group uniform in 1949). You needed to be at a safe distance to flush and there wasn't much distance to be had in the tiny water closet. As for the printed toilet paper, an education in postwar politics and the ideological preferences of one's hosts could be had close up, depending on whether the newspaper cut into squares was the conservative *Figaro,* the popular *France-Soir,* or the communist *L'Humanité.*

Food may not have been plentiful in Paris that year, the water closets retrograde, but signs were afoot of burgeoning political and artistic energies, of life rewritten. Streets were renamed after the military heroes of World War II, and on their walks through the Latin Quarter the students found plaques commemorating Resistance heroes who had died fighting the Nazis. The avenue d'Orléans marked the path of the Allied army that had liberated Paris;

it was now the avenue du Général Leclerc. In the heart of the city, it wasn't unusual to see a commemorative gathering for a Resistance group or an association of deportees, its members still rail-thin and worn by sorrow.

Despite its austerity, 1949 was rich in cultural achievements. French women had been exercising their right to vote for five years, and France was considering new ways to live and new ways to think. Simone de Beauvoir published the two volumes of her *Second Sex* in June and November. To support the flourishing of a proletarian culture encouraged by a powerful French Communist Party, Pablo Picasso was making posters and drawings for peace rallies. His dove, which became an international logo for peace, first appeared on posters for a communist-sponsored peace congress in April 1949. It wasn't always clear how his modernism would harmonize with the realist aesthetic of the party: "One must rip and tear reality," he said to Françoise Gilot, his companion during those early postwar years.[26]

World War II was only beginning to enter into cultural memory, and the 1949–50 season was a turning point: in the spring of 1950, Anne Frank's diary became a French best-seller.[27] The book managed to reassure readers that the experience of coming of age was universal, all the while moving them with the knowledge of her annihilation by the Nazis. Faced with the story of Anne Frank, knowing that millions of Anne Franks—children of their generation—had been lost, every young person alive, every European especially, felt the shock of having *survived*. For the American women abroad, the sense of life's preciousness was contagious. And in a city where nearly every family was marked by the experience of war, Jacqueline Bouvier's host family, the de Rentys, was no exception.

Jacqueline's mother had made contact with the de Rentys through the Franco-American Vagliano family, who summered in Newport and whose daughter Sonia was married to a Frenchman whose mother was the comtesse de Renty's best friend.[28] Connections were made, letters exchanged, with the result that the comtesse reassured Janet Auchincloss she would take special care of her daughter. One of her own daughters, Claude, who was close to Jacqueline in age, had spent a year of study abroad herself, at Wellesley and Mount Holyoke in 1947–48, and was finishing her studies at the Institut d'études politiques. Jacqueline got the largest bedroom and special attention from the comtesse, who also made space that year for two other American students. One of them was Susan Coward, whom Jackie knew from New York.

The comtesse de Renty's home was a second-floor apartment on the avenue Mozart in the sixteenth arrondissement, in the western part of the city. It was a street that had been developed for the gentry at the turn of the century, with its own small businesses and grocers and butchers, where a young woman accustomed to country estates must have had an unfamiliar sense of public social space. Jacqueline exited the Jasmin metro station onto a large square, walked past the newspaper vendor and gazed up at her art nouveau apartment building with its green glazed bricks that glittered in all seasons, a welcome respite from the soot-covered stone of the neighboring structures. She entered through a wooden door into a huge lobby and central courtyard with marble tile, Greek columns, and a winding wooden staircase, an art nouveau eclecticism that was once modern and now looks almost kitsch. Inside the apartment were four bedrooms, two parlors, a dining room, and a kitchen with the traditional wrought iron "cage" beneath the window for keeping food fresh. There was a back staircase for the servants, exiting onto the inner courtyard—the *escalier de service* found in most apartments in the wealthy sixteenth arrondissement. The comtesse de Renty, her daughters, and their boarders lived simply, with one toilet and one bathtub. The great social leveler across neighborhoods in Paris was the cold. The de Renty apartment had a gas heater, which conked out regularly. The students bundled up in shawls and sweaters to do their nightly homework.

They were lucky to be there, because there was an acute housing shortage in Paris. American students who lived with families rather than at Reid Hall nearly always found themselves in a household that had lost someone during the war and was struggling to make ends meet. "Bourgeois ladies who had lost their men, but not their apartments, moved into an unheated maid's room, leaving the rest for some embassy undersecretary whose rights were morally and economically better grounded," quipped the expatriate writer Stanley Geist in a 1948 article in Sartre's *Les temps modernes*.[29] The postwar housing arrangements made for strange bedfellows: Arthur Schlesinger, who became one of Kennedy's closest advisers, had been posted in Paris during the first months of the Liberation by U.S. intelligence, assigned to analyze Resistance movements. His own lodging offered an unexpected site of analysis, for it turned out that his landlady was the sister of the collaborationist newspaper editor Jean Luchaire, soon to be executed for treason by de Gaulle after one of the show trials of "the purge."[30] Although the sister of a notorious collaborator, the landlady was named Fraenkel and had been married to a French Jew. Parsing these networks was a history lesson more vivid than anything offered at the Sorbonne.

Jacqueline Bouvier's host family had a history as complex and tragic as any in postwar Paris. The comtesse de Renty and her husband had been members of the conservative Resistance group, Alliance. The Resistance is usually identified with the two movements of communism and Gaullism. Alliance was an eccentric resistance network with an unusual genealogy: it was founded by a fervent right-wing nationalist named Georges Loustau-nau-Lacau, a former member of the Vichy government and an Army man, who had hoped Pétain would serve as a shield against Hitler but ultimately sided with the British, organizing an intelligence network among upper-class nationalists that proved extraordinarily vulnerable. Because of the kind of intelligence work that Alliance did—classic espionage—and perhaps because its upper-class recruits were less practiced at subterfuge than other social groups, they suffered more arrests and deportations than almost any organization in the Resistance.[31]

The de Rentys were deported with other members of the resistance on the last convoy out of Paris, August 15, 1944—a week before the city's liberation. The comte de Renty was taken to the German slave labor camp, Dora. Confined to a part of the camp called Ellrich, he worked on the construction site of an underground factory for building the V1 and V2 missiles—Wernher von Braun's brainchild. It meant digging through rock—the equivalent of digging through a mountain. He died after four months.[32] The comtesse de Renty survived the women's camps at Ravensbrück along with some of the most distinguished women of the Resistance: Anise Postel-Vinay, Denise Jacob (sister of the future cabinet minister Simone Veil), Geneviève de Gaulle (the general's niece), and Germaine Tillion. Unlike the men who emerged from the war as Resistance heroes—Jacques Chaban-Delmas, Maurice Schumann, François Mitterrand, de Gaulle himself—these women had no ready access to political power in the years following the Liberation. There was the difficult time of basic recovery, after which they returned to their ordinary lives, usually with limited resources.[33] Stanley Geist's light-hearted portrait in *Les temps modernes* was not inaccurate: women like the comtesse de Renty were renting out rooms because it was one of the few respectable ways to supplement an income. But unlike Geist's cartoonish characters, the comtesse did not retreat to a maid's room; her warm presence was keenly felt by all her guests. She rarely spoke of Ravensbrück to her own children, and never of Ellrich. Her daughter Claude, who had spent the war years with relatives in the country, remembers that her mother wanted to focus on the present, to enjoy a France of reliable rituals and high culture. Providing a home for American students was a way to offer up this France to young people who could appreciate it—and the elegant young Jacqueline Bouvier was a charming guest who accompanied her host mother on expeditions to the porcelain museum at Sèvres, to Madeleine de Galéa's collection of dolls in her private home in Auteuil, and to the Louvre. Jacqueline was secretive, Claude remembers, and perhaps that secrecy, born of her own private sorrows, blended well with a family that had so much to forget.

The holidays brought more opportunities for travel. Mary Ann Peyser went all the way to Israel to see the Jewish state in its second year of existence. Martha Rusk planned a trip to Austria and Germany, and, to her surprise, Jackie asked to come along. "Are you sure you want to travel third class again?" Martha asked her friend, whom she considered upper crust, and Jackie reassured her that it wasn't a problem.

Martha spent Christmas with friends of her parents in a partially bombed-out building in Vienna, the kind of semi-ruin that had become rare in Paris but was still quite common in Austria and Germany. She met Jackie in an elegant hotel. Their next stop was Munich. For these young people who had followed the news of the U.S. Army's liberation of the camps, it was impossible to be in the Bavarian city without thinking of Dachau, only ten minutes outside the city limits—a place that by its very location raised the issue of the complicity of the German people. How could the local populations have ignored deaths in the tens of thousands, right under their noses?

By Christmas of 1949, the Federal Republic of Germany was only seven months old, operating under the watchful eye of an Allied High Commission.[34] The Dachau camp had not yet become a full-fledged museum, and parts of it were still being used by the government as an internment camp for Czech refugees, as well as a site for trials of the Nazi camp guards. It was an easy trolley ride from town.

On the trolley car, Martha and Jacqueline met a young GI who, to their surprise, knew nothing about Dachau. He decided to accompany them. Their visit coincided with one of the first debates on what was to preoccupy both Germany and France for the next sixty years: how to commemorate what had happened. Dachau was the first Nazi concentration camp; as early as 1933, the Nazis were using it for political prisoners. In a second phase it became a center for slave labor and a site for medical experiments. Some 41,500 prisoners were murdered at Dachau. They were worked to death, killed in experiments, or died of malnutrition and typhus. Some were gassed off-site; some were cremated in the camp's ovens. Over fifteen thousand inmates had been buried by the Nazis on a hill on the outskirts of the camp, the Leitenberg. American liberators used the same mass grave for 5,400 more corpses they found inside the camp.

An announcement that the Bavarian government was going to bulldoze the Leitenberg, erasing any reminder of its existence, was greeted with outrage. The French government sent a series of observers to Dachau, including a delegation of French survivors. Among them was Edmond Michelet, deported for his role in the resistance movement Combat and now the French minister of justice. Michelet and his group were appalled by what they saw. Signs read, "Entry prohibited—infested area" and "No trespassing—danger of infection." There were neither memorials nor notices explaining the meaning of the cemetery. In early December, before Martha and Jacqueline left for Germany, French newspapers had reported the bitter polemic between local German authorities, who accused the French of being subversive communists, and French survivors, who accused the Bavarians of planning a cover-up. On December 16, just before Jacqueline and Martha visited the camp, a kind of peace was made: Dachau was rededicated as a site of memory in the presence of German members of parliament, journalists, foreign diplomats, and representatives of the Allies.[35]

From her visit to the site, Martha Rusk remembers a white-washed room with drains and an oven. Many details faded in her memory, but not the sense of a sanitized space, the emptiness. The poplar trees that former inmates had planted in a grove outside the main crematorium had not had time to grow. As she and Jacqueline and the GI got on the trolley to go back into town, she remembers saying over and over, "What were they thinking?" The young American soldier who had accompanied them was stunned.

Munich itself was in ruins, with plans for reconstruction barely under way in 1949, but the city had kept its beer-hall feeling, which added to the horror of the Dachau visit. Jackie and Martha spent New Year's Eve in a nightclub with a group of young men, friends of friends of Jackie's.

It was a new year. Several young women from the Smith group sat in an amphitheater at the Institut d'études politiques, listening to the great historian and geographer André Siegfried lecture from his book *The Soul of Peoples,* which would be published that spring: "All Americans," he wrote, "have an innate confidence in their future, in the future of their continent. A hundred years ago in Europe, in the middle of the dynamic nineteenth century, we had a similar faith in our destiny, but we've lost it."[36]

Siegfried's vision—a mix of ethnography, a long view of history, and what we would today call "cultural studies"—took on all of American civilization as one grand landscape. He could not account for the state of mind of individuals, certainly not that of Jacqueline Bouvier, who was born into wealth and whose fate now depended on her own wits—or so it must have seemed, since her father had lost his fortune and she could not rely on an inheritance from her stepfather. The Vassar girl and toast of high society had a sense of her own worth but little security. She was on a quest in Paris, shoring herself up for the next act, on which much depended. The genteel de Renty apartment, with its well-worn antiques, its cold, its shared bathroom, its studious calm, was her backstage. And the sense of living in a space where someone was missing, where a father was missing, not through negligence or scandal, but because a real tragedy had come to pass—all this must have endeared the de Rentys to Jacqueline in ways that were unspoken. The trip to Dachau, in particular, had given a reality to the nightmare her Parisian host mother never mentioned. She was a different person now from the girl who had sung "La vie en rose" on the *De Grasse.*

It's safe to say that the thirty-four Smith students on the Paris program, witnesses to European recovery, were also searching for answers to the great questions of life. Simone de Beauvoir was struck by the plaintive tone of the Yale students she had met on her 1947 college tour: "We want to go to France, my friend and I," a young man told her, "to discover what our problems are. We feel that we have them, but we don't even know what they are. How should we resolve them? From France, with some distance, I hope we will see things more clearly."[37]

Brenda Gilchrist, one of the Smith girls in Jacqueline's group, sent me a snapshot from her year in Paris that seemed to her to sum up their quest.

2. Cordelia Ruffin Richards and Blaikie Forsyth Worth from the Smith College Junior Year in Paris, behind an *Interdit* sign (1949). Photograph courtesy Brenda Gilchrist.

Two of her friends, Cordelia Ruffin and Blaikie Forsyth, stand on a Paris city street behind a *Sens interdit* ("Do not enter") sign on a tall post, a red circle with a thick white line across it. It has since become an international symbol, but it was exotic then. She wrote a caption for the photo on the occasion of their fiftieth reunion:

> Two juniors stand behind an *Interdit* sign in Paris. We (I include myself, the photographer) must think this a knowing, witty pose, layered with innuendo. Long enough in Paris by the late fall 1949, we now successfully read the language of street signs, roam the squares and parks, drink *vin chaud* in cafés with Sorbonne students. We are *un peu* sophisticated: our French improved by living in French families and our esthetic sense enlivened by the regal, Beaux-Arts buildings and urgent literary and artistic life around us. We are determined to keep our American schoolgirl look, however. Avoiding any hint of Parisian chic, notebook in hand we face the city with insouciant intelligence and expectation.[38]

Her friends Cordelia and Blaikie had kept their college look: they are wearing the requisite white anklets with long skirts; their hair is waved tightly to their heads; their New England coats are thick and buttoned tight. Blaikie stands in the shadow of the sign, her head tilted out of the way of the metal post, her gloved hands clasped in front of her double-breasted camel coat. Her tall friend Cordelia, to her right, holds a spiral notebook in one hand, straight from the Smith College textbook store—most likely a notebook for lists of new French words, class notes, monuments visited. Although the photo is playful, they are nonetheless paying homage to the *Interdit*, the forbidden way: what have they decided is forbidden to them as American girls in Paris? Where won't they go?

The Reid Hall girls of 1950 appeared, to the disinterested French observer, well dressed, even distinguished. As journalist Henriette Nizan put it in a Marshall Plan newsletter, there was "something Bostonian" about them.[39] Madame Guilloton, who directed the Junior Year in Paris in its second postwar season, 1948–49, wrote home in despair to the Smith College president.[40] She had set up the same honor system for outings at Reid Hall as the girls were accustomed to observing in their dorms in Northampton: groups of two or three, a card filled out and signed, the requirement being that they return directly after the performance, concert, or meeting in time not to miss the last metro at 12:15 a.m. Translated to Paris, the Smith system was an utter failure. Among the 1948 group, close to 90 percent went out unauthorized and returned to Reid Hall at two or three in the morning, to the consternation of the *gardien*. In 1949–50, Jacqueline's year, a few French families were once again enlisted to lodge students, just as they had done before the war, and it was up to them to monitor the conduct of their resident *demoiselles*. Jeanne Saleil, the director for the 1949–50 group, had a light-hearted pen in her own administrative reports and was undoubtedly a more forgiving chaperone than Madame Guilloton, whose name must have given rise to a lot of decapitation jokes. And for someone like the comtesse de Renty, who had survived a concentration camp, a 12:15 a.m. curfew could hardly have represented a high moral bar. At her house, the girls could skip a meal without giving long notice, and they could even receive male guests in the parlor—most other host families allowed young men no farther than the door.[41]

Still, the lives of the Smith women had a different tenor from those of the bohemian American students on the GI bill, the trust-fund babies, even the Fulbright fellows footloose in Paris at the same time. Years later, Jacqueline Bouvier recalled meeting the expatriate writer George Plimpton to go night-clubbing in Paris and thinking how different his smoke-filled rooms were from her cold parlor and layered sweaters on the avenue Mozart.[42]

In considering the behavior of the young American women in Paris that season, it's also important to compare them to their French counterparts— the nineteen and twenty-year-old French girls who had lived through the Occupation in their adolescence—just as they would compare themselves to one another. There's a sense in the existential literature from the immediate postwar era that the young French women who had survived the war, who had suffered losses, were reckless in their desires. In Beauvoir's roman à clef *The Mandarins,* twenty-two-year-old Nadine, mourning a Jewish lover killed in the war, has her way with her parents' friend, the charming writer Henri (modeled on Albert Camus), by getting him drunk enough to bed her. Not to start a relationship, she tells him the next morning, just to break the ice. In a famous Georges Dudognon photograph from the 1950s, *chanteuse* Juliette Greco, darling of the *cave* scene with her chopped-off bangs and long tangled hair, leans over the disheveled bed to pick up the needle on her record player. Her tiny room at the Hôtel La Louisiane, complete with empty saucers and bottles, record jackets, and a photo of Miles Davis on the wall add up to a recipe for existential bliss. That was the fiction.

The average French girl may have been just as sheltered and virginal as her older sisters had been in 1939, but the public image of her womanhood had radically changed. French women had made do for four years without their husbands and brothers, several million of whom had spent at least part of the war in prisoner-of-war camps; women like the comtesse de Renty and so many others had risked their lives in the Resistance; and with the Liberation, France began a new era, by granting women the right to vote and serve on juries. These were new privileges, which Smith women took for granted.

With their quaint group outings and curfews, the Smith group in Paris seem at first glance not much different from Smith girls who had gone abroad in the 1930s. At the same time, their independence was astonishing compared to today's students abroad, who, with their cell phones, remain in constant contact with their parents. In 1949, months could go by without any phone contact at all between the Smith girls and their families in the States, and letters took several weeks to reach their destination. One of the girls from the 1949–50 group needed surgery. She made all the arrangements and had the procedure done in Paris without ever consulting her parents.[43]

Nonetheless, the American students were what the French call *encadrées*, literally "framed," taken care of and kept in line when they weren't keeping themselves in line. There were many places the Smith girls couldn't go and wouldn't have gone—they weren't among the drunken young women standing on tables and stripping at the Tabou bar, whose photos showed up in *France-Soir*.[44] They weren't living in cut-rate hotels. That didn't mean their lives weren't changing. Experience, that year, took place just as much through their imaginations, and through spectacle, as it did through their deeds.

"If you want to understand how life changing an experience the junior year in Paris was for those girls, look at the theater," said Danielle Haase-Dubosc, director of Reid Hall from 1975 to 2010. Mlle Saleil took the girls to play after play, reporting in a letter to Benjamin Wright, then president of Smith College, how happy she was that the students were seeing both the latest productions and the "good old classics"—Molière, Corneille, Racine, Marivaux.[45]

The Smith women remember going constantly to the theater, but two plays stand out in their memories. *Ondine,* Jean Giraudoux's version of the German romance about a mermaid in love, starred the magnetic Louis Jouvet, who, with his aquiline nose and stiff posture, his inimitable diction, was unlike any man they knew. In Molière's *Fourberies de Scapin,* Jean-Louis Barrault played the scoundrel under Jouvet's direction. They saw *Ondine* in revival at Jouvet's Athénée in the fall of 1949, when they had scarcely adjusted to Paris. It was fortunate that Christian Bérard's stage sets were so enchanting, since they could barely understand any of the dialogue. Like Mr. and Mrs. Smith in Eugène Ionesco's *Bald Soprano*—another revelation of the 1950 season, a spoof on the "Assimil" method for learning English— they were still reacting to the reassuring sounds of fixed phrases in this new world, where, for the first time, they were truly immersed in the language they were studying. For the Smith girls of those years, mastering French gave them an almost religious sense of mission. They would no sooner have said a word to one another in English than committed a crime.[46] Indeed, they were convinced that if they spoke one word of English, Mlle Saleil would send them back home, and their parents would lose their money. To speak French together, no matter how artificial, was their solemn oath.

It was a year of rituals. If theater and French itself were foremost, the ritual of religion was always with them in the background. Paris was not Paris without the sound of church bells from every quarter—the angelus, morning and evening, bells for weddings, bells for funerals. Not even a diehard atheist could be indifferent to the aesthetic miracle of the Gothic cathedrals—Notre-Dame and the Sainte-Chapelle in the heart of city, Saint-Denis to the north, Chartres a few hours away. Nothing could be farther from the simple interiors of a classic New England community church than the kaleidoscopes of stained glass, the flying buttresses, the chapels within chapels. The countless biographies of Jacqueline Bouvier say little about her religious education, and it's not clear she attended mass during her year abroad. But whether she did or not, living in a country where a Catholic education was shared by so many, and where Catholic places of worship were on a par with great works of art, represented yet another important shift in consciousness for an American Catholic girl raised knowing she was part of a religious minority.

: 29

The Faubourg

In March of 1950, Jacqueline Bouvier was photographed at a party with a group of Parisian friends—the well-born gentlemen and ladies of the Faubourg Saint-Germain.[47] Social class in postwar Paris was carefully delineated, and these young people were ever so slightly higher than the de Rentys in the delicately differentiated caste system of aristocratic French society. Jacqueline's host sister Claude did not attend their parties. Like the de Rentys, they had what the French call "names with suitcases" or "names with drawers"—the family names hinged with the preposition *de* that connotes the aristocracy by linking a family to its land—and for this crowd the land was still very real. There was Louis de Gontaut-Biron and his future wife, Chita, the art historian; Sabine de Noailles of the great de Noailles family, who would soon marry Nicolas Wyrouboff, who'd been with the Free French in London and was starting a career in refugee work. One of the Firmin-Didot brothers, of the great family of printers, was at the party, and the eldest Béghin daughter, heir to the sugar fortune.

They look surprisingly modest in the photo, and wholesome—the women have shortish hair, and in their evening gowns of chiffon and lace, they are cute, not glamorous. The young men wear tuxedoes, and they look too young to be wearing them. Jacqueline stands alone. She is in the lower right of the photo, at the very front, standing at the foot of the staircase. She is one of only two young women in the photograph dressed all in black, and her dress stands out for its simplicity: a black satin strapless gown, showing off the perfect lines of her shoulders and neck. She is wearing a pearl choker. Several of the young people have their eyes closed, or they're caught grinning at one another, as if they were in the midst of listening to an inside-joke. Some look awkward; a few have a challenging stare, as if to resist their own awkwardness. Jacqueline, on the other hand, is looking at the camera in quiet repose. Directly across from her, the only other young woman wearing black gazes at her with undisguised admiration; this is Sabine de Noailles. Jacqueline is not looking back, and one senses that she feels apart from the others, that she is with the group but not one of them. Perhaps she knows she isn't in on their conversation in some basic way, not part of the large tree of interwoven relations that bind them together. She doesn't look arrogant so much as removed, outside regular time.

30 :

3. Jacqueline Bouvier at a ball at Ledoyen (March 1950). *Back row, left to right:* Sonia Matossian, Roselyne Béghin, Henri de Clermont Tonnerre, Jacques Firmin-Didot, Serge Tessier, and Jean-Pierre Matossian; *middle row, left to right:* Paul de Ganay, Jean de Méré, and Louis de Gontaut-Biron; *front row, left to right:* Sabine de Noailles, Florence de Selve, Hélène de la Motte, and Jacqueline Bouvier; *bottom, center:* François de Riocour. Photograph courtesy Claude du Granrut.

In any case, her beauty is arresting. Even if she had not become Jacqueline Kennedy, she would be the one person in the photo who stands out. At nineteen, she possessed a talent that is as important to being photogenic as physical beauty, and which consists of being able to surrender oneself to the camera. Certainly she was used to posing, most recently at her coming-out party in Newport. If she could have known then how many poses, how many photographers awaited her! It was the dawn of the paparazzi curse, although the word wouldn't exist for a few more years.[48] A debate had been sparked in the French press that very year when photographers invaded the hospital room of the actor Charles Dullin and took photos of him as he lay dying. It amounted to killing the soul, François Mauriac claimed. Where is the harm? reporter Roger Grenier responded, speaking for a younger generation of existentialists who, in the absence of God, saw nothing unnatural about the desire to capture images of life and death.[49]

To look at Jacqueline Bouvier in 1950 is impossible without thinking about the celebrity she became. Faithful to every cliché about life in France, most of her biographers make her Paris year a year of romance, if not all-out sexual passion. From plausible to outrageous or merely nasty, nearly every version of her love life starts with a footnoted source—and adds detail. She was romanced by a writer named Ormonde de Kay; she lost her virginity in a hotel elevator to a man whom Gore Vidal doesn't name but who is identified by a bolder biographer as John Marquand, Jr., one of the founding *Paris Review* writers. (Marquand ended up marrying Jackie's fellow boarder at the de Renty apartment, Susan Coward.[50] If there is a story in that coincidence, no one has told it.) She fell in love with a mysterious government official, a young assistant to the prime minister who is said to have taken her riding in the Bois de Boulogne; she had a crush on an aristocrat; she dated the son of a French diplomat. In at least one version of her French life, she was a regular at the Eléphant Blanc, the jazz club in Montparnasse.

She herself gives a hint, not necessarily of a romantic life, but of a romantic disposition, in a precious document, a bilingual poem she composed on the avenue Mozart and left with Claude, who put it away in a box of photos and letters from Jacqueline that she has carefully preserved. The poem may say more about Jacqueline Bouvier's love for language, her growing mastery of French, than about any love story. The third strophe is charming and clever, with its patterned rhymes and alternating verse lengths:

Who knows why an April breeze	Qui sait pourquoi une brise d'Avril
Never remains	Reste jamais
Why stars in the trees	Pourquoi les étoiles dans les arbres
Hide when it rains	Se cachent quand il pleut
Love comes along—casting a spell	L'amour vient—jetant un sort
Will it sing you a song	Est-ce qu'il vous chantera une chanson
Will it say a farewell	Est-ce qu'il vous dira adieu
Who can tell	Qui peut le dire (Qui sait?)

She set her poem in April, April in Paris—the quintessential romantic month. *Brise* is a resonant word, typical of French poetic diction, as is the phrase for casting a spell—*jetant un sort*. It's hard to tell which version she wrote first, the French or the English, or how she altered each as she went along to make the other work—that was the fun of it, a kind of bilingual crossword puzzle. She copied out the final version in two neat columns on a blank white page, each verse a perfect straight line of the kind French students learn to write by drawing faint lines in pencil with rulers. If there is a message in her light verse, it is that love is fickle and uncertain, but breezy. As for the reality, Claude, who saw her daily, pooh-poohed the romantic tales—there were no great love affairs. But she advised me to talk to Paul de Ganay, who had squired Jacqueline around town. He's in the party photo, grinning, a round handsome freckled face, the life of the party: "One of the very best of the de Ganays," according to Claude.

There are twenty or thirty de Ganays in the *Bottin mondain*, France's social register, which, in itself, is worth a detour. Its abbreviations and symbols, listed in the front of the volume, summarize what counted as calling cards in immediate postwar France: a medal of the Resistance; membership in an association of escaped prisoners of war, in the Jockey Club (the apex of social respectability), the Racing Club, the Automobile Club; abbreviations for various titles, from His Imperial Highness to prince, duchesse and marquis, and still other affiliations soon to be obsolete: the Yacht Club of Algeria, the Metropolitan Circle of the French Empire. A little house represented a château in the country; "h.p." an *hôtel particulier* (a mansion or townhouse in Paris). The Bottin entry for the de Ganays lists Paul de Ganay's mother, Rosita Bemberg, from Argentina. His great-grandmother on his father's side was one of the American Ridgways, Emily.

It is the kind of lineage Proust would have liked. He was fascinated by the slow decline of the aristocracy around the time of First World War, an aristocracy he saw striving to maintain its standing through strategic marriages to Jews, Americans, South Americans, whose influx of capital put new roofs on the châteaux and kept the cash flowing even as they devalued the very currency they were enlisted to maintain. The de Ganays seemed to have proved Proust wrong, though, as if nothing could touch their prestige: you could go directly from their 1950 salons, in town or country, to the memoirs of the duc de Saint-Simon and feel a perfect continuity between the eighteenth century and the twentieth.

By now there is something of a tradition linking American girls abroad to the French aristocracy, if only through housing arrangements and the intense mutual curiosity that is inevitable when Old World meets New. For Jacqueline Bouvier, the hours spent with the de Ganays were a lesson in the history of decorative art, in etiquette, a realization of her grandfather's fantasies that must have charmed and amused her too, for one of Paul de Ganay's best qualities was the very opposite of what Major Bouvier might have expected of a man like him. He was straightforward and down to earth. For Jackie, who didn't make friends at every turn, he must have been the easiest man in Paris to talk to.

Until his death in 2009, Paul de Ganay lived in the mansion on the rue Saint-Dominique in the seventh arrondissement, in the "Faubourg Saint-Germain," the very heart of the French aristocracy, where he grew up. When I went to meet him there in 2007, I found a slim, distinguished gray-haired fellow, a life-long bachelor, unhurried and easy in conversation. For two hours, with an even-handed courteousness, an extreme graciousness that one rarely finds in the modern world, and the accent so peculiar to his class, with its long-drawn-out syllables and guttural r's, he maintained an amused discretion and affection in giving a portrait of his life and times after the war, the crowd, those who were still his friends. It was the beginning of the Marshall Plan, and 35 percent of the French were communists, he explained. (The actual figure is closer to 27 percent, but he had a clear sense of the importance of the communists in postwar French life.) His crowd? A mixture of the grande bourgeoisie, industrialists, and a modern aristocracy, the first aristocratic generation in France to attend universities. Their parents were members of the Jockey Club or the country club in Saint-Cloud. Their family portraits extended back to the kings of France—an ancestry that Major Vernou Bouvier had claimed for himself. When I discussed my visit to de Ganay with Claude de Renty (now Claude du Granrut), describing the works of art and antiques I wish I could have identified, the mild disorder in the the way the furniture was arranged, paintings covering every inch of wall, she gently reminded me that the de Ganay ancestors were counselors to kings. The walls of their châteaux had always been cluttered with relics.

The choicest branches of the de Ganays have never sunk into decadence. They are a vibrant group, active in high finance, traveling between holdings in Argentina and in France. Jacqueline Bouvier had met Jacques Bemberg, one of Paul de Ganay's cousins on his mother's Argentinian side of the family, in 1948, the year Jacques worked on Wall Street and visited the Whitehouses, friends of the Auchinclosses, in Newport. Newport mansions, including the Whitehouses' Eastbourne, or the Auchinclosses' Hammersmith Farm, came as close as a de Ganay or a Bemberg could get in America to a homelike environment. Jacques Bemberg made the connection for Jacqueline to his cousin Paul in Paris, and it shaped her French life. Paul was in a transitional year of preparatory studies at the Sorbonne during Jacqueline's year abroad.[51] After lectures, the two of them used to meet for lunch at the Brasserie Balzar on the rue des Ecoles, down the street from the amphitheater, where the food was more than decent in a time of general deprivation.

Paul de Ganay described Jacqueline Bouvier with a sense of her inherited traits that is both precise and oddly earthy: he remembered her penetrating voice and the way her eyes were "planted" on her face, wide apart.[52] On the weekends she hunted on the vast territory of their château, Courances. He was whimsical about her riding: "Jackie loved *la chasse à courre*." Indeed, when Mademoiselle Saleil asked each Smith junior to tell the most embarrassing faux pas of the year, Jackie's was equestrian: "J'ai monté à poil," she had told her elegant hosts, "I rode the horse naked," instead of "je l'ai monté à cru" ("I rode the horse bareback"). Courances, the scene of her extravagant French mistake, had been requisitioned by the British fieldmarshal Montgomery at the Liberation, and by 1949 had only begun to return to its former social functions.[53]

The comte de Ganay evoked the social world of his crowd of friends in Paris. He was not a little nostalgic when he recalled putting on a tuxedo as often as four or five nights a week to go to "parties" (a word he pronounced in his perfect English accent, acquired well before the age of reason from his English nanny) where everyone was between eighteen and twenty-five, dancing to Claude Luter records and drinking cheap champagne. Even the rich were poor after the war, he reminded me with a touch of pride.

We covered the ground from his lunches and parties with Jacqueline Bouvier in 1949 to his dinner with First Lady Jacqueline Kennedy at Versailles in 1961. Then it was time for me to leave. In the hallway of his *hôtel particulier*, I looked up at an oil painting hung at the top of the stairwell: a portrait of Courances with its glorious red-brick and stone façade. On the wall to my left, above the marble banister, were trophies: a stag hunted down on the family properties in Argentina, a bear his brother killed in Alaska, several elephant tusks. "We're hunters in the family," he remarked, gazing up with me. We exchanged a few niceties about the neighborhood, in which he had resided since his birth in 1929. "It's good to have continuity" he said, and sang the praises of the Faubourg and its conveniences, explaining how the mansion had been divided up among the siblings upon his mother's death. He had chosen the floor with the highest ceilings.

The Amphitheaters

Throughout her year in Paris, Jacqueline Bouvier inhabited several worlds and managed to keep them separate—a talent she would need to maintain throughout her complex life. There was everyday life with the comtesse de Renty and Claude in the modest part of the sixteenth; partying with the de Ganay crowd in the seventh; small seminars and outings through Reid Hall; and classes at the Sorbonne, the Ecole du Louvre, and the Institut d'études politiques. There was her nightclub world with Ivy League writers who were slumming in Paris—Ormonde de Kay and John Marquand—whose importance is hard to measure. At least one biographer places young Jackie Bouvier as an habituée of the famous blue and white salon in the libertine writer Louise de Vilmorin's château at Verrières-le-Buisson—though Claude de Renty remembers her only going once or twice. By the 1949 season, Vilmorin, a legendary hostess, was no longer the mistress of British ambassador Duff Cooper, and not yet the mistress of French minister André Malraux. Jessica Hunt, Vilmorin's daughter from her first marriage to a Texan, was a classmate of Jackie's at Vassar.

4. Jacqueline Bouvier's student identity card photograph (1949). Photograph courtesy Claude du Granrut.

In one of her rare published letters from 1949–50, this one to her step-brother Yusha Auchincloss, Jacqueline describes her Parisian existence with the same vivid enthusiasm shown in her autumn letter from Grenoble, though the sun was long gone, replaced by a meditative Parisian gray:

> I really have two lives—flying from here [the de Renty apartment] to the Sorbonne and Reid Hall, in a lovely, quiet, rainy world—or, like the maid on her day out, putting on a fur coat and going to the middle of town and being swanky, at the Ritz. But I really like the first part best. I have an absolute mania now about learning to speak French perfectly. We never speak a word of English in this apartment and I don't see many Americans.[54]

She had reached a state of immersion, and discipline, and despite the rush of châteaux, hunts, and parties, what she seems to have valued most that year wasn't much different from what her fellow students valued—and it was intellectual, not social. During her senior year, in an essay she wrote for a prize that might bring her back to Paris, she was nostalgic for what the junior year abroad had given her: "I learned not to be ashamed of a real hunger for knowledge, something I had always tried to hide."[55] The social whirlwind was readily available at home, but a life of the mind wasn't, at least not as she knew it in Paris. She and her group from Smith took classes from the great intellectual lights of the postwar era, had access to special exhibits and performances, and were treated to special guest lectures at Reid Hall—thanks to Mlle Saleil.

Jeanne Saleil, in the best tradition of study-abroad directors, combined the qualities of a parent, a spiritual adviser, a chaperone, a professor, and a deluxe tour guide. Martha Rusk remembers her as a tiny woman, bent over, with pepper-and-white hair, dressed in one of her tailored suits, and radiating elegance and joie de vivre. A native of France, a Smith professor in her late fifties, she had just recovered from a nearly fatal bout with acute asthma and was determined that her students seize the day—that they meet not only Sorbonne professors but struggling artists, weavers, and potters. Apart from her academic pursuits, Saleil had her own career as a writer. Her childhood memoir was published in New York in 1949—a droll account of eccentric village life in the Cevennes region.[56] When invited to the Bal des Beaux-Arts, she created an elaborate shepherdess outfit for herself. This impeccably respectable French lady could make or do or find whatever was needed.[57]

Her work with the students in Paris that year left her, as she reminded the college president in her annual report, with no time at all for her own writing. But the students remembered her as a model of intellectual and personal freedom. Thanks to her commitment to give them "the greatest possible advantage of the extraordinary opportunities offered in Paris,"[58] the education that Jacqueline Bouvier came to value so highly was taking place in a continuum of the classroom, the home, and the street. For all her enthusiasm in retrospect about her year of study in France, Jackie Bouvier was a particular source of frustration to the Smith director. Mlle Saleil complained to Martha Rusk about her friend: "Jacqueline is so brilliant, she could be a stellar academic, but she hasn't thrown herself into the intellectual life. Her heart is elsewhere."[59] Perhaps she hoped that Martha would pass the comment along. But like so many twenty-year-old American students in France, Jackie was learning more than she let on. To Mlle Saleil, who was giving so

5. Professor Jeanne Saleil with students from the Smith program in the "Grande Salle" at Reid Hall (1950). Photograph courtesy Smith College Archives.

. . .

much, it wasn't obvious how much the enigmatic student from Vassar was absorbing.

"Every week," wrote Jeanne Saleil to the Smith president,

we have a one-hour discussion on what might be called "la semaine à Paris" [the week in Paris]. When it is a subject unknown to me, I invite lively lecturers to discuss our strikes, our political imbroglios, new architectural trends, etc. And since the masculine element cannot be dismissed here anymore than it is at Smith, I even had the solicitude to invite *Polytechniciens* to a dance given in Reid Hall. With their sword, cape and bicorne, not to mention the white gloves, they are immensely rewarding.[60]

Among the recent graduates of the Polytechnique was a thin young man named Valéry Giscard d'Estaing, friend to many of the Smith group, including Jacqueline Bouvier. It is tempting to imagine the future First Lady waltzing at Reid Hall with the future president of the French Republic. Between the two of them, they had an incalculable number of official waltzes in their futures. For all the Smith group, dancing with the beswarded Polytechnique military students offered a theatrical outlet unavailable at dances with men from Harvard or Yale, or even West Point, and sometimes led to dinner dates.

By day, in small group seminars at Reid Hall, discussions raged over the reigning intellectual fashion, existentialism; over the escalating conflict in Indochina; over the French Communist Party. As the weather grew warmer, the students spent their breaks on rattan chairs in the pebble-lined Reid Hall courtyard or walked a block for coffee at Le Select, where Hemingway, Djuna Barnes, and Fitzgerald had held court nearly three decades earlier, making Montparnasse the capital of the Jazz Age. In 1949 the young women were reading Sartre and Camus, but not Beauvoir, who might have been more useful to them but was probably disdained by their male professors ("Now I know everything about your boss's vagina," François Mauriac wrote to Beauvoir's colleagues at *Les temps modernes* when *The Second Sex* was published—and his gross misogyny was widely shared).[61] Among the guests who came to speak to them at Reid Hall was a controversial American much in the news—a hero for Camus and a figure of ridicule for Sartre. This was Gary Davis, the World War II pilot who had renounced his U.S. citizenship and issued himself a passport as the first "citizen of the world." Mlle Saleil seemed to know everyone.[62]

Jacqueline Bouvier's Smith transcript includes a list of her courses. She focused her studies almost exclusively on art history and literature. For nineteenth-century French literature, she took a small seminar at Reid Hall from the Maupassant specialist Henri Kerst, a professor whose regular job at the Lycée Henri IV involved training elite high school students for the rigorous entrance exams to the Grandes écoles. For aesthetics, her professor was Didier Anzieu, a psychoanalytic theorist of artistic creation, remembered by one Smith student for his final exam essay question, "Do you have the right to commit suicide?"[63] In art history, Max-Pol Fouchet taught a small course on twentieth-century art at Reid Hall. He had edited a magazine called *Fontaine* from Algiers during the war,[64] considered himself an intimate of Camus and a Resistance luminary, and prided himself generally on his connections to everyone who counted. The students were wild about him.[65] Maurice

Sérullaz, a world specialist in impressionism and one of the great curators of postwar Paris, walked the young women through the museums so they could study the canvasses up close. He asked each of them to pick the painting they would most like to take home: Jacqueline and Martha chose the same Corot.[66]

Only one of Jacqueline's classes ventured out of art and literature and into the realm of politics, which was to be so important in her life, and it was held at the Institut d'études politiques (commonly known as "Sciences Po"), an important postwar training ground for a French business and political elite.[67] If, knowing her future, she could have chosen a single course that might guide her in her role as the wife of an American president, she couldn't have done better than Pierre Renouvin's "International Relations since 1870." Renouvin was a pillar of the institute, a fierce pedagogue and searing lecturer who stood before his classes with one empty sleeve—he had lost his left arm at the Chemin des Dames in World War I. Renouvin had begun his career studying the Great War. Influenced by the *Annales* school of history, he was a theorist of political conflict who believed in combining "deep forces"—demographics, geography and climate, culture—with short-term diplomatic history. For the Smith students who elected to do a certificate at Sciences Po, there were other lecture classes from historian and geographer André Siegfried, political theorist Raymond Aron, and Jean-Jacques Chevallier, who taught a course on monarchy, socialist utopias, and racism.

At the Sorbonne itself, the experience of sitting in the "Grand amphi" set the tone. It was an auditorium complete with balconies and seats for a thousand students. The professor sat on a high stage, with statues and an enormous neoclassical mural as his backdrop. This was the ultimate theater of learning, grandiose and also slightly ridiculous, from the moment the professor walked onto his stage, accompanied by the traditional Sorbonne *appariteur*, a kind of classroom concierge in a dark suit, whose job was to announce the master and keep the blackboard wiped clean. The professor sat in a chair and read his lecture, rarely departing from the text.[68] For anyone who skipped class, or simply couldn't bear the monotony of the hour-long recitation, lectures were available for purchase in *polycopiés* in a bookstore on the Place de la Sorbonne, lending themselves to the word-for-word, comma-for-comma memorization that was expected for success on the exams at the end of term. For foreign students, the *polycopiés* were a godsend for figuring out how to spell the many words and phrases they couldn't quite make out—especially proper names. (Imagine names like Eisenhower or Manhattan pronounced in French.) Far less satisfying than the intimate seminars they were used to, these big lectures nonetheless let the students in on the part of French education that was as ritualistic as Catholic mass. They were by turns excruciatingly boring, highly entertaining, and deeply foreign, and the students never forgot them.

After classes, the young women from Smith could be seen strolling arm-in-arm down the Boul' Mich' speaking French, a language that felt increasingly less "put on," and finally nearly natural. By the end of the year they had begun to blend in with their French brothers and sisters. Mary Ann Hoberman remembers how exciting it was when she realized she was dreaming in French. "I knew it was a milestone and that I had taken the language into myself."[69] Jacqueline Bouvier, who had begun the year, like the others, with halting French, was speaking and writing with greater confidence, even experimenting with bilingual poetry.[70]

Reading official reports to college presidents and gleaning whatever we can from interviews today, it is hard to get a sense of what these American students must have looked like to their French teachers. The most evocative essay I've found about them from a French point of view was written by Henriette Nizan, who had a unique understanding because of her own experience of the United States. Nizan's husband, the writer Paul Nizan, was killed in 1940 at the outbreak of war.[71] Henriette, whose own family was Jewish, fled with their two children to the United States, where she supported herself by running the Maison française at Douglass College, Rutgers, and teaching French literature. Later she got work writing French copy to be used in dubbing Hollywood films.[72] Unlike Beauvoir, who stayed for a few intense months, Nizan spent four years in the United States. She knew the background of these American girls abroad, the dorms where they lived and the French departments where they'd taken classes, what they ate and wore before they got to Paris, their jokes and their slang. By 1950 she was back in France, earning her living as a translator and a journalist. One of her freelance essays for the newly established government newsletter on French-American relations might have been fluff, but instead it was full of insight about the various subgoups of young Americans abroad—the GI bill veterans, the intellectual Fulbright fellows, the protected Reid Hall girls.[73]

42 : The first thing that struck Nizan was how much the American students in Paris all seemed to want to be French: they were more worried about

maintaining French tradition than the French themselves. They were the ones who ordered *picon-citron* (orange bitters with lemonade) in the bistros, while the French drank Coca-Cola. The young American men, who tried to look like the garret painters from 1918 they had read about in books, brought the nineteenth-century French mustache back into fashion. And "it was young American girls who influenced young French girls with the fashion for laced sandals and long straight hair, which no one had worn since 1900," wrote Nizan, adding, "they're the ones you see on Sunday at the flea market."

"Without the American students," she concluded, "bohemian life might not have existed for Parisian youth, whom the years of occupation had made into 'realists.' I'm exaggerating, but not much." She was speaking for all of war-torn Paris, but also, one suspects, for herself.

By the summer of 1950, Jacqueline Bouvier and Claude de Renty had developed a comfortable friendship. Claude, a student at Sciences Po, had studied at Mount Holyoke on an exchange in 1948, so she knew more than

6. Jacqueline Bouvier on her summer trip to southern France (1950). Photograph courtesy Claude du Granrut.

most young French people about the United States.[74] The two friends could move back and forth between English and French, exchange observations about student life in both places. They were neither sisters nor roommates, but something in between. In late June, just as news broke of a war in Korea, Jacqueline left Paris with her friend Rosamée Sauvage de Brantes, one of the Faubourg Saint-Germain crowd, to join Alain and Charles du Luart at their cousins' summer place at Beauvallon, on the gulf of Saint-Tropez. Saint-Tropez was still a fishing village, on the brink of its discovery by the Parisian stars. Jacqueline took the train to Lyon next, where Claude met her with her sister's trusty Dyna Panhard, and the two set off on a three-week road trip. Traffic was nonexistent, reservations unheard of and often

7. Jacqueline Bouvier (*center*) on her twenty-first birthday at Borda Berri in the Basque country, leaning against the Dyna Panhard (July 28, 1950). *Left:* Yusha Auchincloss; *right:* Solange Batsell. Photograph courtesy Claude du Granrut.

unnecessary, since Claude had cousins scattered around the countryside. They saw the Renaissance castle at Azay-le-Rideau; played in the *lavoirs*—the ancient outdoor washing pool—at Salers; and hiked in the Gorges du Tarn, France's grand canyon, where they visited a de Renty relative, Madame de la Romiquière, in an ancient hamlet you could only reach by barge. At Borda Berri, near Biarritz, Jackie's stepbrother Yusha and some of his schoolfriends were summering in an old château. Jackie and Claude spent a week with them, dropped them at the train station in Bordeaux, and went on their way. With no schedule, no obligations, they spoke to whoever crossed their paths—farmers and shopkeepers, the occasional de Renty cousin or châtelaine. The contrast with the American countryside was striking: outdoor

8. Claude de Renty on a picnic along the banks of the Loire (summer 1950).
Photograph courtesy Claude du Granrut.

9. Jacqueline Bouvier on a picnic along the banks of the Loire (summer 1950).
Photograph courtesy Claude du Granrut.

washing pools still in operation, châteaux with their blue slate roofs in various states of decay, villages untouched by time, simple food grown close to the place where you ate it, the ubiquity of wine. Claude took pride in showing Jacqueline every treasure, every beautiful place.

What is most striking about so many of these French-American exchanges of 1949–50 is their nearly perfect reciprocity—it is impossible to decide who got more from whom. In the affectionate relationship of Jacqueline Bouvier with the comtesse de Renty and her daughter, as in Henriette Nizan's perception of the young Americans in their intense enjoyment of Paris, there was something more than fun, something deeply therapeutic at work. It was not the kind of recovery the architects of the Marshall Plan had in mind, a recovery made of the loan of goods and services; instead, it was made of the pleasure and relief for these survivors of war in serving once again as a model for a joyous way of life. And for Jacqueline Bouvier in particular, in matters ranging from the intellect to aesthetics, from pleasure to discipline, France—not the imagined France of her grandfather, but the real France she now knew—provided a model she would turn to in every subsequent phase of her life.

....

TWO

Jacqueline Bouvier
The Return

....

Prix de Paris

The *Liberté* brought Jacqueline Bouvier home from France in September, just before her senior year, on a boat filled with celebrities: Hubert Beuve-Méry, who in 1945 had founded the news daily *Le Monde*, was on his way to a meeting of the American Society of Newspaper Editors; Jacques Fath, the couturier who'd designed the big flouncy skirts for women on bicycles during the fuel-deprived years of the occupation, was headed for Seventh Avenue; Sadruddin Aga Khan, a young Persian prince fresh out of Swiss boarding school, was about to start his freshman year at Harvard, where he would make literary history by bankrolling George Plimpton's *Paris Review*. For all of them, the United States represented the exuberant center of post-war freedoms. It's tempting to imagine Jacqueline being whirled around the dance floor by Jacques Fath or the young Aga Khan. She would have had to sneak into first class to do it, since she was in third class, along with a few Smith girls who had spent the summer traveling around Europe. The year abroad had reduced their need for luxury.

Jacqueline Bouvier never returned to Vassar. Instead, she enrolled at George Washington University and finished her studies with a French major. What was expected of a French major in the 1950s bears little resemblance to today's course of study: a class Jacqueline Bouvier took in the fall semester was devoted entirely to French literature of the first half of the seventeenth century. Not the glittering seventeenth-century plays staged for the Sun King at Versailles, as amusing to read today as they were a hundred years ago, but the obscure literature of the recovery from years of religious wars, including the archaic pastoral novel of Honoré d'Urfé, *L'Astrée,* some devout humanistic writings, a few early plays by Corneille, and Descartes's meditations.[1] It says something about expectations for the affluent young women of that bygone era that Jacqueline Bouvier read d'Urfé and Descartes in conjunction with her courses on typing, interior decoration, and the short story.[2]

During the winter of her senior year, at a moment when the peer pressure on college girls to get engaged was most intense, Bouvier acquired a fiancé named John Husted. He was a Yale man turned stockbroker who lived in New York, which gave her a chance to see her father and visit her favorite museums. Their engagement was short-lived. According to more than one biographer, when Janet Auchincloss discovered that young Husted made only $17,000 a year on Wall Street, she quickly discouraged the match. Perhaps she didn't need to discourage it, and Jacqueline was simply bored.

Jacqueline Bouvier, in 1951, was at loose ends. It's intriguing to imagine what her expectations for her life must have been, her sense of possibility. She wasn't an heiress, for her own father had very little to his name. But she had been raised with a sense of a connection to ancient aristocracies, had grown up on splendid estates in Newport and Virginia, enjoying the leisure activities of the rich. She had attended the best schools, and had come out as the queen of the debutantes with the cream of Newport society. It must have been confusing. She was neither a poor little rich girl nor an aristocrat; nor was she a Gigi or an Eliza Doolittle who had to climb out of her social class. If she had expectations of grandeur, she kept them at bay, for there were no guarantees.

Eager for a job after graduation, she asked her stepfather's friend, Allen Dulles, to shepherd her application for an entry-level position at the CIA. Her request might have been nothing more than a conversation at a cocktail party in McLean, near her stepfather's Virginia estate, but whatever ensued was enough to make her think she might not be available for other work.[3] She would have been in good company, for the agency was recruiting on college campuses—especially the Ivy League and the Seven Sisters. Martha Rusk remembers the opportunity of a job at the CIA as a privilege, responding both to her sense of duty and her desire for intellectual adventure: "We all planned to work, and the CIA was elite, it was Ivy League, it was smart." Martha and Virginia Lyon were recruited right in Northampton, in their senior year, for an annual salary of $2875.[4] They went straight to the French desk, in a temporary office building on the edge of the reflecting pool, and they took an oath never to say what they were doing. Virginia Lyon had lodged in Grenoble with a family whose son was an army officer repatriated after the defeat at Dien Bien Phu, not guessing that what she learned at the dinner table might be part of her working life two years later. International institutions and publications that received CIA funding, conflicts in Algeria and Indochina: there were plenty of subjects that called on the knowledge of French and politics and history they had acquired in France. Bill Donovan, the legendary "Wild Bill" Donovan who had helped transform the Office of Strategic Services into a postwar intelligence agency, crossed Martha's path in the corridor and waxed avuncular with the idealistic girl from Smith: "You see, we Americans have been wrong to think it isn't nice to spy. We need to catch up with the rest of the world!"

How many other students from the Smith study abroad programs joined the CIA? The CIA recruiters came to campus in the spring of their senior year to interview them. Virginia Lyon thought there might have been ten recruits, including students from the Geneva and Paris groups and others who hadn't been abroad. (There were three of them from the Paris group alone; Martha Rusk remembered "a goodly number.") They worked with a sense of purpose, for they believed that France was teetering on the brink of communism.

Whatever the status of her CIA application, Jacqueline Bouvier didn't join Martha and Virginia by the reflecting pool. She had another postgraduation plan underway, closer to her passions. Compared to the CIA job, this one was a long shot. She entered *Vogue*'s Paris Prize competition.[5] The process was rigorous: you had to submit a personal essay, a short story, and several sample feature articles for the magazine. The winner would get six months working at the Paris *Vogue* office, followed by six months at *Vogue*'s New York headquarters—the start of a career in journalism, a chance to live in Paris and be paid to live there, a chance to write and to participate in the world of high fashion close-up.

Jacqueline Bouvier's application to *Vogue* is full of apologies and false starts, almost as if she were trying to dash her own chances. She missed the deadline and wrote in October to ask if she could still be considered. Then she asked for an extension, explaining that she was only just learning to type and the girl she had hired to type her entry was busy with homecoming. In April, upon learning she was a finalist, she wrote to say she could not attend the dinner party for finalists at the Cosmopolitan Club because of her comprehensive exams. She flew up for a private lunch instead on April 30, and wrote again on May 7 to Miss Mary Campbell, coordinator of the prizes, to apologize for her poor performance at lunch. (Mary Campbell, a legendary figure at the magazine, was known for championing young Catholic women and for her aristocratic sense of women's work. She liked to hire Seven Sisters' graduates who were content to earn "pin money," and her talent scouting was part of Seventh Avenue lore: "I can tell by the way a girl ties her scarf," she used to say, "whether she belongs at *Vogue*.")[6]

In her letter of May 7, Jacqueline Bouvier poured out her heart. She was so sorry she hadn't answered any of the questions about her future, and that she had run off early to visit with her ailing father. What she needed to explain was that the lunch with the *Vogue* staff had altered her view of magazine work, and set a new course for her future aspirations. Her letter to Miss Campbell has the breathless tone of the newly converted:

> I had vague little dreams of locking myself up somewhere and turning out children's books and *New Yorker* short stories, and I shied away from working on a magazine because it seemed that the few of my friends who did work on magazines went in with grand ideas like mine and ended up doing pretty routine things with not much hope of advancement. That is the state of mind I was in when I met you for lunch. But then listening to you and Miss Phillips and Miss Heal—I was so impressed. . . . In the four days since I've been home I've been thinking very hard about "my career" and it has changed from vague ideas of puttering around, to something very definite, and I am so relieved to have decided on something definite that I can start working for: In ten years, or 20 if it takes that long, I would like to be a top editor in Condé Nast— and for two reasons. I think when you have several bents, none of them pronounced enough to make you a great novelist or painter, and you love

keeping up with new ideas, a magazine is the ideal place to work. And of all the magazines I can think of, Condé Nast is the one that fits in with the things I am most interested in, and it has such esprit de corps, everyone seems so keen about what they are doing, that I can't imagine ever becoming seriously discouraged with your work.

Then came the surprise: "I am not eligible for the first prize." After all that! She wrote that she was committed to take a job at the CIA, "a special job on a certain project . . . it would only last 3 months, from October till January." All she could hope for was that when she finished the CIA special project, there might be a position available for her at *Vogue* in New York.

The editors might have decided she was spoiled, unreliable. Instead, Jacqueline emerged the winner of the prize among a field of 1,800 applicants—certainly the only contestant who had promised in advance to turn them down.

What could have been enticing enough in her essays to keep her candidacy alive despite apologies, delays, and protestations? Imagination, European taste, an exquisite sense of detail must all have been high on the magazine's list of qualities. Her essay for *Vogue* offers a snapshot of a young French major who has absorbed the lessons of her year abroad and her literature classes, whose standards of beauty and grooming are at one with her social class and her times, but whose sense of culture and geography are still, after a year away from Paris, firmly centered across the ocean.

For the required five-hundred-word feature story, "People I Wish I Had Known," Bouvier chose three Europeans, two of them Parisians: Charles Baudelaire, Oscar Wilde, and Sergei Diaghilev—a French poet; a British playwright (and Parisian expatriate); and ballet's master choreographer, an itinerant Russian who made his mark on avant-garde Paris. What is immediately striking to any reader of the essay is what it reveals about her analytic disposition: even when evoking the poet Baudelaire or the playwright Wilde, she is an essentially visual person. Images always matter more to her than words—or, rather, they impose themselves before words do. She doesn't quote Wilde; she culls images from his poems and colors from the stage sets for his plays: "the yellow liquid light pools in the street"; "the candybox spillings of pinks and mauves." With Baudelaire, it's synesthesia or the crossing of the senses that interests her, the "perfumes green as prairies." The Diaghilev section is weaker, if only because it remains abstract.

Some of her concentration on the visual was strategic; after all, she was writing for a magazine that traded on images. But her attraction to the look of things—what the French since the seventeenth century have called *le paraître*, appearances—was deep in her nature, and it wasn't an interest in her own looks so much as the glance outside herself that counted.

The most significant line in the essay is the last—she has a gift for pleasing endings. "If I could be a sort of Overall Art Director of the Twentieth Century," she concludes, "watching everything from a chair hanging in space, it is their theories that I would apply to any period, their poems that I would have music and paintings and ballets composed to. And they would make such good steppingstones if we thought we could climb any higher."

Overall art director, sitting on a chair hanging in space: whether she knew it or not, her thinking was very much in line with the theories of André Malraux—the man who, as de Gaulle's minister of culture, would become, in ten short years, her *chevalier servant* in Paris. In 1945, this adventurer and author of *The Human Condition* and *Man's Fate* had abandoned his work as a novelist to concentrate on politics and aesthetic theories. In 1947, Malraux published his influential essay, *Museum without Walls*, or in French, *Le musée imaginaire*. A century ago, it begins, even the most cultured men had rarely seen works of art outside their own national context: Baudelaire had never even visited Italy! Now, thanks to photographic reproductions, works of art could be appreciated for the first time across centuries and across nations, instead of being confined to discrete collections in national museums. The result, Malraux concluded, was a revolution in influence: your view of Rembrandt was changed by looking at Renoir, and the fact that Rembrandt lived a few centuries before Renoir didn't matter.[7] Malraux's idea was very much in the air both at the Sorbonne and at Reid Hall during Jacqueline Bouvier's year in Paris, where her kaleidoscope of aesthetic experiences added up to a museum without walls in just the sense Malraux intended. In her essay for *Vogue*, she was transmitting part of his idea, but, better than that, was also conveying her own yearning for aesthetic achievement, which was deep, and genuine: "they would make such good steppingstones if we thought we could climb any higher."

In the self-portrait required by *Vogue*, a shorter "Feature" in addition to the essay on "People I wish I had known," Jacqueline Bouvier describes herself as though she were standing outside herself—as though she were still sitting on that chair hanging in space—with an objectivity that is unusual for a young woman her age. There isn't a hint of vanity in anything she writes. She is amused by her failings, interested in her shortcomings. The only thing she leaves out is her own beauty:

> As to physical appearance, I am tall, 5′ 7″, with brown hair, a square face and eyes so unfortunately far apart that it takes three weeks to have a pair of glasses made with a bridge wide enough to fit over my nose. I do not have a sensational figure but can look slim if I pick the right clothes. I flatter myself on being able at times to walk out of the house looking like the poor man's Paris copy, but often my mother will run up to inform me that my left stocking seam is crooked or the right-hand topcoat button about to fall off. This, I realize, is the Unforgivable Sin.

An unforgiving mother, a flaw—her wide eyes—and a body that needs clothes: it was the perfect set up for the surprise she must have created when she appeared in person for her interview and for the photo shoot with the *Vogue* prize committee, dark and elegant in black cashmere, with a triple strand of white pearls around her neck.

After the self-portrait came "a plan of beauty care suitable for a college girl." Jacqueline Bouvier's plan gives us an even fuller sense than her self-portrait of the strict education she received from her mother, who had a laser vision for crooked stocking seams, in a milieu where, from the sound of it, a girl's good name could be made or lost on a missing button. Decades before teeth-whitening systems, she recommended brushing teeth once a week with a peroxide rinse because "nothing will be counted against you faster than a dingy smile." Putting on lipstick was a five-part procedure: powder the lips, apply lipstick, blot, powder, and apply lipstick again. She offered dire warnings to the potential *Vogue* readers about the life-long stubble that would ensue if one shaved instead of using depilatory cream on one's legs. (The French mode of waxing had apparently not reached U.S. shores.)

The judges were convinced from the beginning: "She is definitely a writer," wrote one of them in the first round of grading; "she has the editorial point of view. . . . My only worry is that she might *marry* one day—and go off on one of those horses she speaks about."

A short story was the final requirement in the contest. The editors were won over by "The Violets," with its evocation of a grandfatherly character who resembled her own grandfather, Major Bouvier, author of the false genealogical treatise, *Our Forebears*. In a Park Avenue apartment where a patriarch has just died, the heirs are squabbling over his possessions. The granddaughter narrates: "Both my father and my aunt wanted the yellow damask Louis XVI sofa." "I had never seen death before," she writes, "and was ashamed that it made no more of an impression."

One disinterested person finally comes to her grandfather's wake—an old law partner, who arrives clutching a bouquet of violets he got at the corner because the florist shops were closed and he remembered that "Dick always liked violets." Her aunt complains that the violets don't belong, and drops the bouquet onto the floor. In the final lines of the story, Bouvier conveys through her senses the difference between empty conventions and meaningful gestures:

> I picked up the violets and put them to my face. They smelled cool and raindrops were still on them. They were a Christmas present to my grandfather from someone who had really cared about him. I stood listening to the swish of traffic in the rain outside and feeling the wind blow through the window. Far away I could hear chimes, from St. James church, over on Madison Avenue. I knelt on the bench beside the coffin and put the violets down inside, beneath my grandfather's elbow, where the people who came to close the coffin would not see them.

She explained in her self-portrait for *Vogue* that she had grown up reading Chekhov and Shaw on the windowsill of her room when she was supposed to be napping. Her sense of bittersweet endings and perfect details owed something to them but was also deeply engrained within her own personality. At twenty-one, Jacqueline Bouvier, who has seen her grandfather die, has already acquired an acute sensitivity to the theater of mourning with its necessary gestures of tenderness.

Vogue seemed such a natural path for her that it is difficult to imagine how she could have considered turning down the prize. Her May 1951 letter to Mary Campbell gives the official reasons: First, her mother wanted her to stay close to home in the Washington, DC, area (and presumably far from her father in the New York area). Second, she was committed to the CIA job she had angled for—though she was positive she could get free of her commitment. (It's the job market equivalent of "I have to wash my hair, even though I'm positive it's not dirty.")

Is it possible she did work for the CIA on a three-month special project? When queried under the Freedom of Information Act about a record of her employment, the CIA responded that there was none. Someone looking for a smoking gun might persist with the fantasy that she was recruited for a covert operation on account of her international society connections (after all, the OSS was nicknamed "Oh So Social"...), but it would take some serious fabulation to argue that Jacqueline Bouvier's specific skills, in 1951, corresponded to what the intelligence agency needed, or even that the CIA would have invested in a costly security clearance for such a short assignment.[8]

Finally came this wistful remark, made apropos of returning to Paris for *Vogue*: "I have already lived in Paris for a year and become so satiated with it, and so miserable when I came back home, that I would rather not go back for a while."

Paris brings with it pleasures so intense, and leaving is so difficult, that it's almost better not to go in the first place. It's the sort of argument one can find in every expatriate writer from Henry James to James Baldwin, a reference to a deep dread and desire for European pleasures in which one's good sense might be forever lost. But in Bouvier's letter to Campbell, coming on the heels of two other excuses, it sounds feckless. In trying to make sense of her various changes of heart toward *Vogue,* some of her biographers claim that she wanted the prize, but that her mother didn't want her stuck in a "mare's nest" and pulled in the reins at the last minute. Others argue that the decision to turn down the prize was all hers—she was holding out for marriage.[9]

As a substitute prize, perhaps a reward for obedience, Jacqueline's mother and stepfather offered her a summer tour of Europe with her younger sister, Caroline Lee. It must have been a shock to return to the place where she had lived for so long in the de Rentys' French cocoon, where she had thrived in the scholarly intensity of the Smith and Sorbonne courses, now as a tourist, with her younger sister in tow. The sisters kept a diary and a sketchbook for recording their antics—which included, this time, an account of infiltrating dinner dances in first class on their transatlantic crossing. Jackie did the drawings and Lee the poems, all tongue-in-cheek and full of references to flirtations and scandalous acts such as wearing shorts instead of the prescribed skirts, hats, and white gloves.[10] They had a long list of people to look up, an international haute bourgeoisie, similar to the people they frequented at home.

The girls leased a Hillman Minx and took to the road. In Poitiers, the gateway to southwest France, they visited Jacqueline's junior-year friend Paul de Ganay, who was doing his mandatory military service. She and Lee made a sensation with the young officers as they entered the military compound in their strapless sundresses. De Ganay joked with his commanding officer that he was engaged to both of them.[11] After France came Italy, where they paid a respectful visit to the art critic Bernard Berenson, then Spain. It was their grand tour. At the back of the scrapbook, under the heading "Dreams of Glory," were their two faces, pasted onto royal portraits: "Caroline, Duquesa de Bronxville" and "Jacqueline, Fille Naturelle de Charlemagne." Their mother needn't have worried about Jacqueline becoming a permanent expatriate, though Caroline Lee would eventually find, in her second marriage, her Polish Prince Radziwill and spend much of her adult life in Europe. Jacqueline became, for a time, the symbol of American womanhood. For now, that future was less than a speck in their imaginations.

Jackie Kennedy, née Bouvier

Two years after the Bouvier sisters' jaunt across Europe, Jacqueline married John F. Kennedy, the newly minted senator she had charmed at a Washington dinner party over a plate of asparagus. During the first six years of her marriage—rough years by all accounts, including her husband's near-fatal spine surgery and her own miscarriage—she felt very much at odds with the Kennedy clan: *une pièce rapportée* is the tongue-in-cheek expression in French for someone who has married into a family but isn't quite of it—literally, a "patch." In 1958, John Kennedy was beginning to plan his campaign for the 1960 presidential elections. For the young Mrs. Kennedy, French major from George Washington University whose only real job before graduation had been brief service as an "inquiring camera girl" for the *Washington Times-Herald,* France was no longer a long-term destination; instead it was an imaginary port of refuge, reached through books. In the summer of 1959, Arthur Schlesinger, already JFK's trusted adviser—the same Arthur Schlesinger who had done intelligence work on the Resistance during his own postwar stint in Paris—visited the Kennedys' summer compound at Hyannis Port and wrote, with a touch of condescension, that the young senator's wife "was lovely but seemed excessively flighty on politics." She asked naïve questions that were irritating, although she was "intelligent and articulate" on other issues. He remarked that she was reading Proust.[12]

Schlesinger was only half-right about her naïveté, for nothing could have better prepared an American political candidate's wife on the campaign trail than Proust's wicked knowledge of human desire, social and sexual, his understanding of the making and breaking of careers. The likelihood of a 1950s or '60s political wife gaining the intellectual respect of her husband's colleagues was slim, whether they noticed her reading Proust or Sartre's *Nausea*: in that milieu, the pursuit of literary culture was comparable to interior decoration. A year later, when the routine on the 1960 campaign trail became too brutal, Jacqueline Kennedy immersed herself in another classic, an eighteenth-century precursor to Proust in the realm of society's deconstruction: "She had the *Mémoires du Duc de Saint-Simon* in French," wrote Kenneth Galbraith, another New Frontiersman who had lived abroad in the late 1940s in England and France and Italy, and who was exceptional in his understanding of Jacqueline's qualities. "She would take no part in the day's political persuasion. . . . But she had a deeper purpose: it was she, not the more trusting J.F.K., who would observe, hear and render judgment on the politicians they would encounter. . . . She made no conscious decision to analyze them; she simply took for granted that it was her job."[13]

For fifty years, bitter about an aristocracy consisting of bastard children and scheming mistresses, the duc de Saint-Simon prepared his posthumous vengeance on the court of Louis XIV. Historians never tire of saying how inaccurate his version is, tainted by bitterness and resentment, and literary historians never tire of quoting his vivid and catty portraits, such as this, one of many pages that would accompany Jacqueline Kennedy throughout her life:

> Mme de Montespan was mean, capricious, and temperamental. Not even the King was spared her arrogance. It was said that to pay her court was to be court-martialed, and the saying became a proverb. It is true that she spared no one, and often her only aim was to amuse the King. Since she was infinitely witty, nothing was more dangerous than to be the butt of her ridicule.[14]

It's easy enough to see what the duc de Saint-Simon might have represented to the daughter of the philandering "Black Jack" Bouvier and the wife of a powerful man with an equally wandering eye. One of the great themes of

Saint-Simon's memoirs was the rivalry among the king's mistresses—he relished recounting how Madame de Montespan, the favorite, was eventually ousted by her own protégée, Madame de Maintenon, a felon's daughter-turned-teenage-wife of an aging, crippled poet, turned devout Catholic. For a soft-spoken but mischievous Jacqueline Kennedy, Saint-Simon and Proust were models of the cutting remark, the elegant slur, the devastating description that surpassed anything she had known in girls' school. And when the tension became too great, she could, according to at least one of her biographers, rival them in devastating one-liners.[15]

The Kennedy administration had its own aspiring Saint-Simon in the person of writer Norman Mailer, who, like Schlesinger, like Galbraith and like Jackie herself, had cut his teeth intellectually in Paris, in 1948, studying—or not studying—at the Sorbonne on the GI bill. Reminiscing in a 1962 essay in *Esquire* about his visit to the Kennedy compound at Hyannis Port during the 1960 presidential campaign, he gave the impression of someone who had been unsettled by the qualities of the young president's wife and was eager to show his readers that he had not been seduced. Nothing, he let his reader know, had escaped his eye; when she let him know there was hard liquor available as well as iced tea, "something droll and hard came into her eyes as if she were a very naughty eight-year-old." (He had recently been arrested for drunk and disorderly conduct and must have assumed, with more than a touch of paranoia, that she was eager to make a joke at his expense.)[16] A remoteness Mailer ascribes to her (she was "moody and abstracted") was the same quality that Galbraith considered an essential contribution to John Kennedy's political success—her skills of observation, of watching from her suspended chair, of watching and knowing that she was always being watched.

Schlesinger put it this way, years after her death: "She observed upper class conventions, but underneath a veil of lovely inconsequence she developed a cool assessment of people and an ironical slant on life. One soon realized that her social graces masked tremendous awareness, an all-seeing eye, ruthless judgment, and a steely purpose."[17]

A Signifying Wardrobe

Is there any other figure in American political life about whom you could say there is a genealogy of her clothes—a genealogy that begins, like so much else, in Paris? For Jacqueline Kennedy's style, you have to begin with Elsa Schiaparelli, the Franco-Italian designer and author of the color known as "shocking pink." (In Paris, clothes designers are considered "authors" who "edit" their collections.) "Never fit the dress to the body," Schiaparelli preached: "train the body to fit the dress." Instead of the breathy chiffon that was popular in the late 1940s, Schiaparelli believed in imposing solid fabrics that held their own. Out of Elsa Schiaparelli's atelier came Hubert de Givenchy, her assistant. In 1952, Givenchy opened his own shop, first on the rue Alfred de Vigny, then at the epicenter of chic, the avenue Georges V. Audrey Hepburn knocked on his door in 1953, looking for clothes to wear in *Sabrina,* since Edith Head's extravagant Hollywood costumes overwhelmed her small frame. The Givenchy-Hepburn-Sabrina triad adds up to a funny connection between Jacqueline Bouvier Kennedy's clothing style and a movie whose subject is the magical romantic consequences of studying abroad in Paris: Sabrina, the main character of Billy Wilder's 1954 film, is the waiflike daughter of the chauffeur to the Larabees, a family of tycoons, and she dreams about David Larabee, the boss's playboy son, who is barely aware of her existence. Off she goes to Paris in her pigtails and polka dots to study French cooking. When she returns to Long Island in a Givenchy suit and white cloche hat, exuding Parisian aura, the playboy makes a play for her, and then the workaholic son, solid and wise, falls for her in turn. The film ends with the vision of the beautiful sophisticate on board the *Liberté,* where the good Larabee son joins her—presumably for their honeymoon in Paris. Givenchy and Audrey Hepburn were a match: his straight lines and unadorned fabric were perfect for her small-boned delicacy and natural elegance.

During her husband's campaign for the presidency, Jacqueline Kennedy wore a slate-gray Givenchy wool shift dress and overblouse with a band of fabric just above the waistline, decorated with a simple bow. It came from Givenchy's ready-to-wear boutique—a democratization of haute couture that was one of the first of its kind. Her Givenchy shift was a model for dress after dress to come, although the fabric became thicker and the colors more daring. What in Audrey Hepburn's look had been *gamine* took on, in the First Lady's interpretation, a patina of timelessness, without ever becoming staid or drab.

In the United States, in the 1960s, showing an allegiance to things French was very different from taking after the British, for Britain was considered part of the national heritage, whereas France, the Louisiana Purchase notwithstanding, was always considered exotic, and also aloof from a shared history. Aloof because France's immigrants had not arrived en masse at Ellis Island. If there were French people to be found in New York and Boston, they were on Park Avenue and Beacon Hill, not on the Lower East Side or in the heart of Brooklyn or the Bronx. The French of Acadia or Louisiana or northern Maine—the poor working-class French who were just as much victims of class prejudice in America as Puerto Ricans or Italians—were not part of the urban American melting-pot story. Jacqueline Kennedy's penchant was not, in any case, for the immigrant Frenchness of her nineteenth-century ancestors; it was for the French of over there, and it never ceased to raise suspicions. The suspicions focused on her clothes, her food, even the furniture she collected for the White House.

The suspicions about her clothes surfaced as early as the presidential campaign, in the form of a declaration of war by John Fairchild, the editor of *Women's Wear Daily*: "Those smart and charming Kennedys—Jacqueline, wife of the senator, and his mother Mrs. Joseph Kennedy, are running for election on the Paris couture fashion tickets. Together the two Kennedys spend $30,000 per year for Paris clothes and hats—more than most U.S. professional buyers."[18]

By the time of the Inauguration events of January 1961, Jacqueline Kennedy had found a solution to her dilemma. An American designer named Oleg Cassini could adapt the French look she loved, ensuring that whatever she wore would be considered American. If she bought a French designer outfit from time to time, people would think it was a Cassini. His presence was important not only in the symbolic realm but in real politics; American clothes meant union-made clothes, and the International Ladies' Garment Workers' Union was a force to be reckoned with.

Of White Russian and Italian descent, born in France and raised in Italy but speaking French as his first language, Cassini was a delicately mustachioed man-about-town, a Seventh Avenue regular excluded from the pantheon of what Fairchild called "the fashion intellectuals."[19] His brother Igor (pen name: Cholly Knickerbocker) wrote the society column for the Hearst newspaper chain, and it was he who had chosen Jackie as Debutante of the Year in 1947. Igor and Oleg were playboys who surrounded themselves with beautiful women, actresses and heiresses, in settings like the El Morocco and the Stork Club. The most prominent women Cassini had dressed were movie stars: his wife Gene Tierney and Grace Kelly. He had learned from the movies, he later wrote, that clothes had to tell a story.[20]

A letter from Jacqueline Kennedy to Oleg Cassini in December 1960, during the inaugural preparations, set the tone for their dealings: playful, flirtatious, and full of French—French phrases, French cultural references—the idea being that Oleg Cassini would be a beard for Jacqueline's French fashion sense, allowing her to become a made-in-the-U.S. French fashion plate:

> I always thought if Jack & I went on an official trip to France I would secretly get Givenchy to design my clothes so I wouldn't be ashamed—but now I know I won't have to—yours will be so beautiful—That is *le plus grand compliment* I can give you—as a designer anyway! XO Jackie.[21]

Cassini became not only her designer but also a keeper of her fashion secrets, protecting her from charges of excessive Francophilia and extravagant spending. He sent the bills directly to her doting father-in-law, Joseph Kennedy, so they would not appear on any official document:

> I refuse to have Jack's administration plagued by fashion stories of a sensational nature—& to be the Marie Antoinette or Josephine of the 1960s—so I will have to go over it with you before we release future things. . . . There just may be a few things we won't tell them about! But if I look impeccable for the next four years everyone will know it is you.[22]

There had been a vast change in Jacqueline Kennedy's tone since she wrote her hesitant letters to the *Vogue* staff in 1951. No longer the dutiful Bouvier daughter or Auchincloss stepdaughter, she was, at age thirty-one, a grande dame, exacting, well informed, with her taste and role models firmly in place:

> Put your brilliant mind to work for a day—Coats—dresses for public appearances—lunch & afternoon that I would wear if Jack were President of FRANCE—très Princesse de Rethy mais jeune.[23]

You would have to have been a regular reader of European society pages to know anything about Liliane, princesse de Rethy, the second wife of former Belgian king Leopold who had the same raven-haired elegance as Jackie. "If Jack were President of FRANCE": Well, at least she didn't say King!

Her letters to Cassini are revealing not only for the sea change in her self-confidence, but for the sense they give of how closely she was following French culture. A January 1962 letter refers to Alain Resnais's film *L'année dernière à Marienbad*. She was ahead of the American public, for *Last Year at Marienbad* wouldn't be released in the United States until March of that year:

> You must see "les Dernieres années à Marienbad" [sic], all chanelish chiffons. I saw a picture of Bardot in one—in Match or Elle in black—but mine could be red, covered up in long sleeves—transparent. That and a drapy dress like jersey would be fun for a change.

During the White House years, she faced the constant challenge of staying connected to the French things she loved without appearing to have abandoned American design—or American garment workers. Now every object she bought, every item of clothing she wore, was analyzed and judged. This was true both of her clothes and of the White House décor. None of it prevented her from devouring French history and novels, or watching avant-garde films.

The cat-and-mouse game between Jacqueline Kennedy and *Women's Wear Daily* continued, with John Fairchild throwing accusations of foreignness and then bowing to the inevitable, so that she became, in his pages, "Her Elegance." Compared to the Bay of Pigs, the Algerian War, and the escalation of U.S. involvement in Vietnam, this was a silly skirmish without much meaning. Except that it said something fundamental about what it meant to be an American in 1960, how rigid the definition was, how unknowing and defensive. A country assuming its status as a world power was still afraid of not being itself.

The gown Jacqueline Kennedy wore to a concert at the Armory the night before the Inauguration was a subtle declaration of identity, in an era when identity was always under the surface of the melting pot. She and Cassini designed it together. The dress was made of satin silk twill, a fabric of sheen and density that is often used for ties because it doesn't wrinkle. The color was white, which she considered the great ceremonial color. The only decorative element was a little knot of fabric placed artfully at one side of the waist, a signifier of France that wouldn't have been recognizable to a casual observer. This was a "cockade" (or rosette), a ribbon tied up into the shape

10. Jacqueline Kennedy and President-Elect John Kennedy en route to the Armory Inaugural Ball (January 21, 1961). Jacqueline is wearing a gown by Oleg Cassini with a French cockade at the waistline. Photograph by Paul Schutzer / Time and Life Images / Getty Images.

of a blooming flower, echoing the decoration first invented by General La-fayette in 1797. The cockade came to symbolize French revolutionary spirit and often reappeared at times of rebellion and resistance: little cockade pins were sold all over the streets of Paris in the week of August 24, 1944, as the Germans were retreating and Leclerc's army was storming the city. Nor was the symbol a stranger to Washington: James Madison, who had been a minister in France after the French revolutionary terror, still sported a cockade on his hat when he entered the White House. That Jacqueline Kennedy should have chosen this discreet sign of Frenchness for this gown, on this night, said something important about her loyalty both to the French part of her own identity and to the historical link of France with the United States. Cassini, who loved military ornament, had wanted to put the cock-ade high on the chest, like a medal, but he dropped it to her waist during the fittings to mark the break from the silk satin overblouse to the overskirt with its train in back. The cockade was almost hidden when she raised her skirt to walk up the steps to the Washington Armory. She was so beautiful in the dress that the soon-to-be sworn-in president asked the driver to turn on the lights in the car so that the people could see Jackie on her way to the musical gala. Not since General Lafayette wore his cockade on his trium-phant return to Washington had the little French symbol made a grander American outing.[24]

Three Days in Paris

By far the best-known chapter in the First Lady's love affair with all things French revolved around her three-day visit to the French capital in June 1961, less than six months into her husband's presidency. "I am the man who accompanied Jacqueline Kennedy to Paris," said her husband at a press conference, after her public relations triumph, and the quotation stuck to her legend. But few Americans know about the letter she wrote to de Gaulle after the trip, which she began by saying she had the impression of hav-ing lived through a dream. She wrote in French, "Everyone has his hero in history. But they are almost always in the past—like Louis XI, Louis XIV, Napoleon—about whom you spoke to me. I had the privilege and honor and the good fortune of meeting mine." She apologized for writing so per-sonally, and hoped he would forgive her French mistakes—of which there were none.[25]

Her fluency was celebrated. When French journalists came to the White House to interview her on the eve of her departure, the *New York Times* speculated in its announcement of the presidential trip that the French wanted to test her skills.[26] Her French wasn't native, but she spoke with the same perfect control she exhibited in English. She pronounced her *r*'s with a gentle whisper, and she knew how to cover up a small uncertainty about the subjunctive, or the order of indirect-direct objects, so that you could hardly hear a mistake.[27] Months of work on the Smith year had taught her to write well, with a classical simplicity, a sincerity that non-native speakers can often bring to French.

In its coverage of the Kennedy trip, *Paris Match* described the first couple as the perfect Franco-American alliance, deploying the classically gendered terms that had prevailed since the Revolution, with the United States playing the role of the masculine cowboy, France the feminine aesthete:

> While he's interested in documents about the Civil War, she studies the French eighteenth century, her great specialty. At the movies, he wants to see action films, like *Alamo* or *Spartacus*. She prefers the "intellectual" films of our avant-garde directors.[28]

During the visit, French newspapers praised the American First Lady on every count, reporting that she had dismissed her official interpreter in order to speak to de Gaulle directly. She had played a large role in planning the events, suggesting a ballet performance at Versailles, since her husband would not understand a play, asking that the trip include museum visits, and specifying that she would like to meet André Malraux and be seated next to him at one meal. She sent ahead a list of French friends to be invited to the various receptions.[29] At the Hôtel de Ville reception, the welcoming event, were the de Renty family, the du Luarts, and numerous de Ganays. Also there was a Bouvier first cousin from Long Island, who was working in Paris and who, with his perfect French, stood in for the Bouvier ancestors.

In a remarkable show of loyalty, she invited Mademoiselle Saleil, the beloved study-abroad director, who had returned to Reid Hall for the 1960–61 season. In January 1962 she would invite her again to an even grander event: a dinner at the White House in honor of Malraux.[30] "This is the woman who taught me to love France." With this phrase she introduced the Smith College professor of French to Malraux, novelist and theorist of the arts, now de Gaulle's minister of culture. It was a mark of affection and an expression of thanks for what neither teacher nor student could have guessed a little more than a decade earlier—that Jacqueline Bouvier's studies under Mademoiselle Saleil's direction were a vital preparation for her starring role on the world stage.[31]

At the Elysée dinner, she was seated according to the strictest protocol, between General de Gaulle and the first in line of succession to the presidency, Gaston Monnerville, the grandson of a slave from Cayenne, a hero of the Resistance, and president of the French Senate. Three years before the passage of the civil rights act in the United States, it was an indication, if only on a symbolic level, that the laws of inclusion and exclusion were different in France. Malraux was seated next to the wife of the U.S. ambassador to France.[32]

Claude de Renty, now Claude du Granrut, was invited to each of the Kennedy events: the City Hall Reception, the dinner at the Elysée Palace, and the gala in the hall of mirrors at Versailles. Claude wore a Dior to Versailles, while Jacqueline wore a Givenchy with a bust of embroidered flowers. On this occasion, only a French couturier would do. The celebrated hairdresser Alexandre de Paris did her hair in a style he named, with a good dose of historical pretension, "Fontanges 1960." It referred to one of Louis XIV's mistresses, the duchesse de Fontanges, who, when her hair got disheveled at the hunt, used to sweep it up with one of her garters. Instead of a garter, Jacqueline's hair was bound with diamond brooches from Van Cleef and Arpels.

Kennedy and de Gaulle disagreed on Algerian independence and a host of other problems, and a few years later the proud French nationalist would ask the American military bases to leave France. For that one night at Versailles, real politics were suspended as the French rehearsed their historic grandeur and the United States played the game of supplicant guest.

The next morning, delighted to respond to an official request, André Malraux escorted Jacqueline Kennedy to the Jeu de Paume, where they stood together contemplating Manet's *Olympia*, that great study of black and white.[33] Malraux was in fragile emotional condition, having just lost his two sons in a car accident. "She's good at talking about books, even the ones she hasn't read," writes Olivier Todd in his 2011 biography of Malraux, perhaps unaware of her career as an editor and the public auction of her personal library of three thousand volumes.[34]

More than one book has been written about Jacqueline Kennedy's successful plot to bring the *Mona Lisa* to Washington and how she enlisted Malraux to secure the precious loan.[35] She remained in regular contact with the French minister of culture after her 1961 visit to France; Malraux, for his part, saw his connection to her as a chance to do de Gaulle's bidding in the realm of the arts.[36] In the dog days of August 1962, Jacqueline wrote a long letter in French to Malraux, which might have been lost for posterity if Malraux's daughter Florence hadn't saved it among her family papers. Jacqueline Kennedy addressed him as "Cher Monsieur le Ministre," an odd form of address that amounted to a common translation of the ordinary American way of starting a letter. ("Monsieur le Ministre et cher ami" is what a French friend might have written.) The letter is astonishing for its spontaneity, for the relaxed tone she allows herself—and for its circumstances.

That August, Jacqueline was vacationing in Italy without the president.[37] The events behind her letter were dramatic. In the wake of a plane crash at Orly that had killed 106 citizens of Atlanta on their return from a museum tour of Europe, Malraux had decided to send the American masterpiece *Whistler's Mother* to the Atlanta Museum, as a memorial to the dead and homage to the city.

Having received news of the loan, she took it upon herself to thank Malraux. But she wrote far from the White House, in her vacation villa at Ravello, on the Amalfi coast, south of Naples. It was unusual for a First Lady to vacation separately from her husband, but even more unusual to communicate with foreign ministers in her own informal handwriting, on resort letterhead.[38] The letter confirms the fact that not far behind the childlike whisper she affected in public—the feathery voice that had become part of her public persona—was a strong and independent woman who intended to keep on living her own life while her husband ran the country—and that life meant time for Europe, time to read, and spaces to retreat from the world of events:

> I'm a bit detached from current events here—the Russian cosmonauts had been in the air for three days before I discovered they were there—a state of affairs which is not without its charms—but neither is it propitious for arranging something as important as your offer of Whistler's Mother to the Atlanta museum.[39]

There are enough mistakes and cross-outs and digressions in this letter to indicate that no secretary, no native speaker of French, no White House official oversaw it or touched it up. She wrote in her round, clear hand, a combination of longhand and printing. Parts of the letter concern questions of protocol: Who should announce the loan of *Whistler's Mother*—Jacqueline, Ambassador Alphen in Washington, or Malraux himself? Parts of the letter are personal, anecdotal: She had always been ashamed of wanting to spend her old age in Florence, and now she knew that she was right. And why should she be ashamed if Whistler had said the same thing? What a pity he wouldn't be there. She was waiting for "La Mère" with the greatest impatience and joy, she said, and she was "proud of that rebellious American who painted it." In the life story of the American artist who had abandoned his country for Europe at the age of twenty-one was the delicate shadow of her own road not taken.

"Que la France est généreuse": she found a charming rhetorical turn—what poets call an apostrophe—to thank not just Malraux, but his country, for their generosity. She signed off by telling the minister of culture that he should be the president of all organizations dedicated to Franco-American friendship. This last remark was a classic diplomatic compliment, a formal and knowing conclusion to an informal, intimate letter of friendship, written in a spirit of joyous complicity. It's in a genre of international diplomacy that was all hers—one example among the many letters she wrote to Malraux and is supposed to have written to de Gaulle as well.[40]

Very few of her letters are available, but this one to Malraux (along with her thank-you note to de Gaulle) gives us insight into Jacqueline Kennedy's communications. Relegated to the sphere of culture and entertainment, she applied herself to her task with dedication, with a lightness of spirit, and with charm. Who is to say, in an era with different expectations for women, whether she could have equaled, in quality and effect, the free-floating cultural ambassadorship she enjoyed.

La Maison Blanche

One of the First Lady's accomplishments in particular marked the Kennedy years as a period of aesthetic achievement, and it too, had a French inflection. Jacqueline Kennedy restored the White House. Not only did she restore it, she made the process of restoration into a public history lesson, and televised her efforts. As with the planning and execution of her wardrobe, she shuttled back and forth between French and American advisers: Sister Parrish was the official designer and Henry Du Pont the historical adviser, but she brought in Stéphane Boudin from a French decorating firm when she wanted advice she trusted.[41] As it turned out, France was present in nearly every room of this most American of houses.

After the British burned the White House during the war of 1812, the mansion was restored by President James Monroe. Monroe had served as minister in Paris for many years and had lived in a showy estate in the north of Paris, in what is now Clichy. Along with Thomas Jefferson, he was the most Francophile of American presidents, with a glamorous New York wife and daughter who spoke French with him at home. He refurbished the White House almost entirely from French sources. Although he wanted mahogany furniture, by the time the order had gone to Paris, Napoleon was ruling and Empire was the reigning style, which meant that gold leaf was added to almost everything he ordered, doubling the cost. Monroe's expenses provoked a financial scandal, which surfaced indirectly during Jacqueline Kennedy's 1961 televised White House tour in the form of a quip by journalist Charles Collingwood: "Empire furniture, not American empire!"

In her televised tour, an enormously successful undertaking with an unprecedented home audience, Jacqueline Kennedy insists, again and again, on the importance of reclaiming, through purchases and donations, the American furniture that might once have belonged in the house. Her goal, she explains, is to contribute to American history, to fill the White House with American furniture, so that Americans understand that "our craftsmen are as good as the Europeans." It is touching to see her refer to a piece of furniture made for Joseph Bonaparte's home in Philadelphia by his cabinet-maker Bellanger—a colleague of her great-great-grandfather Michel Bouvier, though she doesn't mention this.[42] The French radio archives contain a shorter French version of the same tour, recorded on the eve of her 1961 trip to France: Jacqueline shows a remarkable knowledge of specialized French vocabulary for candelabras, chandeliers, and upholstery, and she lingers on paintings by Renoir and Cézanne.[43]

In the American version, the First Lady doesn't dwell on impressionist masterpieces, though Monroe's French candelabras get two long close-ups. Her diction is peculiar, sounding like her husband's Boston drawl ("here" is "he-ah," "china" is "chiner," and so forth). The tour is conventional, even dull, until Collingwood asks her a single, pointed question, about the role of government and the arts. "That's complicated," she answers, in a voice that is soft, but penetrating, and she adds, "The White House should have the most beautiful things." She says it quickly, with conviction. It's the same tone she took with a French journalist who interviewed her for French television during her husband's presidential campaign. Asked if, as the potential future wife of the president, she thought she might help improve French-American relations, she answered, with a laugh, "Je n'ai pas cet orgueil," I'm not that pretentious. It was a beautiful retort, a line that might have come from one of Corneille's tragic heroines or the princesse de Clèves.

French people are often startled, even amused, by the kind of formal language that comes out of the mouths of American students. It's because, especially in Jacqueline's generation, French usually comes to them through the study of literature and not through the language of the street.[44] For most American students of French, until they went on their junior year abroad, there was no French-speaking street, only great books.

Jacqueline Kennedy would always be too French. Her social secretary Letitia Baldrige remembered an irritated JFK phoning her office in the midst of the Bay of Pigs crisis to vent: "He had heard from several congressmen that we were getting too Frenchy and too international, and why weren't we more American, and nobody could read or understand the menus." What the hell was *Potage aux vermicelles,* he wanted to know. Baldrige told him it was "consommé with little things squiggling in it."[45] Kennedy remarked that a few of the Congressmen might understand "consommé," so they should use that word, and change a few other things too. "I just don't want any more persons in this house being too French," she remembered him muttering.[46]

In the Saint-Simon-style sketch that appeared in *Esquire* following the White House tour, Norman Mailer attacked Jacqueline Kennedy from the other side—the bohemian left—of the cultural divide. He thought her taste appallingly middlebrow. Instead of inviting Robert Frost and Sinclair Lewis to the White House, she ought to be bringing Henry Miller and the beat poets. To Mailer's credit, and in the spirit of the subjective New Journalism he had launched, he also confessed his longstanding fascination with Mrs. Kennedy. After they had met at Hyannis Port in 1960, he'd written to her to say that he was planning to write a biography of the marquis de Sade. He had fantasized that this eighteenth-century topic would endear him to her but then realized he had overstepped his bounds, and was confirmed in his fears when she didn't write back and his formal request for an interview was declined. For all his aggression and evident sexism, Mailer is in many ways Jacqueline Kennedy's least condescending analyst. He gives her the benefit of her quiet power and uncanny intelligence; as a figure, she seems to challenge his descriptive powers, bringing out both an aggressive frustration and a tenderness in his own writing, when he refers to "the delicate, muted sensitivity one feels passing across Jackie Kennedy from time to time like a small summer wind in a good garden."[47]

Without a new interview to draw on, Mailer devoted his *Esquire* sketch to a critique of her performance on the televised White House tour, which became an occasion for him to hold forth on America and on the possibility of American history—the country, he complained, was living "in that airless no man's land of the perpetual present," suffering with "no roots by which to project ourselves forward, or judge our trip." The White House tour, which could have helped matters, did the opposite: "it inflicted the past upon us, pummeled us with it, depressed us with facts."[48] If he was attacking Jacqueline Kennedy, it was because he thought he had heard her real voice that afternoon in Hyannis Port—not the childish whisper but the voice full of mischief and challenge. "I like her, I like her still," he wrote, but on the White House tour "she was a phony—it was the cruelest thing one could say, she was a royal phony."

In his 2001 essay, "Jacqueline Kennedy in the White House," Arthur Schlesinger reports that Jacqueline Kennedy privately agreed with Mailer's assessment.[49] It's an intriguing statement that begs some questions. Did she tell Schlesinger as much after watching herself on television in 1961, or was she thinking back to her White House persona later in life, when she had come into her own power? Schlesinger doesn't say. But whether it was in the 1960s or much, much later, her critical distance from her own performance was true to her character.

Editing

No memory of the thousand days that Jacqueline Kennedy spent as First Lady—neither her glittering artistic dinners nor her adventures in historic restoration, her travels, her elegant persona—will ever equal the place she will hold in history riding in an open car next to her husband in Dallas, on November 22, 1963. There is a famous photo of her sitting in another open car, in another Chanel suit with covered buttons, gazing upon her husband with a knowing affection, as he gazes back. These are the before-and-after images that split the American century in two.

About her demeanor, and the funeral she organized, Charles de Gaulle is often quoted, in American sources, as saying that "Jacqueline Kennedy gave an example to the whole world of how to behave." The anecdotes on the French side are different. De Gaulle is supposed to have told his closest friends, referring to the heroine of Racine's best-known tragedy, that Jacqueline Kennedy was "Andromaque for a day." In their private audience at the White House, she took a daisy from a nearby bouquet and handed it to the French president, wanting suddenly to show him her appreciation.[50] The gesture has the ring of truth, for it echoes the simple gesture of affection in her short story about a grandfather's funeral, "The Violets."

Her grace consisted in her ability to move with an equal sense of what mattered and to whom, from the public funeral, with its historic symbolism and ceremony, to the most private rituals. In her husband's tomb she placed a letter, a piece of scrimshaw, and letters from her two children to their father. Her youngest son was barely old enough to write.

Several months later, Jacqueline Kennedy sat in her Georgetown home for seven interviews with Arthur Schlesinger, Jr. She spoke for posterity, as a witness to her husband's presidency. The tape recordings were sealed and deposited in the Kennedy Library. In these conversations, Jacqueline Kennedy is fiercely loyal and irreverent, delighting in political gossip with Schlesinger. Though he has little interest in her role, she lets him know that she translated ten books for Kennedy about the French Empire. That she fed her husband lines from de Gaulle's memoirs to nourish his speeches, and he took her advice (de Gaulle's "All my life, I have had a certain idea of France" became, in Kennedy's 1960 announcement of his candidacy, "I have developed an image of America . . ."). But 1964 was also a high point for American irritation with Gaullist nationalism. Only a year earlier, de Gaulle had vetoed England's entry into the European Common Market, for fear of American influence. Now, after Kennedy's death, Jacqueline recalls her husband's annoyance with de Gaulle and escalates her own. De Gaulle may once have been her hero, a rhetorical model, and a courtly host, but he had become "that spiteful man." She was squarely in her husband's camp: "You know, basically [JFK] didn't like the French, and I loathe the French." She wanted her children to experience that marvelous way a foreign language had "doubled [her] life," but it was Spanish, the language of our hemisphere, she wanted them to learn. Was she disavowing her past? Or did she feel the need to underline how loyal she was—not too French after all?[51]

Five years later, she took off her mantle as widow to marry for a second time. Whatever the public imagined, her escape from the United States was far from frivolous: She left the country with her children two months after the assassination of Robert Kennedy, retreating to the armored world of the Greek shipping magnate, who offered freedom from her role and protection for her children. In addition to his other real estate on land and sea, Onassis had an apartment on the avenue Foch and his own special table at Maxim's.

Jacqueline Bouvier Kennedy, now Jacqueline Kennedy Onassis, crossed over to what many considered the dark side of her cosmopolitanism. She became, in the public mind, a socialite and a jet setter, more European than American. It appeared as though she were purposefully embracing every suspicion every Congressman had ever had about her—"too French and too international," exchanging her Massachusetts preppy for a Greek satyr.

The marriage lasted for seven years, through rumors of estrangement, until Onassis's death in 1975. Then a new phase began. It is tempting to understand this as her "authentic" phase, giving credence to an idea that was in the air in the 1980s and that Carolyn Heilbrun wrote about so convincingly in her book *Writing a Woman's Life*: a woman's true life begins after age 50, when she lives less for her husband's career and more for herself. "It is perhaps only in old age, certainly past 50, that women can stop being female impersonators."[52] The idea of women as female impersonators has a history. Everyone in New York remembered Truman Capote's 1975 article in *Esquire*, "La Côte Basque," an exercise in scurrilous gossip about the rich ladies of Manhattan in which he observes Jacqueline Onassis and her sister Lee having lunch at the celebrated French restaurant. He refers to Jackie, in the "phony" tradition begun by Norman Mailer, as someone so typed and hyped that all that was left of her was "an impersonation of herself."[53] Gloria Steinem, in a classic essay on feminism, suggests that women have something to learn from watching female impersonators, who could teach them "the many ways in which we have been trained to be female impersonators, too."[54]

In 1975, at the age of forty-six—just four years shy of the mythical threshold—Jacqueline Onassis took her first job in New York publishing.

It was in some ways as though the long delayed job at *Vogue* could finally begin. Her initial position was as an acquisitions editor for Viking, but when Viking published a novel based on the fictional assassination of Ted Kennedy, she quit in protest and took a job at Doubleday, where she thrived. Here, in her work with authors, she could put into practice her own aesthetic activism, and she became the person she had fantasized about in her essay for *Vogue*: "a sort of Overall Art Director of the Twentieth Century, watching everything from a chair hanging in space"—in an even more immediate way than when she had remodeled the White House and learned to say, "that's so complicated!" if anyone asked her a risky question.

The men who first hired her imagined her as a magnet for celebrity authors, the kind of useful acquisitions editor whose charm could turn a lunch conversation into a contract. She worked her way up through the system, starting with a windowless cubicle like any junior editor, then advancing to an office with a window, and eventually getting a small Xerox machine and the freedom to pursue projects of her own design.[55]

It turned out she was serious about the work itself. She had a discerning eye, an infallible sense of structure, which had been apparent in her courses on the short story at George Washington University and in her *Vogue* prize essays. She held her authors to standards that could make historical subjects accessible and appealing. She neither competed with them nor harangued them nor thought she was necessarily right. Her colleagues were surprised, for she was not supposed to be this good.

She relied on her taste, her contacts, her knowledge of culture in acquiring manuscripts, and, as a result, many of the books she edited had a direct or indirect connection to her past. In 1985 she published art historian Olivier Bernier's *Secrets of Marie Antoinette,* an edition of the queen's letters. Bernier introduces the letters by evoking the famous scene on the Rhine, where the young Austrian princess, that ancestor of all women students abroad, is stripped of her garb by the severe duchesse de Noailles, who dresses her for the French court. The duchesse de Noailles's twentieth-century descendent was Sabine de Noailles, one of Jacqueline's friends in the Faubourg Saint-Germain. (Sabine is the sweet young girl in the other black gown, gazing at young Jacqueline Bouvier in the photograph taken at the Restaurant Ledoyen in 1950.) In 1991 came *The Diary of a Napoleonic Foot Soldier*— not at Waterloo, like her great grandfather Michel Bouvier, but in the wilds of Russia.

She encouraged her stepfather's cousin Louis Auchincloss to write a novel narrated by a fictional duc de Saint-Simon, which he dedicated to her with this inscription, "For Jacqueline Kennedy Onassis who persuaded me that Versailles was still a valid source for fiction." Three years later, Onassis published Auchincloss's *False Dawn,* his portraits of women in the age of the Sun King. She had challenged him to make every chapter a novel, to imagine the people in their settings, from her favorite, Louis XIV's cousin "La Grande Mademoiselle" with her "big red nose and ungainly walk," to Madame de Maintenon, the king's pious mistress whose bad reputation had been long sealed by Saint-Simon's catty memoirs.[56] We can imagine the sympathy Jacqueline Kennedy Onassis must have felt for Auchincloss's effort to restore dignity and grace to a woman whose own letters told a very different story than had Saint-Simon. "Once one has dispelled the myths about Madame de Maintenon and settled down to enjoy her," Auchincloss wrote, "there is considerable pleasure to be derived. . . . She strips Versailles of its glamour; she goes straight to essentials. She is never impressed with the great world. She is never vulgar."[57]

From time to time, Jacqueline Onassis's own literary voice emerged in one of the books she acquired. The short introduction she contributed in 1979 to a collection by the turn-of-the-century photographer Eugène Atget shows the same writerly qualities she had had since girlhood as well as a sensibility born of three decades of reading and travel in France:

> In the city parks we feel Atget's humanity. He photographs with tenderness and melancholy. In the Tuileries, the park chair, as French as the croissant, lies overturned beside a leering faun. In the Luxembourg, the fountain has become a family gathering place. We find these photographs troubling because we can connect to them. The time is bourgeois here, and our grandfathers sit in black serge suits along the paths laid out by kings and queens.[58]

She had never written so beautifully, with such measure and economy, gesturing delicately to the reader with a few well-chosen details. "We find these photographs troubling": "troubling" is a Gallicism; in French it comes from the poets and playwrights of her favorite seventeenth century, from the romantic frustrations in *L'Astrée,* the pastoral novel she studied in her senior year—and from Racine. It means perturbing to the soul, confusing. She understands the layers of the city, the way that paths laid by kings are now trodden by ordinary folk. As you look at Atget's pictures of middle-class men in their suits, you can begin to see the shine on the worn fabric. True to Jacqueline Onassis's sense of the world, she has zeroed in on cloth as a sign of social class.

Although French subjects were far from her unique preoccupation, one could summarize her contribution to American letters of the period by saying that she made the seventeenth and eighteenth centuries in France, and especially the lives of aristocratic women, come to life, not by making them more glamorous, but by bringing them down to size.

The last book she edited was a history of Paris after the Liberation—her Paris. The authors were the British couple Antony Beevor and Artemis Cooper. Cooper was the granddaughter of one of the most sensational couples of mid-century British society: Duff Cooper, British ambassador to France in the late 1940s, and his wife, the great beauty Lady Diana Cooper. Duff Cooper had shared a mistress—the writer Louise de Vilmorin—with André Malraux, Jacqueline's partner in artistic exchange. During her junior year in Paris, Jacqueline had visited Louise de Vilmorin's famous blue salons at Verrières-le-Buisson, thanks to her Vassar connection to Vilmorin's daughter Jessica. Lunchtime conversation between Jacqueline Onassis and the Beevor-Coopers would have been enlivened by these connections; her publication of their book might have been considered the fruit of her social network. At the same time, *Paris after the Liberation* was a smart acquisition, since Artemis Cooper had access to her grandfather's as yet unpublished journals, which gave an uncensored and often hilarious bird's-eye view of diplomatic life in Liberation-era Paris, including excruciatingly dull evenings with Charles and Yvonne de Gaulle, attempts to keep the Duke of Windsor from making horrendous political gaffes, and scenes of the desperate trade in cigarette butts outside the Hôtel Ritz.[59]

Remembering their work with Jacqueline Onassis, Beevor told a British journalist that he had expected a vapid fashion icon and found "a smart woman who took her role as editor at Doubleday seriously." He and Cooper were trying to finish their book for the fiftieth anniversary of the Liberation, but there was something wrong with the final chapter. They were both stumped: "We sent it to Jackie, and this was three weeks before she died, so she was very ill indeed, and she put her finger on it straight away. . . . She said, 'what you've got to do is bring your three themes together in a crescendo where they come together naturally.'"[60]

76 :

Chapter Two

Paris after the Liberation ends with a short chapter entitled "Recurring Fevers," referring to communism, Gaullism, and artistic and literary movements—projecting forward through each of these themes from 1944 to 1949 to the events of May 1968, which mark, for the authors, the failure of radical thought to "overcome the bourgeoisie." Whether or not Onassis agreed with them, she had helped them find an ending that put their own political perspective into sharp focus, that drew them out of charming anecdote and observation into an assessment of the world born of the Liberation. It was the kind of ending that readers could argue over and that made the book not just a finely drawn portrait but a statement.

Her friends from the publishing world like to tell about the time a guard at the Century Club was preparing to scold a woman who was sitting on the grand staircase in the entry. As he approached, he realized it was Mrs. Onassis, lost in a book.[61] The anecdote is all the more satisfying since women were admitted to the club only in 1987, after a fierce legal battle. There she was at the threshold, bucking convention, and probably too absorbed in the pleasure of reading even to realize she was bucking convention. This was Jacqueline Bouvier in the last two decades of her life.

Retracing Her Steps

Biographers are content when life comes full circle, when they can gesture back to early themes and see them realized. Sartre, in *The Words,* joked that every biography of a great man inscribes his talent in earliest childhood: "All I saw was colors!" says the young Raphael when asked about his visit to the pope.[62] For Jacqueline Kennedy Onassis, there is actually some truth in the matter. France and the French language constituted a thread through her life from her grandfather's early stories to the books she edited, to her everyday life in the early 1990s. Her last companion was Maurice Tempelsman, who had grown up in Brooklyn in a French-speaking family of Belgian Jewish immigrants, and had risen to prominence in the diamond industry. He was her trusted financial adviser, then her friend, sharing her passion for literature and the arts. They spoke French together. In 1993, a year before her death, the two of them retraced the steps of her junior year abroad, her summer trip with Claude to the Gorges du Tarn; then to the Rhône, the region of her Bouvier ancestors; all the way to the magic place she had dreamed about as a twenty-year-old.[63] "The part I want to see is La Camargue," she had written

: 77

home from France in the fall of 1949; "they have a ceremony where they all wade in on horses and bless it—La Bénédiction de la Mer." The townspeople of Sainte-Marie-de-la-Mer, in the Camargue, still wade into the sea once a year, armed with their statue of Saint Sarah, and bless the water. In the same town, the bulls come out for the annual corrida, wearing cockades between their horns.

She wrote to Claude from the Concorde, "the space age plane" taking her home: "You can't imagine what happened last week—It brought me so close to you. The years telescoped and it seemed only a moment ago, our summer trip through l'Auvergñe." She and Maurice had traveled by barge in the Gorges du Tarn, and she had found herself on the banks of a strangely familiar deserted hamlet, La Croze. Suddenly it came back: she remembered Claude's aunt, Madame de la Romiguière, who had welcomed them there in the summer of 1950, and she made sure to place a phone call to the elderly woman from her hotel. La Croze was her madeleine, bringing back the young women she and Claude had been, "both of us full of interest in the world, waiting to discover it and our lives."

Though she vowed to come to Paris more often, her letter had the feeling of a good-bye, including the affectionate quip at the end, typical of Jackie: "Much love dear Claude, and thank you for the trip in the Panhard of long ago. I remember your shouting 'Pauvre con' at some poor man you were running down in the streets of some town!"

Jacqueline Onassis was sixty-three years old. She was thinner than usual, the cleft of her collar bones deep, but despite her fragility—the first signs of her cancer—she had the same inimitable profile, the same sporty perfection as always. She had abandoned the armored suits of the Kennedy era for comfortable slacks and sweaters. The familiar scarves she tied around her neck, the big dark glasses, protected her from the insult of cameras as much as from the sun. Her life, in the end, had brought her closer to her 1949–50 Paris classmates, distinguished women who had pursued careers along with marriage and children: Mary Ann Hoberman, the poet, won award after award for her inventive children's books, Marjorie Flory, the junior Phi Beta Kappa scholar, was an editor at *Reader's Digest*, Martha Rusk, the close friend who visited Dachau with Jacqueline in 1950, was an English teacher and fund raiser. Brenda Gilchrist was an editor of art books, an artist and illustrator. Through the privilege of their education, their sense of adventure, they had beaten the odds of the 1950s stereotypes.

Jacqueline Onassis died in 1994, barely a year after her last French trip, surrounded by her family in the privacy of her Fifth Avenue apartment. The woman who had arranged so many funerals was given a quiet funeral mass, to the French melodies of Fauré and Duruflé and César Franck. Her son spoke first, explaining that the family had struggled to choose readings that captured her essence: "her love of words, the bonds of home and family, and her spirit of adventure." In his eulogy, Ted Kennedy reflected on her privacy, recalling "her unbearable sorrow, endured in the glare of a million lights." No eulogy would have been complete without a reference to her brilliant French persona. Kennedy remembered his older brother joking with the French ambassador's wife at a state dinner: "Jackie speaks fluent French," Jack had quipped, "but I only understand one out of every five words she says—and that word is de Gaulle."[64]

As was to be expected, the French—for whom commemoration is an art form—bade farewell to Jacqueline Bouvier Kennedy Onassis as if she were one of them. Valéry Giscard d'Estaing, former president of the republic, recited for French radio his most intense memory of Jacqueline Kennedy, walking into the hall of mirrors at Versailles on the arm of de Gaulle: it was, he said, one of the most beautiful things imaginable, youth and glory side by side. She might have been amused that her old friend from Paris had paired her off, in French national memory, not with her husband or even with gallant Malraux, but with the elderly French president whose tactics had so annoyed her.[65]

As for her own wishes for commemoration, her sense of mischief never failed her, even about the cult figure she had become. "Sell everything" she is quoted as telling her children; "you'll make a lot of money."[66] Onto the auction block went every French book, every knickknack from her Fifth Avenue apartment, illustrated programs from productions of the Ballets Russes, books on châteaux and decorative arts, on Versailles, biographies of Proust and Victor Hugo and Wharton and James and Malraux and Napoleon and Madame de Lafayette, her copy of Major Bouvier's *Our Forebears*. Someone thought it was worth paying $42,500 for her book of French verb conjugations, complete with schoolgirl sketches of elegant ladies.[67]

I first visited Claude de Renty, Jacqueline Bouvier's host sister, in 2007. Claude was now Claude du Granrut. Her husband, a distinguished lawyer and former head of the Paris bar, was the son of a Resistance fighter who, like Claude's father, had been killed by the Nazis. Both were active in defending the memory of the Resistance. When her children were grown, Claude had entered politics—local, regional, and European. She served as assistant mayor of the town of Senlis and as a trustee of Mount Holyoke College, where she had spent her own year abroad the year before Jacqueline Bouvier came to stay in her mother's Paris apartment. She had stayed in touch with Jacqueline throughout their lives and had attended her funeral in New York.

I sat at the kitchen table of Claude's country house in Senlis as she stood at the stove, a powerful woman in taupe silk, concocting a perfect hollandaise sauce for the first spring asparagus. She talked about her own education at Sciences Po, her political career, her aspirations for Europe, her memories of Jacqueline:

> Her letters to us were perfunctory during the first years: birth announcements, formal things like that. But in the last years they became warmer, much more expansive. . . . "It was the happiest year of my life," she wrote me about the time she spent with us. Throughout everything, the years of glory and the years of distress, her memory of France was a little corner, an agreeable little corner where she was free.

Claude showed me the album she had prepared to send to Jacqueline's grandchildren, Rose and Tatiana and Jack, composed of all the snapshots she had saved of Jacqueline on their road trip in 1950. The best one is a close-up of Jacqueline on the banks of the Loire, on their last picnic. She's wearing shorts and waving a bottle, with what looks like a big piece of baguette wedged between her teeth. More than the elegant picture in the black strapless ball gown at Paul de Ganay's party, this casual snapshot captures something precious—the spirit of an American girl in France who still had the luxury of hamming for the camera.

Chapter Two

THREE

Susan Sontag

1957–1958

If Jacqueline Bouvier's France is outside her, a kingdom of forms, an aesthetic longing, Susan Sontag's is all interiors, an exploration of self, a zone of intense sexual freedom and discovery. Jacqueline Bouvier's imaginary Paris is the Parc de Sceaux, the Luxembourg Gardens; it is any number of perfectly manicured spaces where the young American student could dream her own dreams as she walked along what she would later call "the geometric paths laid out by kings." Susan Sontag's Paris is tiny maid's rooms up seven flights of stairs, cheap hotels, and smoky cafés. Two tall, dark beauties with thick manes of hair, one fine boned, the other a pillar of vitality. One with an odd indifference to her beauty, performing it effortlessly from her earliest youth; the other tortured, self-conscious, struggling to reconcile body and mind. That their relationship to their bodies, the image they projected to the world, couldn't have been more different is obvious even in their hygiene. While Jacqueline Bouvier worried about the whiteness of her teeth and avoiding stubble on her calves, Susan Sontag had to remind herself to wash. Her "to-do list" from 1957, written on the eve of her departure for Europe, includes this admonition: "Shower every other night."[1] The favorite novel of Sontag's youth, Djuna Barnes's 1937 *Nightwood*, was set in an expatriate Paris made to order for her deepest longings, and it sang the nobility of dirt: "The French have made a detour of filthiness—Oh the good dirt! Where you [Americans] are of a clean race, of a too eagerly washing people, and this leaves no road for you."[2] Sontag knew, by the time she was sixteen, which road she would take, and it led her, in the course of eight short years, from Arizona to Paris.

Longing

The vast difference between her Paris and Jacqueline Bouvier's was due to much more than the passage of time between 1949 and 1958. It was a difference of privilege, of disposition, and of longing.

For Susan Sontag there was no junior year abroad. As in so many aspects of her life, she got herself to Europe on her own steam. She had dreamed of making the trip since she was seventeen. When she finally went, she was twenty-four, married, with a five-year-old son. Neither husband nor child went with her.

The draft of a short story she began to write in France sometime in early 1958 gives a clue, not to what really happened, but to the feelings and memories of her marriage that she was able to draw on after she took leave of her family. In the fictional conversation between her two married characters, both academics, a husband tells his wife that they can live in Europe as soon as they get grants together. It will never happen, the wife replies, she is sick of waiting, sick of promises of next year and next year and next year:

> "We'll sit in this rat hole on our asses growing eminent and middle-aged and paunchy—"
> She stopped, aware that it was not "we" she meant, and that this attack was entirely unprovoked.

As soon as the narrator gets on board the ship, her passion returns:

> She felt a savage desire to come to Europe, and all the myths of Europe echoed in her mind. Corrupt Europe, tired Europe, amoral Europe. She,

who had been used to being precocious, at twenty-four felt stupidly lumpishly innocent, and she wanted that innocence to be violated. I have lived in a dream of innocence, she whispered to herself as she watched the wrinkled moon-spattered ocean night after night on the boat. My innocence makes me weep.[3]

There's an echo here of Henry James—the heavy innocence of the American—of Fitzgerald's dangerous Europe and James Baldwin's Europe as a place of savage desire, a place of immorality and hence, for the outsider, of moral freedom. Jacqueline Bouvier had hinted at the dangerous pleasures of Europe, but for her the hint was merely a trope, a turn of phrase she used to turn down her *Vogue* Paris prize. Sontag was serious. With her lovely metaphor, the "wrinkled moon-spattered ocean," she gives a glimpse of the writer to come, waiting to shed her scholar's cocoon in the only place that would let her.

Reading Gide in Tuscon

Sontag was born Susan Rosenblatt in New York in 1933, in the depths of the great depression. Her father was a fur salesman; he died on a sales trip to China when she was five. Susan suffered from asthma, which may be why her mother moved the family of three—herself, Susan, and her younger sister Judith—to Arizona.

She told the French writer Chantal Thomas that the hot dry skies, the unpaved streets of her early childhood, her widowed mother, lethargic and depressed and addicted to alcohol, stretched out on the sofa, paying paltry attention to her daughters, made her dream of the energy of cities, of New York and Paris, from the time she could read—at the age of three. One of the first books she read was a biography of Marie Curie, who became her idol. Before she discovered literature, she dreamed of becoming a scientist or a doctor; childhood, she decided, was something to get over with.[4] Judith, three years younger, seems to have been too young to provide a hedge against her loneliness. When Susan was thirteen, her mother remarried and moved the family to Los Angeles. The new husband was a military man, Nathan Sontag; the children took his last name. Nothing that Susan Sontag has written gives the sense that her stepfather was difficult or unkind. Her mother, on the other hand, remained mercurial and violent. It is difficult to imagine Susan as she must have been in 1947, a reader of Gide and Rilke at North Hollywood High in an era of sock hops and drive-in movies. With her head in the classics, her eyes on Europe, she was already separated from her milieu by an imagined century and an imagined continent. She hurried through high school and left home definitively when she was fifteen, attended UCLA briefly, then Berkeley, then the University of Chicago—a wunderkind, graduating three years ahead of herself at age eighteen. Her ambition, from one university to the next, was to recreate herself: to become the person she later called "a self-Europeanized American."[5]

Her intellectual mission coincided with her sexual awakening. At Berkeley, in the summer session of 1949, she met the person who is called, in the posthumously published diaries edited by her son, "H."—the discreet abbreviation for Harriet Sohmers, an Upper-East-Side New York rebel she met at the U Cal Textbook Exchange and who, as a pickup line, asked her if she had read the lesbian cult classic *Nightwood*.[6] Harriet introduced Susan to the lesbian and gay bar scene in San Francisco: to the Tin Alley, the 299, 12 Adler, the P.D., the Red Lizzard (a men's gay bar). Euphoric writing came to Sontag with the realization that she could live a life of sexual passion, that she wasn't condemned to teaching, or library work—the assumption being that the life of the mind excluded bodily pleasures. "Everything begins from now" she wrote on May 31, 1949, "I am reborn." Her diaries record drunken nights, the ecstasy of sexual abandon, with Harriet as her mentor.

"Femme to H and butch to L," she notes, as she tries different women, different sexual roles.[7] In her diary, she makes lists of gay terminology by theme: the names of bars, the slang for sexual roles and types—as though the homosexual world were another country, for which she was drawing a map. Throughout her life, she would enter a new world by recording its contours, its manners, its important people, creating her own grammar in the form of lists. It's the system she used to write her undergraduate literature papers, the system she used again when she got to Paris. Even her brief attempt at drafting an autobiography was in the form of lists.

Aside from the lists that dominate so many of her notebooks, Sontag's journals abound in portraits—physically vivid, sociologically astute, and often mocking. She liked to pick up on a flaw, a silly physical trait. Typical of this genre is a sketch of Anaïs Nin that a young Susan Sontag wrote during her time at Berkeley after attending a lecture given by the writer in San Francisco. She focused on Nin's voice:

She shines and polishes each syllable with the very tip of her tongue and teeth—one feels that if one were to touch her, she would crumble into silver dust. Her theory of art was preciously intangible (discovery of the unconscious, automatic writing, revolt against our mechanistic civilization).[8]

As a young woman, she could be hard on older women intellectuals, from Anaïs Nin to Simone de Beauvoir, but there was one woman writer who never garnered her scorn. This was Djuna Barnes, the American in 1920s Paris who became Sontag's literary mascot—her imaginary escort to intellectual and erotic life in Paris. She writes about *Nightwood* for the first time in April 1949:

> That is the way I want to write—rich and rhythmic—heavy, sonorous prose that befits those mythic ambiguities that are both source and structure to an aesthetic experience symbolized by language.[9]

These are heady thoughts for a girl barely out of high school, echoing the dogma then in vogue—the rhetorical criticism of Kenneth Burke, the archetypal criticism of Northrop Frye—that she was inhaling at an astonishing rate, in and out of class.[10] This single sentence on Barnes shows a feature that would emerge as Sontag's great strength as a critic: the ability to adapt a style, a metalanguage, to make new ideas seductive and powerful, so that the reader wants to understand the newness that their author has mastered. At the same time as *Nightwood* was entering her literary pantheon, she and her friends considered their romantic entanglements a parody of Barnes's world:

> I found myself sitting with three women: one named C, a lawyer, around 34 years old, "distingué" as H kept repeating, born and brought up in California, who had a fake British accent which periodically became noticeable and then was snatched back into her unconscious, and a Crosley car. . . . H told me she'd lived with her for two months, until C bought a gun and threatened to shoot them both. . . . The other two women were a couple named Florence and Roma . . . H had had an affair with Florence . . . At one point C began to laugh and asked us if we realized what a parody of *Nightwood* all this was. . . . It was, of course, and I had, with much amusement, thought of that many times before.[11]

Nightwood revolves around a trio of female lovers and the freakish, omniscient, transvestite gynecologist who narrates their impossible passion. And although this highly unrealistic novel ranges geographically from the unnamed woods of North America to decadent aristocratic settings in Italy and Vienna, its French center is recognizable and specific: the Place Saint-Sulpice in the sixth arrondissement of Paris; more specifically, the Café de la Mairie, still a great spot for people watching, with its chairs spilling out onto the sidewalk, and the little Hôtel Récamier, once a typical bargain Parisian hotel. The experimental writer Georges Perec chose the Place Saint-Sulpice for one of his famous observations in the literary exercise he called "An Attempt at Exhausting a Place in Paris." In October 1974, he sat in three different cafés on the Place and recorded what he saw and heard: pigeons, numbered buses, church bells, women with grocery bags, the most banal signs and signals imaginable.[12] For Barnes, the Place was the backdrop for extravagant tropical interiors, wild drunken stalking, and oversized emotions. In the most famous chapter of *Nightwood,* entitled "Watchman, What of the Night?" Barnes left the realm of fiction for argument, polemic, praising Europe and life after dark over American orderliness. For Sontag, Barnes's novel acted as an invitation to visit Paris, to drink in that café and sleep in that hotel, to abandon American daytime certainties for nighttime European delirium. Which is exactly what she did—after a significant American detour.

Humanities

In the fall of 1949, Sontag left her social and sexual laboratory in Northern California for a more scholarly and competitive environment in the Midwest. She was accepted as a junior at the University of Chicago. She thought Chicago was the ugliest city she had ever seen. As she waited for her dorm room assignment, and with no social circle, she had plenty of time on her hands to contemplate her future.

There was a hint in her San Francisco diaries, a kind of premonition one can only measure in hindsight, about the surprising turn her life would take in Chicago in just a few months. Though the friends whose comments she quotes aren't identified by name—one is a man, "F," and the other simply "E"—the knowing quality of their exhortation gives the impression that they're speaking to her from personal experience:

Your only chance of being normal is to call a halt right now: No more women, no more bars. You know that it will be the same thing in Chicago—in the dorm, in school, or in the gay bars. . . . Go out with a couple of men at the same time. Park and let them feel you plus have their little pleasures. You won't like it at all at first, but force yourself to do it . . . it's your only chance. And during that time don't see any women. If you don't stop now . . . [13]

If she didn't stop, she could never stop! It's impossible to tell from her diary if her friends' admonitions were tongue-in-cheek, menacing, or merely strategic. She did try a few boys in California, and wrote, with a mixture of relief and regret, that bisexuality was not an option; she knew who she was.

And yet her San Francisco friends' warnings about the homosexual temptation continued to dog her in those first lonely months in Chicago. In a bookstore, she thumbed through William Stekel's *The Homosexual Neurosis* and recorded in her diary its theory that all humans were originally bisexual. The theory, she added, had been successfully put into practice only once in world history—by the Greeks. And the Greeks, in the intellectual world of the University of Chicago, were the center of the universe.

The *coup de théâtre* came a year later, in the form of a one-liner on December 2, 1950: "Last night, or was it early this morning?—I am engaged to Philip Rieff."[14] Three months into her third semester at Chicago, after a ten-day courtship, she married her sociology instructor, an Anglophile Jewish intellectual with the looks and manners of an Oxford don. He worked on Freud. "A bleeder," she called him, after their marriage had gone bad—"an emotional totalitarian," needy and depressive.[15] Everything that was dark and intense in her was wan and proper in him. Their intellectual connection was, by her own description, overwhelming. In one of her short stories, a barely disguised portrait of her married academic life, she describes a couple so intent on conversation that the husband followed his wife into the bathroom so as not to interrupt the flow of ideas.[16] This is not a standard honeymoon complaint. Sontag had had platonic relationships before with male friends, substituting for the sexual realm a vigorous exchange of ideas. Rieff, who was several steps ahead of her in the university hierarchy, introduced the precocious undergraduate to the world of intellectuals with diplomas and teaching positions. His own friends never quite understood what had brought the couple together: "Did you hear," the famous quip goes, "Philip has married an Indian."[17]

No one who has read the first volume of Sontag's diaries can fail to be struck by the strange disconnection between her joyous acknowledgment of lesbian sexuality in San Francisco and her Chicago marriage to Rieff. It was, as the French might say, "like a hair on the soup" (*comme un cheveu sur la soupe*). She doesn't say in her journal that she is climbing the social ladder, or that she is afraid of failing at the university without a male consort who doubles as a mentor, or that the intellectual intensity she enjoys with Rieff compensates for a lack of sexual passion, or that it's nice to be adored. There is just this cryptic phrase: "I marry Philip with full consciousness plus fear of my will toward self-destructiveness."[18] Only a few lines in a letter to a college friend the previous spring break give a hint of the financial drama behind her decision:

> My mother is finally and completely penniless after all these years of anticipa-
> tion—My father's estate is no more, Uncle Claudius having this past month
> definitely lost the whole business (through drink, horses, mis-management,
> chorus girls and bank fraud). He needs all his money to keep from going to
> jail—there is no more for us. The consequences of this: my mother must
> go to work and will probably have to sell the house. I should work this next
> quarter, certainly this summer and next school year, and unless I retain my
> scholarship, I cannot return to Chicago. The direct consequences are that if
> I can get there myself, through earnings, scholarship, or whatever—I go to
> Europe in fifteen months—just get my BA and run![19]

There were very few study abroad programs available to an American student in 1950. She might have applied to Smith, or Sweet Briar, or Sarah Lawrence, if she had known the possibility existed. But she was moving too fast from one institution to another, and, more important, there was no money for anything extra—she was dependent on her Chicago scholarship and whatever support she could get on the side. She worried again in May of her junior year: "My comp [comprehensive exam] performance is really mediocre: the price of my folly will be postponing Europe."[20] The desire to get to Europe was foremost on her mind in the months before her marriage: "If I can get there myself, through earnings, scholarship, or whatever—I go to Europe in fifteen months." Instead, she married, and her dream of living in Europe was reduced to a transatlantic wedding trip with Philip in July and August 1951, after her graduation.[21]

Sontag's most significant literary achievement as an undergraduate was her term paper on Barnes's *Nightwood* for Humanities 3B, important enough to generate several entries in her diary. Written in her junior year, the spring of her mother's financial crisis, it was tantamount to an imaginary form of expatriation for a student who felt grounded, as well as a form of nostalgia for the homosexual life she was hoping to put behind her but couldn't—she had just been with Harriet on her winter break in New York. The paper was her opportunity to reread the queer novel from a cooler academic point of view, to see what remained. Her college copy of *Nightwood* (conserved in the UCLA archives) is full of marginalia, some in her hand, some in Philip Rieff's. At some unknown date she had allowed her husband to mark the novelistic territory that had once belonged to Harriet.[22]

The student of literary criticism at the University of Chicago had lost none of her enthusiasm for *Nightwood*. As she would do again and again in her controversial career, she began an argument by taking issue with an intellectual giant. This time it was T. S. Eliot, the poet and critic whose foreword had launched *Nightwood* in 1937 and who was responsible for its publication. Eliot connected the novel's "quality of horror and doom" to the tradition of Elizabethan tragedy. For Sontag, there was nothing tragic about *Nightwood*, and nothing Elizabethan:

> Horror and doom do pervade *Nightwood*, but I would suggest that, stylistically, the book is much closer to the fin-de-siècle writers like Huysmans or Wilde. *Nightwood's* [illegible word] and passion have no affinity to the "wholesomeness" of an Elizabethan tragic plot; it is Pater's style, rather than Marlowe's or Webster's, that Miss Barnes' hyper-conscious refinement of perception resembles. Whereas, in English Renaissance tragedy, the doomed characters are unambiguously exalted by defeat and death, the subject of *Nightwood* is dissolution, and moreover, as we shall see, the paradox inherent in dissolution.[23]

Much has been written about Sontag's precocity, which is in full evidence here, along with a dose of pedantry. She is right that Barnes's hallucinatory style has more in common with the decadent writers of the turn of the century than with any Elizabethan tragedy; Eliot's comparison is an odd one. She is right, too, that the decadence, the physical dissolution, even the animalistic combat of the final pages of *Nightwood*, unrealistic and barely

Susan Sontag: 1957–1958

decipherable, have a triumphant, almost orgasmic feel rather than a tragic one. She argued that through the force of its language, *Nightwood* succeeded in making something noble from what was dissolute and debased, and something high from what was low.

She had chosen none other than Kenneth Burke as adviser for the paper. Burke was a revered figure at Chicago and most recently the author of *A Rhetoric of Motives*. Mellowed at the age of fifty-four beyond his Greenwich Village youth, a farmhouse critic from Vermont,[24] who still combined a passion for rhetorical analysis and social theory with his creative work as a poet, Burke had no PhD, nor even an undergraduate degree, since he had dropped out of school to be a writer. Teaching college without a college degree was rare—but Burke was Burke. From Sontag's point of view, his offbeat credentials were perfect. As her biographers have remarked, "Burke did more than teach Sontag; he fathered her conception of the literary life." Later she remembered how thrilling it was to learn that Burke had once shared an apartment in Greenwich Village with Djuna Barnes: "You can imagine what that did for me."[25] *Nightwood,* with its insistent symbols, its overwrought language, and its anti-institutional charm, was a perfect text to explore under the guidance of a teacher who bathed in the aura of her favorite author.

When it came to literary criticism, Kenneth Burke more than made up for his lack of diplomas in rigor and method. Sontag's college notebooks from the University of Chicago illustrate the workmanlike method in which Burke trained his students. He asked them to construct a lexicon of key terms to serve as scaffolding for whatever literary text they were analyzing, which enabled them to stop relying on plot descriptions, to reach deep into language. Before taking on *Nightwood,* she had written a shorter paper on Conrad's *Victory* for Burke's Humanities 3B, and she was so thorough in her index of terms that he had to remind her, in the course of several typed pages of comments, to pay some attention to the major characters, for they, too, were helpful and revealing.[26]

Her preparatory index for *Nightwood* included its "essence words"— prehistory, shadow, odor of memory, racism memory, and forgotten experience—which were interwoven with other functions—sleep, night, sea, bottom, womb, and always, she added, lesbianism, "seeking its essence in the ultimate image of pure beast, equated with infancy in the sense of both childhood and speechlessness."[27]

But on the subject of the novel's lesbian plot, Sontag was less thorough, and her own language turns slippery: heterosexual relationships where the women are stronger then the men seem to "anticipate" homosexuality. Sontag uses the old Freudian term "inversion," which harmonizes nicely with the upside-down universe of the novel: night for day, beastly for artful, dirty for pure.

What the young college junior doesn't see, because she can't yet know, is that the novel stands as a premonition of her life to come. The main character of *Nightwood*, Robin Vote, marries the weak Jewish aristocrat Felix, has his baby, then leaves Felix and returns to Paris with a woman, Nora Flood. Susan Sontag married Philip Rieff, gave birth to their child, David, and left them both five years later for Paris, for a life that echoed the one Djuna Barnes lived with Thelma Wood on the rue Saint Romain in the 1920s, the life that inspired *Nightwood.* All the things that interested Sontag at the most private level—sexual role playing among women, the loss of boundaries between lovers, the presence of aggression and cruelty in sexual practice, a life lived at night, from bar to bar—these surface in Barnes's novel as well as in Sontag's diaries. When Sontag says she wants to write like *Nightwood,* she also means she wants to live like *Nightwood.* As a young woman, an undergraduate student, she put that ambition on hold and wrote instead about the novel's forms, at one large remove from her own desires.[28]

Despite what she might have repressed in writing it, Sontag's paper was unconventional enough to create controversy among the humanities faculty at the University of Chicago. Burke was enthusiastic, but the second reader didn't like her paper at all. A third humanities professor, called on to adjudicate, "liked it even less."[29] So the humanities staff called on a fourth reader, who had himself written about *Nightwood* and happened to be visiting the campus—a friend of Burke's from his Bennington College days named Wallace Fowlie. Fowlie was a convert to Catholicism who had studied with T. S. Eliot at Harvard. He was a fervent Francophile, a lover of the avant-garde, and an aesthete.[30] Sontag's argument dazzled him.[31] The drama of the disagreement, the administrative confusion and revolving readers, the threat of failure and ultimate triumph through outside intervention, were certainly more satisfying to an ambitious young student with avant-garde ambitions than if her paper had simply sailed through the system with flying colors.

Soon after graduating from the University of Chicago in 1951, Susan Sontag accompanied her husband to Cambridge, Massachusetts. Rieff had a job at Brandeis, in nearby Waltham. Their son, David, was born in 1952.

When David was three, Sontag began the PhD program in philosophy at Harvard.[32] It would be philosophy, not literature, that finally drew her toward an academic career and toward Paul Tillich, the protestant theologian and German émigré. After her preliminary exams (she reported being ranked first among all the graduate students in her cohort), she won, with Tillich's support, a fellowship from the AAUW to continue her study of "the metaphysical presuppositions of ethics" at the University of Oxford. She negotiated her departure carefully: Philip's parents would take care of her infant son while she was away.

She arrived at Oxford after her moon-spattered ocean crossing only to find the university atmosphere there stifling. The men in England reminded her of Philip: "There is a type—the male virgin—lots of them in England, I suppose."[33] She attended lectures by J. L. Austin, the philosopher of language, and worked on her short story about a woman who, like her, was stuck in England:

> The atmosphere was too much like the one she'd known in America—the tense careerism of the academic world, the talkativeness of it. She felt sick of talk, of books, of intellectual industry, of the inhibited gait of the professor.[34]

There was plenty of time, during lectures, to scribble on the cardboard back cover of a stenographic notebook the address of the place to get student meal tickets in Paris or a list of the different brands of anise-flavored liqueur—"Pernod, Ricard, Berger"—and what happens when you add water, through the mysterious chemical process the French call *louchissement*. As Austin explained speech acts, Sontag prepared for a new life: "Pastis always yellow," she wrote; "add water, they turn white."[35]

What finally got her out of England, and off the straight and narrow path to a PhD? It was simple: Harriet Sohmers had dropped out of Berkeley and was living in Paris. Whether it was Harriet who came to England to get Susan or Susan who went to Paris to find Harriet, their reunion was decisive. The couple spent Christmas together in Paris. Instead of leaving after Christmas holidays, Sontag stayed through summer.

Paris with Philip, Paris with Harriet

Sontag had visited Paris as a tourist, in 1951, the summer after her marriage, in what may have been the first chance for the couple to take a honeymoon. When she and Philip got into their taxi at the Gare Saint-Lazare, she told the driver "La Sorbonne, s'il vous plaît!" because it was the only place in Paris that seemed familiar. Those were her first real French words. She liked to recall in later years that she and Philip had stumbled into the Hôtel des Etrangers, not knowing it was the same hotel that had sheltered the young rebel poet Rimbaud after Verlaine's wife had thrown him out of her house. They were terribly timid, and they didn't speak to anyone—it was their "mute summer."[36]

Now she was back, six years later, living a much different life with Harriet. Yet the city she lived in was virtually unchanged from the one she had seen in 1951, or from the Paris of 1949 that Jacqueline Bouvier had known. Since very little on the Left Bank had been destroyed by German bombs, there was little new construction in her orbit. On the outskirts of Paris, Orly Sud had replaced Le Bourget as the main commercial airport. To the west of the city, on a straight line with the Champs Elysées and the Arc de Triomphe, the most celebrated new building of 1957–58, the CNIT, was under construction. It was a vast exhibit hall made of vaulted ceilings that looked like a wave, or a scarf blowing in the breeze. There was as yet no metro line to reach it, and it was well outside the beaten tracks of American students in the city.[37] The only new construction Sontag would have seen involved the transformation of the old wine markets on the left bank of the Seine, destroyed in 1944. Work began in March 1958 for a science campus for the University of Paris, which desperately needed lab space and classrooms. The Sorbonne was bursting at the seams, and students were pouring into France from what Rosemary Wakeman calls "the crumbling French empire."[38]

Here was the sign of the real change for France, and it was deep. France had lost Indochina in 1954; in the same year it began a hopeless war to keep Algeria French. There were plenty of indications of a crisis, but you had to know where to look for them. Boris Vian's song about a deserter, written during the debacle at Dien Bien Phu, was censored by the government. For good reason: by 1958, there were nearly half a million French troops in Algeria, draftees from the mainland. Amid the grand upheavals and the influx of colonial students, came a more modest alteration of the Paris landscape, which had a direct effect on the lives of Harriet and Susan—the opening

11. Susan Sontag (*center*), Harriet Sohmers (*right*), and Harriet's sister Barbara on the Pont au Double, walking toward Notre Dame (1958). Photograph, by an unknown Paris street photographer, courtesy Harriet Sohmers Zwerling.

of the Beaux Arts, the Mabillon, and the Prince, three student restaurants where a full-course meal with wine could be had for fifty cents.

Life in Hotels

The Paris of 1957 remained a series of neighborhoods as distinct as separate villages. The difference between Jacqueline Bouvier's sixteenth arrondisse-ment with its shops and respectable apartment buildings, Paul de Ganay's Faubourg Saint-Germain with its enormous mansions standing behind the grand esplanade of Les Invalides, and the bohemian Paris where Susan Son-tag dwelled was vast, though the three neighborhoods were separated by only a few miles. In December 1957, as soon as she arrived in Paris, Sontag wrote:

> Saint Germain des Prés: Not the same as Greenwich Village, exactly.... No rupture of national identification, and mal-identification.... The café routine. After work, or trying to write or paint, you come to a café looking for people you know. Preferably with someone, or at least with a definite rendez-vous.... One should go to several cafés—average: four in the evening.[39]

A map of Sontag's Paris would include the cafés and bars, the hotels and apartments of the fifth and sixth arrondissements, in the neighborhoods known as Saint-Germain-des-Prés and the Latin Quarter. In Saint-Germain-des-Prés, defined loosely by the church of the same name, were the pub-lishing houses and the great literary cafés—the Deux Magots and the Flore, where Beauvoir and Sartre had spent the Occupation years, staying warm as they wrote over three-hour cups of ersatz coffee. The Latin Quarter, only a few blocks to the east, was the student neighborhood around the Sorbonne and up and down the Boul' Mich, with its dozens of bookstores and cheap restaurants.

The Left Bank was the capital of literature in a city that still considered itself the literary center of the world. In his 1949 *What Is Literature?* Sartre joked about how closely knit the community of French writers was: "With a bit of luck, a busy American might meet us all in twenty-four hours."[40] He might have added that a busy Frenchman could meet the Americans in 1950s Paris even faster, in those winding streets between the Seine and the Luxembourg Gardens. Harriet did her writing and translation in a minuscule *chambre de bonne* "in a very posh apartment building, six hard flights up with a view of the rooftops," in Saint-Germain-des-Prés, near the Bac metro stop.[41] When Susan arrived, the two friends stayed ten days together at the Grand Hôtel de l'Univers on the rue Grégoire de Tours, closer to the Odéon metro, and then moved back to Harriet's regular lodging at the Hôtel de Poitou on the rue de Seine, behind the Ecole des beaux-arts. Later they borrowed a larger apartment on the rue des Boulangers from Harriet's mathematician friend Sam.

Sontag's friend Annette Michelson had started out in a room at the Hôtel des Carmes, a student place near the Panthéon, with the standard sink and bidet. By 1949 she had moved off the beaten track with her companion Bernard Frechtman; Frechtman had bought an apartment on the rue Joanès in the fourteenth arrondissement from the outlaw writer Jean Genet, who preferred hotel life. The walls of the former Genet apartment were covered in dark burlap, and there was no kitchen, so the couple ate in restaurants as if they were still living in a hotel.[42] Frechtman, Genet's agent and biggest supporter, was translating Genet's entire oeuvre into English. Annette was writing art criticism. Sontag's neighbors included poet Allen Ginsberg, part of her crowd if not an intimate. He was closer to the river, living with his boyfriend Peter for next to nothing in the Latin Quarter rooming house that came to be known as "the Beat Hotel" at 9 rue Gît-le-Cœur, a decrepit place with Turkish toilets on every landing and a single bathtub for forty-two rooms.[43] Iris Owens, an English major from Barnard who wrote pornographic novels under a pseudonym for Girodias's Olympia Press, lived nearby. Her *Woman Thing* took place almost entirely in a hotel room on the rue Monsieur-le-Prince in the Odéon neighborhood. The scenery was interior, the rhetoric tongue-in-cheek (example: "His prick was bruising her thigh, as massive and stony as the steeples of Chartres").[44]

There's rarely a published account of Parisian intellectual life in the 1950s and 1960s—French or American—that doesn't involve hotel rooms. Rents had been strictly controlled between the two world wars, discouraging the construction of new housing, since there were no profits in the offing for landlords. At the Liberation, Paris found itself with a population about to explode. In the absence of available apartments, people rented hotel rooms by the month, single rooms with toilets down the hall and, with luck, a gas burner for cooking oatmeal or making an omelet. The other possibility was to live in a maid's room: any apartment building of standing had a top floor (usually the sixth or seventh) with a mansard roof and tiny spaces where the servants had once resided. With the slow democratization of Parisian society there were fewer live-in domestics, and their quarters were turned into cheap rentals for students—often with a shared toilet. For showers, you had to go to the *bains-douches* that existed in most neighborhoods. Not far from where Sontag and Sohmers were lodging, on the rue Mouffetard at the southern end of the Latin Quarter, was a bathhouse called Le bain des patriarches. Ginsberg and Burroughs and Corso, in their Beat Hotel, could have a bath with advance notice if they paid extra for the cost of heating the water.[45] That much hadn't changed since the Smith juniors made do with a bath a week in 1949.

Both Sontag and Ginsberg, looking back on their years in Paris, describe a material world that was unmistakably French, and a social world that was essentially American. Sontag's French was elementary—literally. Elementary French 1a, 1b, and 1c at the University of Chicago emphasized reading, followed by a qualifying exam: "A one year course with fluent and accurate reading of standard French as the major objective. Secondary emphasis upon oral-aural abilities. Special attention to aspects of French culture and civilization," according to the College catalog.[46] Sontag might have been able to read a little, but she'd had no significant high-school French (at Hollywood High she'd taken Spanish), no long-term preparation for life abroad; compared to the students on the Smith Junior Year in Paris, her French barely existed.[47]

"We were in an enclave of our own 'cause our French wasn't that good," Ginsberg remembered.[48] Their freedom was also a source of isolation and financial struggle. No host mother prepared their meals; no immersion was refining their French; they had no Mlle Saleil to integrate them into the cultural life of the city. For Ginsberg, as for thousands of expatriates since, Paris was a place where you fell into a life of time-honored rituals, from gathering food in the open market to figuring out how to keep yourself clean, operating in a universe that had little connection to the French people who paraded before you on the street, distant apparitions.

"I came to Paris in 1957 and I saw nothing," Sontag told a French journalist ten years later, when she returned to the city as the author of a novel in translation, responding smoothly to questions asked of her in French: "I stayed closed off in a milieu that was in itself a milieu of foreigners. But I felt the city [*j'ai senti la ville*]."[49]

: 97

Harriet Sohmers had been living in Paris since 1950, working on and off for the *Herald Tribune*. You could consider her part of the population of writers and artists and journalists who identified themselves with the beat generation abroad. Edward Field has described her, a young beauty with blond hair and Prince Valiant bangs, hawking the paper on the streets of Paris. He speculates that it was her slender image, her haircut, and her resonant American voice that inspired Jean-Luc Godard to cast the Iowa actress Jean Seberg as Patricia, immortal in her pixie haircut and striped boat-neck T-shirt, calling out "Paris Herald Tribune" on the Champs-Elysées in the early scenes of *Breathless*.[50] If it's true, Susan Sontag had an intimate connection she never realized to the New Wave cinema that helped launch her career as a critic.[51]

Sohmers was doubtless a shrewder, wiser person than Godard's fresh-faced, innocent, and pregnant girl abroad. She modeled for artists, picked up a translation here and there, and painted and wrote for her own pleasure. She had steady work from 6:00 p.m. to midnight at the *Herald Tribune* offices on the rue de Berri on the Right Bank, after which she would cross the river and end the evening in one of the clubs or bars in Saint-Germain-des-Prés. In 1953 she contributed, in a modest way, to the literary history of modernism. Through her circle of friends, she made a connection with the editor Maurice Girodias, Henry Miller's publisher, who had inherited his father's press, Obelisk. The mission of Obelisk, and later of Olympia Press, its successor, was to publish English-language books in Paris that couldn't pass the censor in the United States. Girodias published "db's"—dirty books—along with modernist masterpieces like Beckett's *Watt* and Nabokov's *Lolita,* which he acquired through a combination of cunning and the existence of a morally rigid British and American literary market. The Americans in Paris knew they could write or translate for him if they were broke. Harriet translated the 1787 version of Sade's *Justine: The Misfortunes of Virtue.* Sade's elegant, eighteenth-century French is difficult to render even for the most practiced translator; Harriet's translation ("And is not the object of this so wise law the sacrifice of one to save a thousand?") never transcended the awkward exchange of word for word, and lacked the erotic charge of the original, which relies on a coy back-and-forth between cool philosophical banter and orgiastic description.[52] In the same year, Girodias commissioned a translation of the longer and more graphic 1791 version of *Justine* from Austryn Wainhouse (who used the pseudonym Pieralessandro Casavini), which appeared under the title *Justine, or Good Conduct Well Chastised.*[53] There was a certain logic to this division of labor: Sohmers, the lady, got the relatively tame version of *Justine*; Wainhouse/Casavini the hard-core sequel.[54] Wainhouse revised his Sade for a new edition in New York in 1965 and went on to do a whole series of translations; Sohmers's career as a translator, inseparable from her Paris adventures, began and ended with *Justine.*[55]

The world of American writers in Paris was small: Harriet's expanding circle of acquaintances included the young men on the rue Gît-le-Cœur, the *Herald Tribune* staff, and African Americans who met down the street from the Senate at the Café de Tournon, whose brightest light, in 1958, was James Baldwin.[56] Sohmers and Baldwin had even written for the same magazine—*New Story*. Before Susan joined her in Paris in the winter of 1958, Harriet had had a passionate love affair with a Cuban actress and playwright, María Irene Fornés, who had pride of place in her conversation—and became a troubling imaginary third in her relationship with Sontag. Harriet had introduced Susan to the bar scene in San Francisco. In Paris there were more bars, and many more scenes.

With Harriet Sohmers, Susan Sontag left the mental universe of Chicago critics and Oxford philosophers, and joined a world of expatriate beats. But can a woman be a beat? There is nothing more masculine, more macho, in American culture, than the beat poets of the 1950s and '60s—Ginsberg, Bowles, Kerouac, Corso, wild men with women hanging on their every word, or bonded to one another in sexual adventures of their own. Joyce Johnson has written movingly of her life with Jack Kerouac: she was a writer too, but an invisible one at his side.[57] As she describes her milieu, there would have been no decent role for someone of Sontag's ambitions, at least not in the company of men. What Sontag and Harriet shared with the beats was geography, and addresses. They all ate at the Café des Beaux-Arts on the rue Bonaparte, where you could get a three-course meal with wine for a few dollars, sitting at a communal wooden table covered with paper. They drank at the Old Navy on the boulevard Saint-Germain, where, to this day, Godard's lead actress Anna Karina still has her afternoon drinks, and at the Monaco—William Burroughs's spot at the Carrefour de L'Odéon. There was a difference in literary status, of course. Ginsberg and especially Burroughs were established anti-establishment writers, whose experiments with form were already famous. Ginsberg had left for Paris just as his poem *Howl* made headlines for surviving an obscenity trial. Sontag was a graduate student, with no books to her name; Sohmers, for all her talent and flair, had more genius for living than for art.

Paris for the beats, as historian Barry Miles has written,[58] provided an escape from conformism and puritanism that neither San Francisco nor New York could offer. For Sontag, Paris was something more immediate and more profound—an unexpected break with marriage and the demands of motherhood. The separation from her husband was bold enough. More radical was the fact that she had left her son behind. What she wrote about him (which has appeared with the publication of her diaries by the adult David Rieff) is heartbreaking:

> I hardly ever dream of David, and don't think of him much. He has made few inroads on my fantasy life. When I am with him, I adore him completely and without ambivalence. When I go away, as long as I know he's well taken-care-of, he dwindles very quickly. Of all the people I have loved, he's least of all a mental object of love, most intensely real.[59]

Real, therefore unreal.

Sontag was not part of a community of lesbians in Paris, as Djuna Barnes had been before her, or even as she and Harriet had been in San Francisco. She was not inclined to community. Yet the feeling that surfaces in her diaries, despite her amorous suffering, is her sense of relief and belonging: "It was so good to be home, as it were—to have women instead of men, interested in me."[60] A year earlier, James Baldwin had published *Giovanni's Room*, the story of an American expatriate in Paris who finally confronts his homosexuality. Two decades earlier, Barnes, her muse, hadn't shied away from depicting women in love. But when Sontag experimented in her journals with a short story based on her affair with Harriet, she made her into a man named Hazlitt. She was not interested in representing queer life in fiction. Perhaps she believed that the life she was enjoying could appeal to men and women alike, to heterosexuals and homosexuals, for it was defined, in true expatriate fashion, by what it wasn't: a social straitjacket.

A Method of Her Own

In the winter of 1958, along with her passion for Harriet, Sontag had fallen hard for French. If Jacqueline Bouvier's bilingual poem suggests youthful affection for her second language, Susan Sontag's notebooks document a more obsessive love.

Stories about learning languages have some common elements: the dog-eared grammar book, the beloved or feared teacher, the hilarious accounts of embarrassing mistakes, the various life experiences that push someone into another language in the first place, from the economic and social necessities of exile to the tongue-loosening effects of falling in love. Like love, language acquisition may be too complex, too emotional a process to be explained by a behavioral science, which is why memoirs—Nathalie Sarraute's *Childhood*, Vladimir Nabokov's *Speak, Memory*, Alfred Kazin's *A Walker in the City*, with their novelistic sense of accident and detail, come close, if not to the science, at least to the art of immersing oneself in a new language.[61]

What is unique in the case of Susan Sontag and French is that she did not entrust her language learning to any method or textbook, to any classroom, or even to the vagaries of experience—she constructed her own method.[62] She took care to save the vocabulary lists she kept during her year in Paris. They are part of her archive at UCLA, pages upon pages of spiral notebooks, neat columns of words with French on one side, English translations in parentheses, and the occasional outlying term in the margins. At first glance they have no more importance than laundry lists. For her, they were an act of will.

In a standard French grammar book—say Mauger's *Cours de langue et de civilisation française*, the text used for years by the Alliance française, or Pierre Capretz's *French in Action*, with its '60s New Wave aesthetic—vocabulary is presented thematically: for Mauger, the family, the dinner party, the outing in the country; for Capretz, the Franco-American flirtation, the detective novel, the stroll through the Luxembourg Gardens. With no purpose other than to instruct herself, Sontag tailored her vocabulary lists to correspond to her own life in the bohemia of 1950s Paris. There are separate pages in her diaries devoted to such topics as keeping clean, sex, talking to children, insulting sobriquets, telling stories and jokes, types of people, and mental aptitudes.

Because her Harriet was an American, pillow-talk language learning was out. There was no French love affair on the horizon—not yet—or even many French friends in her circle. Nonetheless, and perhaps with a touch of regret, Sontag studied the nuances of amorous expression, setting out the subtle differences between the verb "to love" with and without an adverb, and how to apply it to people versus to things:

Aimer bien = to like (for persons)
Je l'aime bien = I like him
Aimer bien = to like all right (of things)

"Je l'aime beaucoup," she explains to herself, "is MORE than 'Je l'aime bien' but LESS than 'Je l'aime.'" An alternative to talking about liking or loving someone is the time-honored French double negative as a positive: "Il [n']est pas mal (of physique or character)," meaning "he's nice"—"il est sympathique." At the top of her love page, she added the strongest case: "s'éprendre de = fall in love with."

Along with these lexical nuances of love in the city of love, she construct-ed a who's who, a lexicon of her ambitions: names of publishers, theater critics (Robert Kemp and Jean-Jacques Gautier are labeled "big wheels"). On one page she parsed out the daily and weekly newspapers and maga-zines and their political leanings ("*Combat*, left wing started by Camus; *Le Figaro*, pro-American Catholic conservative"); on another, sites of her pleasures: gay and lesbian bars, jazz clubs, drag shows. In the late 1950s, her Paris could still lay claim to the cross-dressing Paris of 1930s Mont-parnasse, photographed by Brassaï at the Monocle Bar and celebrated by Djuna Barnes and painter Romaine Brooks. The lean, short-haired, mon-ocle-sporting women made famous by the Monocle were parodies of the wan British men that Sontag had left behind at Oxford. Every bar and club in Paris had its constituency: working-class lesbians went to La Montagne, on the rue de la Montagne Sainte-Geneviève; Le Tabou, upstairs on the rue Dauphine, and the Club Saint-Germain on the rue Saint-Benoît were the centers of postwar jazz, consecrated by figures like Claude Luter, Boris Vian, singer Juliette Greco, and American jazz genius Miles Davis. It was an alcoholic Paris: "Met H at the [Café] Flore afterwards, and had 5 or so whiskeys at the Club St. Germain and the Tabou," Sontag wrote on January 12, 1958: "Not stupefied drunk, but enough to get with the so-so jazz we were hearing at the St. Germain, and with the superb sex we had near dawn, in bed."[63]

The most prophetic page in Sontag's self-made grammar—the page she took most to heart—is the one headed "intellectual conduct"—a guide as useful today, in a country where repartee is an art form, as it was in 1958:

Exposer, discuter, raisonner, se couper, en soi, critiquer, contester, signifier, vouloir dire, analyser, très discuté, critiqué, c'est une bonne idée, d'ailleurs, qualifier.

For which she gives the following key:

to explain, expound, to argue, to contradict oneself, in and of itself, to criticize, to mean, to analyze, controversial, critical, It's a good idea. From another point of view; also, on the other hand (d'ailleurs), to describe.

The deliberate, logical, and independent way that Susan Sontag went about learning French was typical of her approach to life. There is always the sense in her lists that she is in the know, with a feel for genre and convention, even if it's antiestablishment convention. Ever the precocious student, she was up on slang (*bidule* for thingamabob, *gougeat* for a jerk, *tantouze* for fag). Her sense of time was sophisticated, too, for a beginning student: early on, she learned to say *la veille* for the day before, instead of the literal and incorrect expression that beginning language students tend to use, "le jour avant." Soon her vocabulary lists morphed into a more general guide to Parisian nightlife, then into an almanac with information about the organization of French territory into *départements* and of Paris into its twenty *arrondissements,* districts that curl around the city like a snail. Typical of her ambition to understand everything about the place where she was living was a note she made to herself early in her stay: "read the Napoleonic code."

Sontag's Sorbonne

A decade later, when she reported on the results of her year of research to the American Association of University Women, Susan Sontag described her fellowship year studying the metaphysical presuppositions of ethics "at Oxford and the Sorbonne" as "perhaps the most valuable single year of my academic life."[64] "The Sorbonne" for Susan Sontag, as for so many American students in the postwar era, was never literally the Sorbonne—if her diary and course notebooks are any indication, she attended no regular classes at the university. You could register at the Sorbonne and get a card that let you into the student cafeterias—that's what Harriet had done when she got to Paris.[65] But registering didn't require going to classes.

There are four mentions of the university in Sontag's diaries, and they are casual. The first, on January 8, 1958, merely notes: "Spent the late afternoon exploring the Sorbonne." In the second, on February 19, Sontag mentions a cocktail party at the home of a Sorbonne professor, after his late afternoon lecture on Claudel. The host was Jean Wahl, a poet and philosopher, and according to Sontag's diary he had three holes in the back of his pants so that you could see through to his underwear. She doesn't say, and may not have known, that he had been stripped of his position at the Sorbonne by Vichy anti-Semitic legislation, had escaped the Drancy transit camp after an arrest, and had fled to the United States, where he spent the war years at Mount Holyoke, an intellectual leader among French refugees.[66] Like the young Sontag, he was a critic of T. S. Eliot's aesthetic vision, and had even gathered some of his wartime poems, written in English, under the title "Four Anti-Quartets." His cocktail party—barring one uncomfortable element, the presence there of the man she called "the disgusting Allan Bloom," who had been Sontag's Chicago schoolmate and was already a champion of the intellectual Right—was in all other respects an ideal setting, which she would try to recreate in New York: a social meeting of minds connected, but not bound, to any university.

On February 26 comes a third mention of the Sorbonne: an extracurricular lecture. Simone de Beauvoir was addressing a group of left-wing students about whether it was still possible to write a novel. The French feminist was at the height of her fame—winner of the Prix Goncourt for *The Mandarins*, and author of *The Second Sex*, the work so fiercely controversial in the 1940s, which had since penetrated the cultural landscape. She was now completing the manuscript of *Memoirs of a Dutiful Daughter*, her account of a bourgeois Catholic childhood. Sontag was as hard on Beauvoir as she had been on Anaïs Nin in San Francisco—and for the same reason: her voice. "Very good looking for her age" (Beauvoir was fifty), "but her voice is unpleasant, something about the high pitch plus nervous speed with which she talks."[67] Perhaps Sontag was anticipating her own performances. On February 27, she mentions the Sorbonne for the fourth and final time, in connection with a concert of Beethoven and Mozart.

Susan Sontag's Paris university, like her method for learning French, her Europeanized identity itself, was largely of her own making. She was a voracious consumer of culture, just not in class. The interesting thing about her insular hotel-room life with Harriet was that it, too, was a window onto culture, since when she was too distraught about their affair, she went to the movies, several movies a day—westerns, Italian comedies, French classics, it didn't matter. "I fled, weeping, into the Métro . . . plunged into a movie," she wrote in March. People usually go to the movies to cry, but for Sontag it was in the dark remove of the Paris theaters that her tears would dry.

At the end of her life, on the centennial of the birth of cinema, she wrote about film as a school for living. She might have been thinking of her Parisian year:

> It was from a weekly visit to the cinema that you learned (or tried to learn) how to walk, to smoke, to kiss, to fight, to grieve. Movies gave you tips about how to be attractive. Example: It looks good to wear a raincoat even when it isn't raining. But whatever you took home was only a part of the larger experience of submerging yourself in lives that were not yours. The desire to lose yourself in other people's lives . . . faces.[68]

Theater was another outlet, an entry for Sontag into French culture, just as it had been for the Smith girls a decade earlier. Sontag may not have met many Parisians in her day-to-day life, but she could absorb Frenchness, in highly condensed form, on the stage. She went to the left-wing Théâtre national populaire to see Pirandello's *Henri IV,* to *Don Giovanni* at the Opéra, to Racine's *Britannicus* at the Vieux Colombier. Racine, she wrote, was more foreign to her than Kabuki theater:

> Emotions are externalized, mathematical. The play consists of a series of confrontations of two or at most three characters (no Shakespearean waste!); the intellectual medium is neither dialogue nor soliloquy, but something in-between, which I found unpleasing—the tirade. No movement, just postures.[69]

Her reaction gives a sense of the enormous cultural gulf that existed then— and still today—between what tragedy can mean in two divergent cultures. Americans raised on Shakespeare, and on a theater that is constantly reinventing and stretching the language, come to French theater with a set of expectations in place, only to find them dashed. Racine's theater draws its power from what is not shown on stage, from what is implied, from the constraints of the alexandrine verse and its refined vocabulary. Racine, so the saying goes, used a vocabulary of only 3200 words (and only 1600 in *Phèdre,* his masterpiece), compared to Shakespeare's 15,000. The idea of restrictions and limits as a foundation for art—as opposed to unbridled originality and expressivity—is the cornerstone of the French-American difference. Pascal Baudry, in his recent study of American and French style, *French and Americans: The Other Shore,* suggests that the French favor an implicit form of communication, Americans an explicit form. He is advising today's global business executives, but he could just as well be talking about the classical theater—or perhaps about the difference between a Catholic monarchy with its privileged secrets and a Protestant democracy striving for transparency.[70] Jacqueline Bouvier, with her careful sense of appearances and aristocratic restraint, had embraced the French difference; Sontag resisted it.

It is poignant to imagine Susan Sontag at twenty-four, all fire and passion in the midst of her own love affair, sitting at the Vieux Colombier on a Thursday afternoon—the time set aside for staging the classics—and, with whatever comprehension she could muster, trying to decipher the betrayal of Britannicus by Nero. Theater décor in the 1950s was stark, and the stage for that particular production of *Britannicus* was, by all accounts, extremely simple, consisting of black velvet curtains whose pleats were made to resemble Roman columns. Agrippina the matriarch wore a velvet cloak and several gold necklaces adorned with pearls and emeralds. Standing still on the stage, she declaimed on motherhood and on the evil that lurked in the heart of her son Nero, who, at the end of the play, has his rival Britannicus poisoned. "J'embrasse mon rival / mais c'est pour l'étouffer" (I kiss my rival, to suffocate him). As in all proper Racinian tragedy, significant actions—the poisoning of Britannicus, the public lynching of Nero's treacherous adviser—take place off stage. If you couldn't understand the telling, you might miss those deeds altogether. In 1958, Roland Barthes—who was to become Sontag's favorite French critic—published his famous polemic against academic criticism, *Sur Racine,* where he puts it succinctly: the Shakespearian question is "to be or not to be"; the Racinian question is "to say or not to say." Junia, the woman who loves Britannicus, must respond to him coldly while Nero, off-stage, is spying on them; she tries to let Britannicus know that Nero is listening by telling him that "walls can have eyes," but he takes her reticence as rejection, and he is wounded.

The disciplined sing-song of the French alexandrine verse—six syllables, a pause, then six more syllables—is at the heart of French literary education: every French schoolchild learns the scansion. Critics of the production at the Vieux Colombier were harsh on the diction. The alexandrine lines, wrote Jean Guignebert for *Libération*, "limped"—that is, they were missing a few of the required syllables, muffled or botched by the actors.[71] Limping or leaping, the quality of the syllables would have made little difference to an unpracticed American ear. Sontag would have to wait for Barthes to meet a Racine she could love.

Exit the Republic

Desperately in love, unhappy—but unhappy in a grand tradition—Sontag spent five months, December 1957 through April 1958, in a whirlwind of cafés and restaurants, movies and plays. When she needed to supplement her modest fellowship, one of Annette Michelson's friends, a young film-maker named Noël Burch who had studied at the Institut des hautes études cinématographiques, got her a walk-on part in Pierre Kast's *Le bel âge*; he

12. Susan Sontag and Jean-Claude Brialy discuss a lantern in *Le bel âge* (movie directed by Pierre Kast, 1958). Author's photograph.

was working for Kast as an assistant director. Kast was a Saint-Germain regular, and his film, based on the novel by Alberto Moravia, was full of recognizable character actors and actresses—Alexandra Stewart, Jean-Claude Brialy, and Boris Vian. Vian, the trumpet player, songwriter, and existentialist-in-residence at the Tabou bar, starred in the film as "Boris," owner of an artsy furniture gallery in Saint-Germain-des-Prés.[72] Susan Sontag appears on camera in a single scene, willowy and elegant in high heels and a long skirt, as she stands before a large paper lantern and discusses its merits with Brialy. She never wrote about the walk-on—she never cared much for autobiography—but it's easy to imagine the experience adding a spark to her romance with French cinema.

One great mystery remains in connection with Sontag's intense stay in Paris in the winter, spring, and summer of 1958. Even given her youth, her absorption in a difficult love affair, and her relative distance from French people, it is astonishing that her diaries—those reflections by a woman who would one day be a fierce commentator on current events—make absolutely no mention of the fact that France, the country where she was living, was on the brink of civil war.

It is no exaggeration to say that the year 1957–58 found France in its greatest period of crisis since the Nazi Occupation. The Algerian war for independence from France had really begun as soon as World War II ended, with a riot in Sétif that turned into a massacre, by the French, of Arab veterans of the French colonial army. In 1954, the Algerian Front de libération nationale had launched an insurrection. By 1957, the struggle for independence was in its fourth year, with the French sending more and more young men to fight the rebels, and the French residents of Algeria becoming more and more desperate to keep Algeria French. It was too late for liberal solutions, half measures, and government promises of privileges and assimilation. The war was spreading quickly from Algeria to France, with the arrests, in February 1958, of 277 Algerian Muslims in Paris, including 102 members of the Front de libération nationale's network; the FLN, in turn, began to target French police. The French prefect Maurice Papon was transferred from Constantine to toughen up the police repression of the Algerian rebels in Paris. The French had begun a policy of torture to break the clandestine networks of Algerian revolutionaries in Paris and Algeria alike, and more and more Algerian "fellaghas" were arrested and sentenced to death. A growing number of French, in Algeria and on the mainland, openly supported

Algerian independence: Sartre most vehemently, and other less-known figures who risked their lives for the cause.

The month that Susan Sontag arrived in Paris, December 1957, an event took place in the Grand Amphithéâtre of the Sorbonne that made headlines in every newspaper. There, in a room that had seen hundreds of public thesis defenses, a defense was held for the first time in the absence of the candidate. Maurice Audin, a young mathematics instructor in Algeria, a communist, had been arrested for his support of the Algerian liberation movement and tortured to death in prison. He was granted a doctorate, with all the traditional language and ceremony, by a committee whose president was mathematician Laurent Schwartz, one of the heroes of the Resistance and now a fervent defender of Algerian independence. Anyone as fascinated by the Sorbonne's intellectual history as Sontag might have taken note.

In the month of February, the month she attended plays by Pirandello and Brecht, read Svevo's *Confessions of Zeno* and Carson McCullers's *Reflections in a Golden Eye,* drank at the Café de Tournon and the Café de Flore, another French communist named Henri Alleg published a slim volume called *La question*—an account of his own interrogation and torture by the French army in Algeria. His book was seized by the government, but the waves it made radicalized a public already weary of four years of an undeclared war.

A few blocks from Sontag's hotel, Allen Ginsberg was sitting in his Beat Hotel, writing to his father on the blue aerograms you folded and pasted closed on three sides about the demonstrations and the FLN bombs exploding and the police with their machine guns on the street. In his diaries that spring, Ginsberg scribbled a satirical ode to Henry Luce, the editor of *Time,* while the magazine was covering the Algerian conflict with Francophobic relish (*Time* later featured both General Salan—the diehard military proponent of French Algeria—and de Gaulle on its covers):[73]

> What strange reporting of the news.
> Benevolent, indifferent, sentient.
> To both Frenchman and Algerian.
> Murderer and Murderee.
> Demo and Republican
> Communist and camp—girlfriends too.[74]

In March a woman awaiting the guillotine was bringing international attention to the Algerian cause: Djamila Bouhired had been sentenced to death by a French court for her participation in the bombing of a snack bar in Algiers. She testified that she had been tortured for days following her arrest, strapped onto an operating table, with electrodes attached to her genitals. The trial itself added to the scandal of her detention when it appeared that the witness called by the French government to testify against her was a mentally ill prostitute.

"Stop reserving this journal so exclusively for the chronology of my affair with Harriet," Sontag wrote on March 24. But she made no mention of Djamila Bouhired, two years younger than she, another dark beauty with thick black hair and sorrowful eyes, who gazed that month from the front pages of the *Herald Tribune*, *France-Soir*, *Le Figaro*, tugging at the political conscience of anyone who looked at her. At her trial, Bouhired had claimed that she was anti-colonialist but not anti-French. Now, after an international outcry, the president of the Republic commuted her death sentence to life imprisonment; she was later pardoned.

The Algerian crisis came to a head on May 13. On that day, General Massu, commander of the French military forces in Algeria, formed a Committee on Public Safety (the phrase had obvious echoes of the French revolutionary terror), and effected a military takeover of the whole of Algeria, wresting control from the French government officials in place. By May 17, mainland France, fearing a takeover by Massu's soldiers, was under martial law, and the threat of civil war between pro-independence and anti-independence forces was part of every conversation. The *Herald Tribune* reported a flurry of phone calls by panicked Americans in France and serious debate at the embassy about whether to evacuate all Americans from the country. The *Herald Tribune*, where Harriet Sohmers worked, had changed its tune along with the rest of France: the references to menacing rebel terrorists early in the year had now evolved into references to menacing paratroopers and generals, the new sources of public fear. The paper quoted a junior senator from Massachusetts, John Kennedy: "In my opinion, the continuing French position in Algeria costs the Free World heavily."[75] He called on the United States to urge France to act in favor of Algerian autonomy. The senator had learned quite a bit about France's colonial empire from his French-speaking fiancée, who had translated Ho Chi Minh and d'Argenlieu for him the year before the French defeat at Dien Bien Phu.[76]

Chapter Three

It's tempting to say that Sontag's silence on these questions was typical of many young women her age, for whom world events mattered less than inner life. But Harriet too kept a diary, and reading it makes it clear how unusual it was for anyone to be able to ignore the events of May. Here she describes her dramatic flight, with Susan, from a city under siege:

> May 20 Strasbourg. Crisis Time in France. People are fleeing Paris. There is fear of a right-wing coup led by the pieds-noirs [French colonists in Algeria]. Last night Sydney Leach nervously invited us to "Come and sleep in the lab tonight if you want to see action"; little groups all over Paris are keeping vigils, preparing for a fight. We hitchhiked out. It's great not to be there tonight while my beloved, free, libertine city is under attack by the *salauds* as Sartre calls them, the right-wingers, paratroops, racists.[77]

Susan and Harriet took to the road at the very moment when it looked as though France was falling apart: in that sense, the events of May were inseparable from their everyday lives. In June, while the couple was in Germany, de Gaulle traveled to Algeria to reassure the French population: "I have understood you," he said, in a promise that turned out to be a death knell for French Algeria, since only a few months later he entered into negotiations with the FLN.

Susan's summer diary gives none of the context of their departure, harnesses no Sartrean vocabulary, has no political commentary. It consists mostly of tour notes, aesthetically inclined—incense in Seville, American soldiers in Munich, donkeys and mountains in Delphi. The future novelist was practicing descriptive writing. Outside pressure came not from politics but from her husband. By July, she notes, Philip was writing her "letters filled with hate and despair and self-righteousness. He speaks of my crime, my folly, my stupidity, my self indulgence."[78] Their correspondence is not part of her archive at UCLA, but it's unlikely she would have responded to him with reports on the crumbling Fourth Republic.

By October, when a new constitution ushered in the Fifth Republic with its greatly expanded presidential authority, Susan Sontag had returned to New York, ready to act on the resolve Paris had brought her. She would miss by one month the opening of Louis Malle's *The Lovers,* a scandalous film whose screenplay had been written by the same Louise de Vilmorin whose blue salon at Verrières-le-Buisson had welcomed Jacqueline Bouvier in 1949. The woman at the center of *The Lovers*, Jeanne, played by Jeanne Moreau, is alienated from her rich, neglectful husband and spends as much time as she can in Paris. She meets the dashing young Bernard on the road when her car breaks down, and invites him home to dinner. What scandalized French Catholics, and Americans even more, was the film's ending. Jeanne beds Bernard in her own house, then leaves her husband and her angelic infant at dawn to take to the road with her lover.[79]

Sontag, too, had taken leave of husband and child to pursue her own road trip. Only she did it openly, with advance notice. Like the New Wave heroines of Malle and Godard and Chabrol, she had operated in that mythical 1958 season outside of history, outside of political time and space—and outside of the traditional family structure that Paris had helped her unravel.[80]

Chapter Three

FOUR

Susan Sontag

The Return

Louis Malle's *The Lovers* gives no inkling of what happened to Jeanne after her flight from husband and child, how long she stayed on the road with her young lover, or whether she saw her child again. There is only a close-up of the lovers' confused faces as they drive off in their car, a hint that their happiness will not last forever. Susan Sontag's escape from home lasted from September 1957 to August 1958, the end of her fellowship period. She returned to New York, greeted her husband at the airport (or dock, we don't know), and told him she wanted a divorce. At least that was how she describes it in a short story she wrote for the *New Yorker* three decades later: "The Letter Scene."[1] The improbable marriage had lasted for eight years.

By the winter of 1959, Sontag had an apartment on West End Avenue, a job at the magazine *Commentary,* and temporary custody of her son David— who remained with her throughout the custody battle she waged against Philip Rieff until 1962. "Being queer makes me feel vulnerable," she wrote in 1959, but also, "My desire to write is connected with my homosexuality. I need the identity as a weapon to match the weapon that society has against me."[2] Her lover, during those first years in New York, was Irene Fornés, the Cuban actress who had lived with Harriet Sohmers in Paris before Susan's arrival and who had loomed so large in Harriet's imagination. Harriet had returned to New York as well, and the three women could be seen together at parties.[3] Harriet joked in later years that Susan's capture of her beloved Irene caused her to turn her back on a whole way of life: she married, had a child, and never slept with a woman again.[4] When Rieff accused his ex-wife of lesbianism in an effort to gain custody of David, Fornés and Sontag, now roommates, presented themselves before the judge in dresses and lipstick, which, in those days of rigid sex and gender stereotypes, passed as an argument for heterosexual normalcy.[5] The psychoanalytic culture of the early 1960s still classified women who wore pants as neurotic, afraid of their femininity. In a photo taken in Greece in the summer of 1958, twenty-five-year-old Susan Sontag was wearing an A-line sleeveless shift, her black bobbed hair defining the strong line of her chin. In the late 1960s, she let her hair grow longer and started to look the way Edward Field remembered her in the time of her ascension to New York prominence, wearing black boots, pants, and turtleneck, a cigarette in one hand, her other hand at the nape of her neck, holding back her thick mane of hair. In the mid-1970s, Jacqueline Kennedy too abandoned the armor of her wrinkle-proof A-line dresses for cashmere sweaters and tweed trousers, outfits befitting an editor. Both women were exquisitely conscious of dress codes. Now it was Sontag, the intellectual, who was setting the look.

The Formalist

A fight for custody, a new lover, a job, and the beginning of a career as a public intellectual: of all of these developments, the last is the most difficult to narrate, although central in its importance. Books read and positions taken *were* events for Susan Sontag. Reading her diaries from 1958, then skipping to the early 1960s, you can't always tell that she has relocated from Paris to New York, for she continues to write with the same passion about the flow of books and the traffic in ideas. Her landscape was what went on in her head.

By 1958, the time of her American reentry, an event was taking place at the level of ideas. The wind from France had changed direction, and there was talk of a New Wave, a New Novel, a "structuralist revolution." Sontag's

American destiny, her story, had to do with the surprising way she seized those changes and made them hers.

On the French side, the existential magic had faded. Sartre and Camus and Beauvoir, who had toured so many college campuses in the late 1940s, were now middle-aged, and important enough to have produced a reaction in the next generation. In philosophy, that reaction came via structuralism, which questioned the humanist commitment of the existentialists in favor of a cooler appraisal of surfaces and forms. In literature, the reaction was spearheaded by Alain Robbe-Grillet, who in 1953 had published a novel called simply *The Erasers*. The existentialists wanted their fiction to carry a message, while the New Novelists set out to banish the traditional features of nineteenth-century realism from fiction, and political and social messages went out the door with the rest. Milan Kundera has referred, horrified, to the late 1950s as the era in which aesthetic values were reduced to linguistics; from the rule of linguistics, it was a short and brutal path to the takeover of the novel by academics. Kundera's list of what makes up a novel—"Story, composition, style (levels of style), spirit, the nature of imagination"[6]—was everything that Robbe-Grillet wanted to jettison, or said he did, in *For a New Novel*, a collection of essays which, along with Nathalie Sarraute's *Age of Suspicion*, set the terms for what counted as new. Sontag, in her 1963 essay *"Muriel, ou le temps d'un retour"* would champion Robbe-Grillet's goal "to suppress the story, in its traditional psychological or social meaning, in favor of a formal exploration of the structure of an emotion or event."[7] But in revising her essay on Sarraute for her 1966 collection *Against Interpretation*, she conceded that the theory produced by the New Novelists was more interesting than the novels themselves, and she would later abandon her enthusiasm altogether.[8]

Robbe-Grillet and the other writers who championed the New Novel had a small, elite following in the United States, consisting mainly of college students, their teachers, and the few readers—Angela Davis would be one—willing to make their way through fiction with no recognizable plot or characters, either out of genuine intellectual curiosity, or for the sake of their allegiance to an international literary avant-garde. The American embrace of avant-garde French fiction makes a funny contrast with the kind of mass following American culture was acquiring in France at the same time: a boy named Jean-Philippe Smet changed his name to Johnny Hallyday and burst onto the French concert stage in 1960, pretending to be an American. He sold millions of records by copying Elvis, with lyrics in French. Hallyday appealed to French youth who aspired to nothing so much as the teen scene that Sontag had fled—the sock hops and drive-in movies of North Holly-wood High.

In a different way from Johnny Hallyday, Alain Robbe-Grillet also owed much of his success to the United States. American professors of French literature loved the New Novel because it lent itself to rich, sentence-level analyses, vocabulary drills, and endless interpretive games. By the mid-1960s, *The Erasers* and *Jealousy* were being excerpted in French literature textbooks, becoming as much a part of the standard classroom curriculum as Balzac and Molière, and despite their apparent difficulty, they were easier to teach. Robbe-Grillet would become the very image of the French writer in America—suave, scandalous, and mysteriously alluring. His American prestige bounced back to France, his success in the American university consolidating his standing in his own country. In 2004 he was elected to the venerable and archaic Académie française, founded in the seventeenth century to protect the sanctity of the French language. The parallel with Susan Sontag is intriguing, for much of her own power and prestige in the United States—her aura—was connected to what she learned, then learned to transmit, from France.

Sontag's acquisition of French avant-garde culture came in phases. It's difficult to say how much of the world of aesthetic games and experiments in form she had absorbed during her time in Paris in 1958 and how much she gathered after the fact, once she became, in New York, the American intellectual who had studied in France. If her journals are any indication, she had seen as many American as French movies during her time in Paris. She had familiarized herself with French productions of Genet, Pirandello, and Brecht, but most of the books she mentioned in her journals were Ameri-can or British, part of a literature of soul-searching in tune with the mindset of an adventurous young woman abroad: Hemingway, Oscar Wilde, Emma Goldman, Carson McCullers, Nathanael West. There is no mention of Rob-be-Grillet or Sarraute in her journals until the 1960s, and although Robbe-Grillet had already published *The Erasers* when she was in Paris, he had not yet gathered his essays in *For a New Novel*, the book that became his mani-festo. And while she had actually participated in the filming of Pierre Kast's New Wave film as an extra, it was because of her friendship with Annette Mi-chelson, who introduced her to Noël Burch—she was only trying to make ends meet. In 1958, New Wave film was in its infancy, so it's not surprising that there is no mention in her diaries of the movement's flagship journal, the *Cahiers du cinéma,* or of the figures who were becoming its most visible proponents. Her essays on Godard and Resnais came much later.[9] What she had learned in Paris was less specific—a way of living, a way of writing, and a cultural acquisitiveness that was not academic. Between her senior essay on *Nightwood,* her studies in philosophy, and her year abroad, she had developed a style of argument and a specific taste for formal play. You could even say that her own reasons for preferring form over plot, difficulty over transparence, were a matter not of taste, not even of trend watching, but of a need to dwell on complex appearances. This predilection for form would end up coinciding with the highly formalist moment in French culture, once the New Novel and the New Wave took root. Sontag's avant-garde formalism would assure her a small but faithful audience of American readers, the sure sense of belonging to a cultural elite, and, most of all, an intellectual agenda radically distinct from that of her American peers.

Identifiable as Paris

In 1960, in addition to her work at *Commentary* and the philosophy courses she taught at Columbia and Sarah Lawrence as an "all but dissertation" MA from Harvard, Sontag set out to write a novel, her own New Novel, which she published in 1963, calling it *The Benefactor.* The AAUW, which had funded her research abroad, reported in 1966 that Susan Sontag "regarded her dissertation as 'a dropped stitch that you just have to go back and pick up' and speaks of completing it soon."[10] Nothing in her early diaries—except perhaps for her teenage desire to write sentences like Djuna Barnes's—hints at a desire to be a novelist. But if she wanted to distinguish herself from academia (hence from her ex-husband) and model herself on her European counterparts—Beauvoir, Sarraute, Duras—a novel was de rigueur, an entry into the world of literature that distinguished her from run-of-the-mill freelance journalists and philosophy instructors who hadn't finished their PhDs.

Like the New Novel, *The Benefactor* aims for an escape from standard linear plots, deep psychology, and realistic settings—but it also mimics an old philosophical genre dear to French literature, which Sontag describes in her journals as "a sub-genre: the pseudo-memoir" and "the French *moraliste*

: 117

Susan Sontag: The Return

tradition."[11] *The Benefactor* is narrated by a man named Hippolyte who lives his life according to his dreams. He has a corrosive relationship with a woman he refuses to love, whom he alternately rescues and attempts to murder. He sells her into slavery in Tangiers, builds a palace for her, watches her die. He marries, then betrays his wife. Germans occupy the city in which he lives, which may or may not be Paris. There are long descriptions of dreams in the novel, and a voice—the voice of the narrator Hippolyte, who, like a character in an eighteenth-century French novel, or perhaps like William Burroughs in the American context, lives on inherited wealth, with the luxury of making his life's work the exploration of his dream life.

"Politics interested me no further than the daily newspaper. In this I resembled most of my generation and class, but I had additional reasons of my own for being un-political," Hippolyte announces in the early pages of the book: "I am extremely interested in revolutions, but I believe that the real revolutions of my time have been changes not of government or of the personnel of public institutions, but revolutions of feelings and seeing, much more difficult to analyze."[12] It was a page right out of Robbe-Grillet, who believed that the writer's truest commitment was to his artistic form, not to politics.[13] For anyone steeped in the history of French literature, there is an almost constant sense of déjà vu reading *The Benefactor*. Hippolyte is, by turns, Gide's immoralist Michel, Huysmans's des Esseintes, Benjamin Constant's Adolphe. While she would have abhorred any old-fashioned autobiographical impulse in her avant-garde phase, Sontag did put something of herself in her main character. Hippolyte is the solitary, solipsistic child sprung from an unremarkable family in the provinces, a loner with an irrepressible sense of difference and a thirst for knowledge coupled with a distaste for the classroom. He is imbued with a sense of sexual alienation.

It would be difficult to overestimate the total incomprehension *The Benefactor* generated among its few American readers, although the reviews give hints. "*The Benefactor* suffers from some of the overly intense subjectivity it describes," wrote a critic for the *Antioch Review,* a publication more likely than most to receive experimental fiction with open arms: "It does not create a world, it only comments, in its brilliant way, on one strangely withheld from our view."[14] The critic for *Time* was appalled. "Identifiable as Prose" was the title of his review—making fun of the book jacket that described the novel as set in a city "identifiable as Paris."[15] *The Benefactor*, he concluded, sounded like a "blurred translation from some other language." Sontag's debut was nonetheless the occasion for reviews in the most important magazines of the day, mainstream and literary: the *Saturday Review*, the *New York Review of Books*, the *Evergreen Review* (a satellite of Grove Press with strong expatriate ties). She had the protective patronage of her publisher, Roger Straus, of Farrar, Straus & Giroux, who was relatively indifferent to her sales and ready to invest in and nurture her talent as a writer and critic over the long haul.

Sontag came of age in a world where experimental writers still had the benefit of the doubt on the cultural stage, especially if they were also performers. "To give no interviews until I can sound as clear and authoritative and direct as Lillian [Hellman] does in the *Paris Review*," resolved the young author, who had once been so critical of Anaïs Nin and Simone de Beauvoir's lectures.[16] She was already aware, in 1965, that what takes place around the publication of a book could be as important as the book itself.

The Great Un-American Novel

Robbe-Grillet had earned his place on the literary scene by attacking Sartre. And Sontag? The American novelists to whom she would have compared herself in 1960, the rivals who counted, were men like Philip Roth, her exact contemporary, or Saul Bellow, ten years older—both Jewish intellectuals educated, as was she, at the University of Chicago.[17]

A notebook from 1960 contains several characteristic lists devoted to American writers: Saul Bellow, Ralph Ellison, James Baldwin, Philip Roth, Herbert Gold, Bernard Malamud, and a single woman, Grace Paley—all of them, in her words, "coming to terms with the American experience," and all of them either black or Jewish.[18] No sign of another contemporary, John Updike, who had just published the very American *Rabbit, Run*.

The comparison with Philip Roth is especially telling. He had arrived in Chicago just as she was leaving, to earn a master's degree in English and to teach freshman composition. He was in Paris in the summer of 1958—her Paris summer—to collect a prize from the *Paris Review* for a story called "Epstein" about the dying embers of an aging Jewish man's desire. It was one of the stories collected in *Goodbye, Columbus*, Roth's first book, which won the National Book Award in 1960 and established him as Bellow's heir.

Roth's stories were full of dialogue, because the people in them, the Jewish people he had grown up with in Newark, were always arguing, complaining, venting, chortling, bemoaning their lot. His stories were full of detail, often grotesque, about the layered sights and sounds and tastes and smells of ethnic America: "Even the smells had lingered," Philip Roth wrote about the black section of Newark, formerly the Jewish section, in *Goodbye, Columbus*: "whitefish, corned beef, sour tomatoes—but now, on top of these, was the grander greasier smell of auto wrecking shops, the sour stink of a brewery, the burning odor from a leather factory; and on the streets, instead of Yiddish, one heard the shouts of Negro children playing Willie Mays with a broom handle and half a rubber ball."[19]

Sontag's prose in this early period is abstract, airy, contemplative, and solitary—even when there are relationships. Here is the voice of Hippolyte, narrator of *The Benefactor*:

> While I was occupied with my initial investigations into what I vaguely thought of as "certitude," I felt obliged to reconsider all opinions which were presented to me. Consequently I felt entitled to one myself. This open mindedness raised certain problems as to how my life was to be guided for the interim, while I questioned content I did not want to lose form.[20]

The quest for a native voice versus the quest for form: that is one way to understand the gulf that separated Philip Roth and Susan Sontag in their writerly pursuits.

What exactly had bitten her? In 2000, when she was interviewed by the French magazine *Les Inrockuptibles*, long after she had turned to writing more conventional historical fiction with plot and character, she said she had felt obligated, for that first literary outing, to write in what she considered the style of the moment. "When I discovered the New Novel, I found it interesting and I thought you were supposed to like it. But in all honesty, I never managed to like it."[21]

She felt obligated, but she hadn't really liked it. A strange obligation, since none of her American peers were doing the same thing, even the ones who had spent significant time in France in the 1950s and 60s. Among the successful expatriate writers of the era were exiles Baldwin and Wright, and the returnees Mailer and Bellow, the latter two having spent their year "at the Sorbonne," Mailer on the GI bill in 1947, Bellow on a Guggenheim Fellowship in 1948.[22] None of them was influenced by French forms. For Bellow, Paris was a place that, by its very remove from home, lent itself to sensual memories of Chicago. European modernism, he once said, "was not the kind of thing that would have come naturally to a kid who had grown up in Chicago in the twenties and thirties."[23] Even the Americans who lived in France for long stretches seemed untouched. For Sontag, modernism—the French modernism of Rimbaud and Baudelaire, fruit of the nineteenth century—was the essential requirement for meaningful intellectual life. To find an affinity group for *The Benefactor,* you'd have to look toward writers closer to the world of American poetry—to Harry Mathews, for example, who was influenced by the experimental French poet Raymond Roussel and by the American poet John Ashbery. Mathews edited the *Paris Review* and eventually settled in Paris. His first novel, *The Conversions,* came out in 1962, a year before *The Benefactor.* There was also Alfred Chester, Sontag's wildly eccentric friend in Paris and New York who wrote a few highly regarded experimental stories before his descent into schizophrenic madness.[24] And there was Ginsberg, her Paris neighbor from the Beat Hotel, who eschewed realism and knew his French poetry—but nothing was more American than the rhythms of *Howl.* Even when Sontag returned to traditional narrative in her last two novels, her prose never came near an American vernacular.

Her refusal of homegrown prose was a conscious strategy. In a journal entry from 1963, Sontag categorizes *The Benefactor* as one of her "meditations on a dissociative fait accompli," which is a way of acknowledging its indirection.[25] The setting is French but not obviously French; Hippolyte believes in impersonal sex; the characters are sleepwalking, describing their subjectivity without inhabiting it. "Homosexuality, you see, is a kind of playfulness with masks," is one of Hippolyte's lines, and it is probably too easy to reduce this first literary effort as the effect of writing in an attempt to hide, or dissociate from, her true desires.[26] What is clear is that Sontag had no desire to write in either a "native voice" or a sincere one. She was striving for the very opposite of her anti-model Bellow, who declared that "the only language that I use is the language of Americans."[27] Sontag had been determined, since she was sixteen, to create a new persona for herself as far from her native persona as possible, and to experiment with a voice that was neither entertaining nor transparent. She was aiming for the Great Un-American Novel, and the result, published on the fragile outer cusp of McCarthyism, was both pretentious and courageous.

American in Spite of Herself

You would think, with its enormous debt to French literary tradition, that *The Benefactor* might have triumphed in avant-garde Paris when it was translated in 1966, but this was not the case.

If American reviewers were complaining that her novel was too European, the French reviewers were not going to let her into their pantheon so easily. Michel Mohrt, acquisitions editor for American literature at Gallimard and a critic for the conservative *Le Figaro,* found it odd that Sontag had taken the voice of a man. "Under a man's mask" was the title of his review, and he emphasized what he called the novel's "sterility" and "onanism." Please write more like a woman, he seemed to be suggesting, and not like a philosopher or a man. *The Benefactor* was reviewed in *Le Devoir,* the Montreal daily, by Naïm Kattan, an Iraqi Francophone writer living in Montreal, who had been at the Sorbonne in 1958 and whose own hybrid background would have made him sympathetic to Sontag's intellectual position. Her novel reflected "the cool world," he wrote; it was detached from science and politics, its emotions strictly controlled. Yet for all its European influences, "it was American reality that dominated in this novel. Susan Sontag treats in fact similar themes to those of Mailer, Bellow, Malamud. First of all the theme of identity." Her opposition to these homegrown writers, he concluded, did little more than prove them right.[28]

It was not a glorious beginning, but it was a beginning. The reviews were accompanied by photos. Sontag looked awkward, even girlish, with soulful eyes and a dark intensity. A French woman journalist reviewing *The Benefactor* with *Against Interpretation* in 1966 called her "an apostle of the avant-garde": "This intellectual has the beauty of an Andalusian, a sovereign ease, a nonchalant, distinguished quality, and dark velvety eyes. . . . Despite her French affinities, I'm bound to say that the hero of *The Benefactor* seems to me closer to those of Updike and James Purdy than to those of our 'new novel.'"[29] Sontag must have been astonished to learn that her Hippolyte had affinities with Rabbit Angstrom!

So it went. The American literary establishment called attention to her by finding her literature impossibly French; the French literary establishment insisted she wrote like an American in spite of herself. It was just the kind of neither/nor position that suited her.[30]

13. Susan Sontag in front of Notre Dame (ca. 1965).
Photograph © René Saint-Paul / Agence rue des Archives.

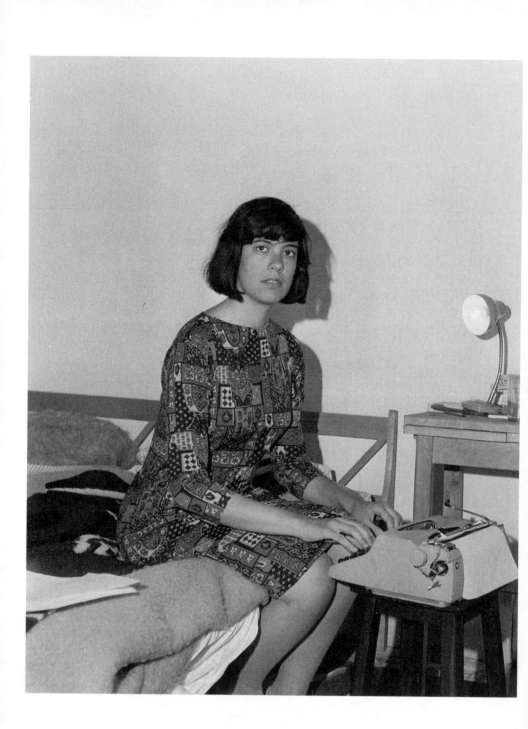

14. Susan Sontag with her portable typewriter in a Paris hotel room (ca. 1965).
Photograph © René Saint-Paul / Agence rue des Archives.

The story of Susan Sontag and France, like so much else about her life, is a story of books first, then of lived experience. The publication of *Against Interpretation*, three years after *The Benefactor*, catapulted her into prominence. From the woman writing under a man's mask, she became the sovereign female intellectual. All the essays had already appeared in article form, primarily in *Partisan Review* and in the *New York Review of Books*, the literary magazine that was coming of age along with Sontag.

Against Interpretation is a strange book when you read the essays in the order in which they are arranged. It starts with an argument for the autonomy of works of art ("On Style") and ends with an argument in favor of the cultural sensibilities of Jews and homosexuals ("Notes on 'Camp'"). "Notes on 'Camp'" has been credited with intuiting the entire field of queer theory *avant la lettre*. Without ever acknowledging her own lesbianism, Sontag became an important defender of a male homosexual sensibility. In between these two bookend essays, *Against Interpretation* contained a series of artistic editorials that might have been called "On France": detailed analyses of a whole panoply of French writers and filmmakers and novelists, from Nathalie Sarraute to Robert Bresson, Ionesco, and Jean-Luc Godard. Sontag had become, in the pages of the *New York Review of Books*, the expert on French topics and on what would go, a decade later, under the banner "French theory." In her foreword to the collection Sontag referred ruefully to her tendency to "assign grades" to works of art—realizing perhaps that she had never quite shed her University of Chicago education, with its emphasis on the evaluation of a canon.[31] In those early years, the French got honors.

The X Factor

With two books in print, life went on—the more and more dazzling public life, the secret inner life. Life and work were tightly combined, yet under the pile of manuscripts, cultural outings, and intellectual connections was a constant buzz of worry, a struggle that preoccupied her throughout the winter months of 1960, in her daily existence with Irene and her son David. She called it "X"—the overwhelming desire to please, to appease, to see oneself through other people's reactions, to spare other people's feelings, to care what they think. Women, she decided, were X; America itself, with its cult of popularity, was "a very Xy country." "X is the scourge," she wrote in February 1960: "How do I really cure myself of X?" She made lists of X situations, X feelings, X characteristics, and finally connected her personal problem to a concept in existential philosophy: "X is Sartre's bad faith."[32] In her ongoing struggle to be a writer, she tried to understand what she had accomplished in *The Benefactor* and where she was going: "Writing is a little door," she wrote in her journal. "Some fantasies, like big pieces of furniture, won't come through."[33] In 1965, in one of her self-designed French lessons, she copied Georges Bataille's preface to his pornographic novel *Madame Edwarda* into her notebook line by line: an epigraph by Hegel on death, a philosophically elaborate definition of eroticism as "a vista of anguish"—philosophical preliminaries for his story about a hooker in a taxicab. Nothing in Sontag's own background connected her to this very Catholic exercise in blasphemy, which was precisely the point: in Bataille, she found the combination of high philosophical seriousness and perversion that she would cultivate in all her early fiction.[34]

Solstice Nights

The year of *Against Interpretation,* 1966, was a triumphant one for the public Sontag. Richard Avedon photographed her for *Vogue* with her son David, now fourteen years old. She had enrolled him in the Lycée français de New York, where he could study history and literature (and even physics and math) in French, enjoying intellectual opportunities she had longed for at his age. She began to return, each summer, to Paris, reveling in the dinner parties that proliferate in June and July, as Parisians suddenly feel the desperate need to see all their friends before they go off for the annual month of vacation.

Paris is as far north as Nova Scotia, so the sun doesn't set until almost eleven in late June. Dinner might not start until ten, when the sky turns a deep blue before darkness descends. Day and night, all summer long, people gather on every terrace. Roger Grenier, who lives on the rue du Bac, has described his own corner café in an eternal summertime: "With the first ray of sun, a crowd mobs the outside tables, while the boulevard Saint-Germain stretches out below like an arm of the sea. This is our beach."[35]

Every summer, there was a different apartment, a different neighborhood with its cafés and restaurants, its newsstand and metro stop, different books and different furniture, usually belonging to a French writer or artist or a full-time expatriate. In the summer of 1966 she was living on the Ile Saint-

Louis, through an exchange with Anthony Glyn, a British expatriate who was enjoying her apartment in New York. A few years later, integrating into the small world of Parisian artists and writers, she borrowed another apartment, whose every square meter must have seemed charmed. It belonged to Alain Resnais, whose films had meant so much to her, and his wife and assistant Florence Malraux, André Malraux's daughter.[36] There was no social register, no *Bottin mondain* for them, as there was for the de Ganays and de Noailles, but the intellectual and artistic elites of Paris were as intertwined, in their own way, as the Faubourg Saint-Germain aristocracy that Jacqueline Bouvier had known.

What was especially meaningful about these Parisian summers for Sontag, as for so many American intellectuals, were the layers of history in every house and every neighborhood—the layers that add up, year after year, with the layers of one's own experiences and friendships. The Ile Saint-Louis, a tiny residential island planted in the heart of Paris, looks over its shoulder at the cathedral of Notre-Dame in one direction, at Paris's city hall in the other. Long before the invasion of tourists seeking Berthillon's sorbets, the Ile had been a village unto itself, a place where aristocrats, hard-up poets and artisans crossed paths. Baudelaire liked to sunbathe on the quai d'Anjou.

Being in Paris in the summer also meant the back and forth of correspondence with New York, where the poet Richard Howard, Sontag's closest literary friend and ally since 1960, kept her up to date about his own work and about the writers who had read her work and would be interested in seeing her in Paris. There was Maurice Nadeau, critic and editor of a brand-new magazine called the *Quinzaine littéraire,* and Roger Caillois, one of Georges Bataille's crowd. Howard asked Sontag to get him the sequel to Michel Leiris's *Manhood* (Sontag had reviewed Howard's translation of *Manhood* for the *New York Review*), Michel Foucault's *Les mots et les choses,* Kojève's *Introduction to Reading Hegel.*[37]

It was the beginning of a remarkable collaboration between Sontag and Howard, an intellectual tag team through which so much French thought was transmitted to American readers throughout the 1960s and 1970s. Howard translated Barthes and Leiris and Cioran; Sontag wrote about them for their new readers. The two were leaders in the conversation that was bringing that thing called French Theory to the United States, made of equal parts of Walter Benjamin, Roland Barthes, Michel Foucault, Jacques Lacan, and Jacques Derrida.

Roland Barthes became a central figure for both of them. A tuberculosis survivor who had forfeited graduate school for the sanitarium, this playful writer was able to maneuver with ease inside and outside the university, mastering the intellectual trends of the moment (late existentialism, semiotics, psychoanalysis), gathering the next generation of writers and critics in his seminar on love at the Ecole pratique des hautes études.[38] Sontag followed every debate in what had become the two leading magazines for French intellectuals—Philippe Sollers's *Tel quel* and Jean Piel's *Critique*. She sent the French translation of *The Benefactor* to the young philosopher Jacques Derrida, who wrote back with encouragement: "Is it true that you are alone and misunderstood in the United States? If it's true, there or here, you should not let it slow you down or set you off course. A certain 'misunderstanding' is often—especially in cases like yours—the best sign, as you well know."[39] She sent *Against Interpretation* to Derrida, who replied with a letter full of praise, enclosing two offprints, his "two last articles in *Critique*," which he said were part of a project also "against interpretation." "My book is called *De la grammatologie.*"[40]

"The hyperactivity of the heroic depressive," she wrote, years later, concering the collector of fine art in her novel *The Volcano Lover.* There had always been something of the collector in her own approach to intellectual life, in her lists and her pride in accumulated knowledge, her voracious consumption of books and magazines, her correspondence with important intellectuals, carefully archived. And, like many a collector, she was never satisfied. "To see more, colors and spatial relationships, light," she wrote on August 20, 1965, and "My vision is unrefined, insensitive."[41] In 1976, she wrote to Fredric Jameson in response to his request for a future contribution to a new journal of Marxist thought, *Social Text,* offering to serve as a kind of cultural scout: "I spend about five months a year in Paris and read a lot of obscure magazines that, possibly, you may not have time or opportunity to look at. And I could read and give you an opinion on articles you are considering. What else? I don't know."[42]

Back in the summer of 1966, Richard Howard wrote to her about the U.S. bombings of Vietnam, about Lyndon Johnson, about the horrors of the war. Paris was full of draft dodgers. For Sontag it would be impossible to remain apolitical. Along with the antiwar movement, the women's movement began to play a role in her public discourse. In 1968, a display ad in the *New York Times* read: "Susan Sontag says Join me in Washington January 15: Thousands of American women . . . will demand that Congress end the war in Vietnam and our social crisis at home. Make Womanpower Political Power."[43]

In May '68—with revolution in full swing in France—Sontag joined James Baldwin, Norman Mailer, and LeRoi Jones in a letter to the editor of the *New York Times,* protesting an Oakland police shoot-out that had killed an unarmed eighteen-year-old Black Panther, Bobby James Hutton, and wounded other party members.[44] In France, the two most politicized New Wave filmmakers, Jean-Luc Godard and Agnès Varda, set their sights on the Panther cause, traveling to Oakland in 1968 to make *Sympathy for the Devil* (Godard) and *Black Panthers—Huey!* (Varda). Jean Genet would follow them. Sontag, for her part, traveled to Hanoi, wrestling with her ambivalence about propaganda. By now she was a spokesperson, someone whose words counted. Her everyday correspondence took on new political overtones: an English professor at the University of California, Irvine, informed her in the fall of 1969 that Marcuse was upset about the Angela Davis case at UCLA, and was talking of resigning if Davis was not permitted to teach.[45] The case against the young black philosophy professor fired for her membership in the Communist Party had galvanized the intellectual world.

For Sontag, like so many social critics of the 1960s, the American war in Vietnam and domestic racism were twin issues that needed to be analyzed together. The white race, she wrote in response to a questionnaire in the *Partisan Review* on what was happening in America "*is* the cancer of human history."[46] She had always been uncompromising in her formalism; aesthetic commitment had now given way to the fiercest political passions.

Hôtel Rothschild

In the thick of those violent, political years, it finally happened. Susan Sontag fell in love with a French woman. You could say it was bound to happen, given summer after summer in borrowed French apartments, her imaginary investment in the city of Paris, in its culture, in the French language; those lists of words and expressions in her diary becoming ever more sophisticated; the reading lists of books and journals; the days she spent hungrily at the Paris *cinémathèque* (where films were both shown and archived), soaking up the history of French film.

They met at the Cannes film festival. Nicole Stéphane was there in 1969 for the screening of Marguerite Duras's *Détruire dit-elle,* which she had produced, and again in 1971 to raise money for a project.[47] Long before she met her, Sontag would have seen Nicole Stéphane on the screen, perhaps in a revival movie house in New York or during one of her outings to the *cinémathèque*—she'd remained faithful to her habit of several movies a day, whether she was in New York or Paris, and she had included *Les enfants terribles*, a film starring Stéphane, on a 1965 list.[48] In 1970, having ventured into filmmaking herself, Sontag noted Stéphane's name in her journal, this time on a list of French producers; Stéphane had become an important person for her to meet.[49] Theirs was the last major romance in which Sontag would play the ingénue: Sontag was thirty-six years old, Nicole Stéphane was ten years older.

Two films owe their magic to Nicole Stéphane: *The Silence of the Sea* (1947) and *Les enfants terribles* (1950), both directed by Jean-Pierre Melville, one of the elders lionized by the New Wave. In *The Silence of the Sea* (an adaptation of Vercors's Resistance novella, published underground in 1942), Stéphane played the young girl who lives with her uncle in a house requisitioned by a German officer. The scene is 1941, and the girl's resistance, in those early days of the Occupation, consists in remaining perfectly silent in the face of this more and more awkward, garrulous, and confessional guest, a stiff German aristocrat with a melancholy taste for German music and a doomed love for French literature. Nicole Stéphane's power is even more obvious today than it was in the 1950s, if only because our culture is quicker to recognize androgynous beauty—in her case, a classical, sculpted face, short wavy blond hair, strength in every gesture. At the age of twenty-six, she was as far as you could get from the baby-faced Brigitte Bardot.

Her greatest role was as Elisabeth in *Les enfants terribles*, the Cocteau novella adapted for film by Melville. Elisabeth is the passionate and possessive sister of Paul, a disturbed boy who's been expelled from school for his playground violence. Paul and Elisabeth live together after the death of their mother in an ever more deranged promiscuity, until an outsider—a young woman named Agathe—falls in love with Paul, and he with her. Elisabeth destroys the couple's relationship by intercepting Paul's love letter to Agathe and lying to each of them. Paul poisons himself in despair, with just enough life in him to unravel the deception and join Agathe in confronting his sister with her betrayal. Elisabeth, unmasked, looks at herself in the mirror with an intensity that Cocteau likened to the Greek Electra. She rages, pulls at her hair, revels in her monstrosity. *Les enfants terribles* ends with the sound of a gunshot, and with a high-angle view of Elisabeth's corpse, the gun lying by her hand.

Offscreen, the actress who immortalized Elisabeth's mad passion was no less compelling. Born Nicole Rothschild, she was a seventh-generation descendant of the British branch of the Rothschild banking family and granddaughter of Henri de Rothschild, the doctor and playwright whose fortune had financed hospitals and funded the research of Sontag's childhood idol Marie Curie. Nicole's privilege was cut short by the war. She escaped Paris in 1942 under the threat of German occupation, armed with false papers for "Nicole Regnier." She and her sister crossed over the Pyrenees into Spain, where, like so many refugees, they were arrested by Franco's Guarda Civil, imprisoned, and released. They reached England via Lisbon, joining the Resistance in London.[50] Melville discovered her after the war in drama school. She made the two great movies with him, and then played a series of minor roles, including Madame Curie in a Georges Franju short. During Sontag's semester in Paris in 1958, Stéphane had appeared on screen as Denise Bloch, a martyred Jewish Resistance fighter, in the patriotic British film *Carve Her Name in Stone*. By 1960 her roles had dwindled, either by choice or because her physical and emotional persona was so at odds with the starlets then in vogue.

Stéphane was thus no longer an actress but a producer when she first met Sontag, and the detail is significant. After an injury from a car accident marked the definitive end to her acting career in the early 1960s, she became an enabler of films for other actresses and writers. She produced *Mourir à Madrid,* a political documentary about the civil war in Spain. With Sontag, she produced a film about Israel and, later, Sontag's staging of Beckett's *Waiting for Godot* in a besieged Sarajevo. She produced the first film directed by Marguerite Duras, based on one of Duras's own novels, *Détruire dit-elle.* Duras was known for her haunting screenplay for Alain Resnais's *Hiroshima mon amour* in 1959, and with Stéphane's support she became a New Wave director in her own right.

Most of Stéphane's film projects were documentaries, but the great adventure of her life as a producer was literary. In 1964 she acquired the film rights to Proust's *In Search of Lost Time,* whose extravagant language and microscopic sensuality did not promise an easy adaptation to film. But she was determined to see the book on screen, and for years she searched for the right screenwriter and director in what began to seem like a wild goose chase.

Luchino Visconti, Harold Pinter, René Clément, Joseph Losey all tried their hands, to no avail. In 1984, she finally succeeded in producing *Swann in Love,* based on the efforts of screenwriters Peter Brook, Jean-Claude Carrière, and Marie-Hélène Estienne, and directed by Volker Schlöndorff. Sontag was surrounded by Proust-bound companionship on both sides of the Atlantic: Richard Howard had taken on the project of translating all of the *Search* into English for Farrar, Straus & Giroux, an all-absorbing task.

These facts of Nicole Stéphane's life and work, however intriguing, can only approximate what she meant to Sontag, how many layers of French, and Jewish, culture and history she represented. For some of their years together, Stéphane lodged Sontag in her apartment on the rue de la Faisanderie, just off the Bois de Boulogne, a more luxurious part of the sixteenth arrondissement than Jacqueline Bouvier's avenue Mozart at the Jasmin metro stop. She had bought the pavilion in the garden of the Hôtel Goldschmidt-Rothschild, a three-story white stucco mansion with mansard roofs belonging to the baroness of that name, a distant relative of Nicole, famous for her collection of impressionist art and for her sheltering of Jewish refugees in the 1930s. Sontag's future intellectual hero Walter Benjamin had even sought the Baronness Goldschmidt-Rothschild's assistance after he fled Hitler's Germany for Paris. Sontag lived over the Goldschmidt-Rothschild garage for months at a time, writing.[51]

From one *hôtel particulier* to another—Nicole Stéphane's world and aura, so different from that of Paul de Ganay's Faubourg Saint-Germain mansions where Jacqueline Bouvier had danced to Claude Luter records in her black strapless gown, was redolent with the Napoleonic ambitions of the Rothschilds, the moral stamina of the Free French, the glamour of postwar cinema, and a postwar political passion firmly on the left. She was a woman of remarkable force of character; *volontaire* is what a French friend called her—willful. She became Sontag's producer, but, more than that, she gave Sontag advice about how to develop her career, encouraged her to write screenplays, and sent her to a French cancer specialist, who saved her life after a first bout with breast cancer in 1975.[52] With Nicole Stéphane, Sontag was finally on the inside of French life, although Stéphane herself—as a Jew, a Resistance fighter with the Free French, a woman disabled by an accident, and especially as a Rothschild—was not really an insider either.

Sometimes Stéphane's advice stopped Sontag in her tracks. In the summer of 1973, Alain Resnais and Florence Malraux were out of town, and

15. Susan Sontag in Paris (1972). Photograph © Henri Cartier-Bresson / Magnum Photos.

their apartment in ethnic Belleville served as a workplace for Sontag and the American expatriate filmmaker Noël Burch. Sontag had acquired the film rights to Simone de Beauvoir's first novel, *She Came to Stay*—the story of a painful love triangle, based on Sartre's affair with two Polish sisters, which deeply wounded Beauvoir. It was a melodrama worthy of Sontag's 1958 Paris hotel life, a potential film noir, since, in a fictional revenge over reality, the story ends in murder. After a summer of intense work, Sontag told Burch she was dropping the project: Stéphane had decided it was bad for her career. Burch was dumbfounded.[53]

Corrections and Queries

From 1966 to the end of her life, Susan Sontag was a transmitter, an adapter, an interpreter, a collector, and a lover of what France had given her. Because of her particular set of intellectual preoccupations, translation was vitally important to her. The translation of her books, especially into French, allowed her to work out her feelings about being understood or misunderstood, to control the reception of her work, to be known beyond the confines of her native language. In a 1982 speech on translation at the American Academy in Rome, she challenged her fellow writers in a kind of declaration of war against translators who appeared to rely on authors not knowing the language of the translation: "My books are translated into at least fifteen languages, mostly badly . . . .my advice to my fellow-writers is to badger these cowards to show us what they are up to."[54]

Hostility was not her only tack—Sontag was capable of untiring correspondence with her translators, much of it affectionate, reveling in the intimacy of the translator-writer relationship. She has conserved, for posterity, pages and pages of letters and faxes she exchanged with various French translators over the choice of individual words, phrases, or titles. They constitute an unusual record of her passion for language. An exchange over *The Volcano Lover*—her historical novel about the collector Lord Hamilton, his wife, Lady Emma Hamilton, and her lover, Admiral Horatio Nelson—shows both arrogance ("French," she said in a letter to her agent, "is the only foreign language in which I am almost perfect")[55] and anxious humility. She worried about the title of her novel in French, just as she had worried about the difference between *aimer, bien aimer,* and *s'éprendre de* in her student notebooks. Was *The Volcano Lover* going to be called *L'amant du volcan* or *L'amoureux du volcan?*

> "The soul of the lover is the opposite of the collector's": first of all, you have convinced me that "amoureux" is better here than "amant." But about the very large question of changing the title: I don't feel competent to have an opinion—though your argument has now created a big doubt in my mind. . . . What you are saying if I understand you correctly, is that "amant" is too specifically sexual (in a broad sense) in French. In English, as you know, it is not. We say so-and-so is the lover of so-and-so, but we also say that someone is a music lover or a lover of travel. I'm glad you brought this up, though I'm now very troubled. What do you think the next step is to decide about this?[56]

The translator she most respected was Philippe Blanchard, who was perceptive and diplomatic in responding to her messages—including, on one occasion, twenty-eight pages of corrections and queries:

> Well, dear Philippe, I wish I could have taken a plane to Paris. It would have been more fun than typing this letter, which has taken me a total of about fifteen hours, spread over two days!

She was worried about verb tense:

> I know that in French, the present tense is often used to describe actions in the past (unlike English), but I still don't want to do it that way. Further, as I've already said, there is the question of consistency. About twenty percent of the time you do say so-and-so DISAIT, and eighty percent DIT. Let's make it always DISAIT.[57]

What she hadn't understood, because the confusion is easy to make, is that DIT in French can be either the present or, spelled the exact same way, the *passé simple*—the historic past. Blanchard responded tactfully, not hitting her over the head with her mistake:

> In several places the "said" phrase was too close to a time-mark to be translated by an imperfect. In these cases, I have kept the passé simple (the idea,

in my previous version, was to use the tense which sounded more natural in the sentence).[58]

Sontag prided herself on being a step ahead of her translators, just as she prided herself on being a step ahead of the trends. In that respect, translations of French work into English and academic enthusiasm for the "French Theory" she had defended were a mixed blessing. Once the structuralist classics had been translated into English and absorbed by English departments—"globalized," as the saying goes—Sontag's particular expertise was no longer news. She moved on from her romance with French literature to other enthusiasms: Eastern European literature (where she worked in tandem with Philip Roth) and writers she took pride in putting on the map: Joseph Brodsky or W. G. Sebald. Her critics have pointed out that by the end of her life she had morphed from a partisan of the avant-garde to a defender of the great work and the great writer, as staid as the University of Chicago professors who had once disapproved of her term paper on *Nightwood*. On that score, a strangely confessional note in one of her interviews is revealing. Seeing the old Paris Gare d'Orsay refurbished as a museum for nineteenth-century art, Sontag was appalled:

> When I visited this new museum in Paris, le musée d'Orsay, I burst into tears. Because we thought it was established what the 19th century canon was. We thought it was clear that Degas was better than Bouguereau. Now comes a new museum which says it is all the same, or that, in fact, the bad art is better than the good art because it is more entertaining.[59]

The problem was that the museum had given academic paintings pride of place by hanging them in the vast salons of the former train station. The curators had relegated the impressionist masterpieces to an attic space on the fifth floor. Sontag still spoke in the uncompromising voice of protest, but now she was speaking with the royal "we" about the triumph of impressionism and the clear division between high and low art. She might have argued that the impressionist paintings belonged in their fifth-floor garret, reflecting their controversial origins. Instead, she spoke about entitlement, position—about privilege earned.

Her trajectory, studied over the long term, is full of astonishing reversals, rebirths, re-evaluations. The young student so taken up with her sexual freedom that she scarcely noticed the Algerian crisis became one of the most outspoken critics of American foreign policy, and shocked the country by looking at terrorism from the terrorists' point of view.[60] The young intellectual who once complained she had no visual sense became the partner first of an iconic movie star and then of a brilliant photographer, Annie Leibovitz, and made an important contribution to the theory of photography.[61] The cancer patient became an influential and consoling analyst of the prejudices against her disease. The woman so troubled by sexual pleasure ("If only I could feel about sex as I do about writing," she had confided to her journal in 1965)[62] wrote about sexual passion between two aging lovers in *The Volcano Lover* with a rare beauty and empathy.

In public life, Sontag mastered the arrogance that Beauvoir had always claimed as a philosopher's basic right. She won her old struggle against X, against appeasement, pleasing others, and earned a reputation for being difficult and imperious, though many people who met her, expecting a Fury, were surprised by her girlish pleasure in things, her need to charm. Her French editor at Editions du Seuil wrote to her in 1980, exasperated after receiving her complaints about the quality of a translation of *Illness as Metaphor*, which had gone to press as she was recovering from chemotherapy:

> Finally, might I tell you this: in nearly 18 years of work as an editor, I have had dealings with many authors, French and foreign, often difficult, but you are the only writer who ALWAYS writes to me (one exception, a letter from you dated November 15, 1978), through the intermediary of your p.d.g. [*president-directeur-général*, French for CEO—in this case Roger Straus]. It can be said without offending anyone that this complicates relations for no good reason. And it is rude.[63]

Roger Straus had even done her bidding when Jacqueline Kennedy Onassis requested a blurb, and the exchange is worth quoting, for the snapshot it gives us of these two women in the world of publishing. In the spring of 1980, Onassis was editing a book of fashion photographs assembled by her friend Diana Vreeland, former editor of *Harper's Bazaar* and *Vogue*. She sent Susan Sontag a portion of the book in advance of publication and asked her a favor:

> It would be so deeply appreciated if you could give a quote for it. . . . If you could see the different ways her original eye treats photographs—cropping,

layout, juxtaposing. Or the photographs she remembered and put here, that we would have never seen. Do you know Paul Haviland? I believe he took about 11 photographs. His *Passing Steamer* looks like a Whistler. And Elsa Maxwell, Callas and her husband in a nightclub is pure Fellini. I think I had better be pulled off this book soon as I am ranting on a bit. Please forgive me. I want to do everything I can to make it a success for her. She is a gallant figure to whom I am devoted—(and it is a great book!).

The letter was addressed to "Dear Susan" and signed "Affectionately, Jackie." It was not Susan Sontag but Roger Straus who replied to "Dear Mrs. Onassis." Susan had handed him her letter and the material "with one foot on the plane to Poland." He explained:

> I did phone to tell you that she is sorry she cannot comply, for besides everything else, she has a standing rule not to comment on any "picture books." This of course has to do with her book, ON PHOTOGRAPHY, and I am sure, and she is sure, that you will understand.

He was returning the material, and wished Mrs. Onassis much luck with the publication of the book. He signed his letter, "Sincerely, Roger W. Straus."[64]

It is difficult to read this exchange and not despise Sontag for ignoring Jacqueline Onassis's fine-grained and personal support of Diana Vreeland's unusual collection—her letter even included a wink by alluding to Callas, Onassis's lover. All was reduced to a "picture book."

Perhaps what is even more astonishing is that these two women, with their different backgrounds and choices, were now traveling in the same circles. Onassis's form of address and signature make it clear that they were on a first-name basis.

If Jacqueline Kennedy's great achievement was to have become a thinking woman in a world where she had been destined for the empty life of a socialite, Susan Sontag's was finally not so different—to have become, from her ordinary Arizona beginnings, the writer described by a French magazine as "the figurehead [la figure de proue] of North American intelligentsia,"[65] above the fray, and above caring much about what Jacqueline Kennedy Onassis represented—not caring, or careful not to show that she did. The same person who couldn't be bothered to respond to Onassis directly, saved for her archives an invitation from Onassis to a cocktail party at her

Fifth Avenue apartment, with a hand-scrawled note at the bottom: "Susan, do stay for supper, Jackie."[66] Only someone who had struggled so hard not to appease would have to make a show of turning so far in the other direction.

At Home in Paris

She may have been known as the ultimate New York intellectual, but Paris was, as Sontag put it, "the alternative capital of my imagination."[67] In Annie Leibovitz's book *A Photographer's Life,* you can see Susan Sontag in her last home in Paris at 2 rue Séguier, a stone's throw from her rooms with Harriet, though now she was living in a classified historical monument, the Hôtel Feydeau de Montholon, a seventeenth-century *hôtel particulier.* In one photograph, she is leaning on a stone wall on the quai des Grands Augustins, looking toward the book stalls across the river. In March, 2002, she performed her last reading at the Village Voice Bookshop just behind the Place Saint-Sulpice, centerpiece of her beloved *Nightwood.* Whenever

16. Susan Sontag on the quai des Grands Augustins near her Paris apartment (2000). Photograph © Annie Leibovitz / Contact Press Images.

she was in town, she spent hours there, perusing the shelves and talking to owner Odile Hellier about what she was reading, had read, wanted to read. In the afternoons, she sat at the Café de Flore, leaning against the wall, writing in her journal, and watching the street. I was walking down the boulevard Saint-Germain when I saw her that March. Her thick mane of hair no longer had the white streak above her temple that made her look like Athena, as Daniel Mendelsohn put it—but she was still unmistakably Susan Sontag.[68] It seemed to me then that she would always be there, or at least that there should always be room, at that café or at another in Paris, for someone like her, writing in a journal to try to make sense of the world.

When she died in 2004, her son David, with no instructions from his mother but knowing her better than anyone else, brought her to Paris to be buried. She resides in the Montparnasse cemetery with so many of the writers whose work she had scrutinized: Beauvoir, whose lecture she attended as a student, and whose novel—the perverse love triangle—she had wanted to bring to the screen; Duras, the New Novelist whose first film had been produced by Nicole Stéphane; Eugène Ionesco, the Romanian playwright she dismissed in *Against Interpretation*; and Beckett, the high modernist who had crossed over from English to French and whose *Waiting for Godot* she had taken to Sarejevo. Sartre is there, too, the critical and political standard bearer of a half-century of French intellectual life. Long after her student year in Saint-Germain-des-Prés, she had managed to live briefly in his apartment on the rue Bonaparte.

"Everything is renewed when you speak in a foreign language, when you live in another country," she told Chantal Thomas on French radio: "I understood my own country living here—obviously by contrast; I am very attached by temperament to the status of the foreigner, to what one learns and one feels when one is foreign. . . . Even though I live there, I don't feel like a New Yorker."[69]

On a 1979 French talk show, she spoke briefly about her origins to her host, Bernard Pivot, before discussing her book *On Photography* in a series of arresting philosophical statements, as photographers Marc Riboud and Robert Doisneau watched in admiration.[70] She had so thoroughly absorbed the French way of understanding her place in the world that instead of saying "I grew up in the American west" or "I was raised on the West Coast," she said what the French would say: "J'ai été élevée en province"—I was raised in the provinces. She spoke, with visible pleasure, as if she had come to Paris

17. Susan Sontag and Bernard Pivot on the television show *Apostrophes* (June 8, 1979), discussing photography. Author's photograph.

. . .

from Bordeaux or Dijon, as if she were truly akin to the characters in Stendhal or Balzac, the Julien Sorels and the Rastignacs, who had nourished her Arizona ambitions; as if she, like young Rastignac, had once looked down at the city from the heights of Père Lachaise and declared, "A nous deux maintenant!"—It's up to you and me now, Paris!

FIVE

Angela Davis

1963–1964

Four years after Susan Sontag and Harriet Sohmers hitchhiked out of a Paris under martial law, a Brandeis sophomore named Angela Davis, passing through the city on a summer tour, celebrated Algerian independence on the Place de la Sorbonne. In that tiny increment of time, something essential had shifted in the attitude of young Americans, both toward themselves and toward their country. For France too, the end of the Algerian war was only the beginning of a fomentation, a questioning of national values that would last beyond the revolutionary days of May '68.

Whitney Walton, in her history of American students in France, defines the generation of 1960s and '70s students abroad as critics, not so much of the country they were studying, but of their own home.[1] You can't understand these students without the larger picture of what international travel had become for Americans. On the one hand, the Hilton hotels, the idea of American comfort available everywhere; on the other hand, the Peace Corps, inaugurated by Kennedy in 1961, where privileged young people were sent to the farthest, least privileged places in the world. For some

Americans, the early 1960s was an era of idealism and service, Vietnam a cloud on the horizon. For young African Americans, for Angela Davis, those years were defined by the life-and-death struggle for basic rights of citizenship.

After a childhood in segregated Birmingham, Angela Davis went north, where she was educated at two institutions compelled by their particular histories to foster progressive education: Elisabeth Irwin High school in New York, many of whose faculty had been blacklisted in the McCarthy era, and Brandeis University, named after a Jewish Supreme Court justice in the immediate aftermath of World War II, and committed both to social justice and to the welfare of the Jewish community. While studying at Elisabeth Irwin on a Quaker Scholarship, Angela Davis perfected her French and read *The Communist Manifesto*; at Brandeis, she immersed herself in French literature and began to study philosophy with Herbert Marcuse. She first traveled to Paris in the summer of 1962, then enrolled in the Hamilton College Junior Year in France in 1963–64, with funding from Brandeis. She graduated with a French major and highest honors in 1965.

French was the first important stop on an intellectual path that led Angela Davis from literature to philosophy, from philosophy to political radicalism and life as an educator. The dramatic events that took place after her junior year in Paris—including a courthouse shoot-out for which she was indicted as an accessory, an arrest, and a murder trial—might have buried all but the vaguest memories of her time in France. Yet France had mattered to her, and would continue to matter, from her teenage years in Alabama to her adult life as an educator and radical thinker.

Gertrude Stein once said, referring to the country where she spent forty-four years of her life: "It is not what France gave you but what it did not take from you that was important." But civil rights was the furthest thing from her mind. Angela Davis's situation as a student of French had little in common with Stein's—or Sontag's or Bouvier's. No one had ever told those women where they could or couldn't eat, sleep, and drink. They might have been unhappy, or worried about an uncertain future; they were not fighting for the dignity of their beings.

Angela Davis grew up in Birmingham, Alabama. To the journalists who interviewed her about her childhood, she said, years later, that the first sounds she ever heard were bombs detonating in her neighborhood during the violent years of white resistance to integration. Along the way to adulthood she discovered French the way children discover a secret language, except that for her, the discovery corresponded to a basic need. In an atmosphere of escalating violence, she found, in French, and eventually through the French, a language through which she could make her demands heard, a prelude to taking up her own voice as a philosopher and political leader. Her voice, in turn, came to resonate for hundreds of thousands of French-speaking people, becoming part of their own language of liberation. The story begins in Alabama and ends in Aubervilliers.

Alabama

Only rarely has Angela Davis evoked her roots: "I have looked for my history in the story of the colonization of this continent and I have found silences, omissions, distortions, and fleeting, enigmatic insinuations."[2] She was born in Birmingham in 1944, the daughter of African Americans who had migrated to the industrial hub of Alabama from two rural counties. Marengo County, her father's birthplace, was founded by French expatriates from Napoleon's army in memory of a victory against the Austrian army in Italy—the same expatriates from the white terror who settled in Philadelphia, including Jacqueline Bouvier's furniture-making ancestor Michel Bouvier.[3] Her mother had grown up a foster child in Talladega County, where, since the 1760s, the Creek Indians had intermarried with Spanish and French settlers.

On her father's side, Angela's grandmother was a loving woman who welcomed the grandchildren on their visits to the farm. Her paternal grandfather, a mystery to the grandchildren, was white.[4] There were rumors that he might have been a wealthy man from Marengo county who had moved to Birmingham to run a lumber business. None of the children knew him but they knew that miscegenation was against the law in Alabama. "If your skin is the color of Angela's," said her lawyer in his closing speech at her 1972 trial, "every time you look at the color of the skin you realize that it's the result of some white master having raped your great-grandmother."[5] Angela's host mother on her junior year in Paris, interviewed almost fifty years after the fact, was convinced that Angela Davis had a French grandparent. That was her fantasy. In the American south, in the 1940s and well beyond the 1940s, the old racist rule of "one drop of blood" held sway: no white person would ever claim black heritage, and no black person was supposed to acknowledge a white forebear. Patricia Williams, in her classic essay "On Being the Object of Property," describes the intolerable inheritance: knowing she was descended from a great-grandmother who had been raped, and owned, by her white great-grandfather meant that she lived the terrible paradox of "claim[ing] for myself a heritage the weft of whose genesis is my own disinheritance."[6] This violent dialectic of inheritance and disinheritance is of a far different order from the aristocratic family tree that Major Bouvier faked and presented to Jacqueline, or the intellectual genealogy that Susan Sontag created in reinventing herself as a European.

Angela Davis's parents, Frank and Sallye Davis, were community leaders in Birmingham. Her father, a teacher and graduate of Saint Augustine's College in Raleigh, North Carolina, owned his own business, a service station; her mother taught school. Sallye was a person of great courage who had run away from her foster parents when they wanted her to work rather than continue her education. She lived at the YWCA until the school principal took her in, and she changed her name from Sally May to Sallye Marguerite because, as her daughter Fania remembers with affection, it was more sophisticated. She graduated from Miles College in Birmingham and got a master's degree at New York University. It's hard to say exactly what that French middle name meant to her. She wanted the world to be bigger than Talladega County, bigger than Birmingham.[7] She gave Angela a French middle name as well—Yvonne.

Sallye Davis was an activist as well as a teacher. She worked with the Southern Negro Youth Congress, which had organized for voting rights in the South since the 1930s. She lobbied her landlords for running water and toilets in the apartment complex where Angela was born.[8] The Davises were among the African American families who bought homes bordering on a neighborhood of whites—hence the bombs planted by the segregationists, thanks to which their neighborhood was nicknamed "Dynamite Hill." There were some fifty unsolved bombings in Birmingham between 1957 and 1962.[9] Angela attended a segregated school—separate and unequal—which she credits with giving her the rudiments of black history missing from the curriculum of white Alabama schools.[10] She knew early on that she wanted to learn French. There was no French instruction at her school, so she got a grammar book and studied on her own, teaching the other children by staying a lesson ahead.[11]

A *History of Alabama,* taught in state schools from its first edition in 1927 well into the 1950s, gives the full measure of the dominant ideology into which Angela Davis was born, with its nostalgia for plantation society, its praise of kind overseers concerned for the health and well-being of slaves—slaves whom the author, a professor of history at the University of Alabama, compares to farm animals.[12] Lest anyone forget a time when "separate and unequal" was considered part of the natural order of things and was, in fact, the rule of law, his rhetoric is the genteel flipside of the violent Ku Klux Klan propaganda.

For a young black woman growing up in the Jim Crow South, the simplest aspects of everyday life were a struggle. The family vacation with no hotel accommodations. The child who runs to the seat behind the bus driver and needs to be coaxed to the back by a terrified caretaker. The separate water fountains. The amusement park or movie house off limits. Fania Davis used to go into white bathrooms, knowing it was against the law and knowing from what her parents had taught her that the law was wrong.[13]

Later, when Angela Davis came into the public eye, the press would portray her as a product of private schools and a French education who had joined the revolution—a child of privilege gone wrong. On the contrary, her political roots in Alabama remained a solid foundation, and her family a source of unity and support. Though she may have been more bookish and more introverted than her parents, she never lost her sense of their legacy through struggle. And her sense of herself as exemplary rather than special, as one among the masses of African Americans fighting for liberation, pervaded everything she did.

In the mid-1950s, Sallye Davis attended NYU summer school to pursue her master's and took her children with her. There young Angela tasted new privileges: zoos, parks, and beaches open to them, Puerto Rican, white, and black children to play with, seats on the bus behind the driver. The return to Birmingham after that first New York summer was a terrible awakening. When she grew older, even the so-called racial harmony of the north was tarnished for her. She heard about the mixed-race couple who couldn't find a place to live, and watched, confused, as her friend Harriet's father, James Jackson, disappeared. He was forced to live underground during McCarthy's witch-hunt because of his political work for the Communist Party.[14] The simultaneous pressures, in her parents' world, of race, political activism,

: 147

and Jim Crow segregation all came together to create a situation in which Angela Davis became an exquisite reader of signs; of "blond-haired children with their mean-looking mothers . . . always crowded around the ticket booth" for the theater where she wasn't allowed; of the words "Colored" and "White," deciphered well before the elementary sentences in the Dick and Jane reader; of the strict line of demarcation between her house on Center Street and the white neighborhood across the street; and of the absolute interdiction of crossing from east to west.[15] Segregation, she said years later in a television interview in France, was not one among many memories of childhood—it *was* her memory of childhood.[16]

It's easy enough to see the destiny of the philosopher in the young Angela Davis, a reader of signs, an inventor of rules and principles for living, a person of essentially cerebral qualities, who valued orderly, rational thinking. In such a world, for such a person, a counterlife of dreams and imaginary travel was an absolute necessity. In her autobiography, written in 1975, Davis explores the state of mind of a black child growing up in the segregated south. It was one thing to learn to deal with rage. You did that to survive. It was another to deal with envy, with wanting to be white—the equivalent of wanting to be your own worst enemy. And yet how natural it was to long for the privilege and freedom that came with being white. The temptation to turn the racism of society against oneself was strong—a conflict white girls didn't have to deal with.

Her first act of resistance was an act of imagination designed to outfox the desire for whiteness by controlling her racial identity:

> I constructed a fantasy in which I would slip on a white face and go unceremoniously into the theater or amusement park or wherever I wanted to go. After thoroughly enjoying the activity, I would make a dramatic grandstand appearance before the white racists and with a sweeping gesture, rip off the white face, laugh wildly and call them all fools.[17]

A writer who would become important to her, the Martiniquan psychiatrist Frantz Fanon, explained a similar emotional temptation in *Black Skin, White Masks* (1952), his analysis of racial psychology in the Antilles. He described a girl in Martinique who emptied a pot of black ink over the head of anyone who dared to insult her but who, as an adult, gave in to the desire to turn white, to bleach herself mentally.[18] In Angela's imagination, there was a theater where she could move in and out of her black self, put on a white mask, but always rip it off in the end. Her mask was only temporary, and strategic.

When she was a teenager, she was able to put her fantasy into action. She found the mask, which came in the form of language, and that language was French. Now at Elisabeth Irwin, Davis had begun intense French classes with a native Frenchwoman named Madeleine Griner. "Madeleine," as the girls called her, was a battle-ax, a WAC veteran and a disciplinarian who specialized in examinations by *dictée*—a cornerstone of French pedagogy, requiring students to write down the sentences exactly as she spoke them, with every point of grammar and spelling correct. Other teachers at the progressive high school were rigorous, but no one was as tough as Madeleine— and if you didn't have an ear for French, you were in trouble. Angela had only her self-designed preparation in the language, and now set herself the goal of excelling in the hardest subject of all.[19]

On one of her visits home from Elisabeth Irwin, the adventure took place. Angela was seventeen, a senior in High School, and Fania was thirteen[20]:

> My sister Fania and I were walking downtown in Birmingham when I spontaneously proposed a plan to her: We would pretend to be foreigners and, speaking French to each other, we would walk into the shoe store on 19th Street and ask, with a thick accent, to see a pair of shoes.

The plan worked:

> At the sight of two young Black women speaking a foreign language, the clerks in the store raced to help us. Their delight with the exotic was enough to completely, if temporarily, dispel their normal disdain for Black people. Therefore Fania and I were not led to the back of the store where the one Black clerk would normally have waited on us out of the field of vision of the "respectable" white customers. We were invited to take seats in the very front of this Jim Crow shop. I pretended to know no English at all and Fania's broken English was extremely difficult to make out. The clerks strained to understand which shoes we wanted to try on. Enthralled by the idea of talking to foreigners—even if they did happen to be Black—but frustrated about the communication failure, the clerks sent for the manager. . . . He asked us about our background—where were we from, what were we doing in the States and

: 149

what on earth had brought us to a place like Birmingham, Alabama? . . . After
repeated attempts, however, the manager finally understood that we came
from Martinique and were in Birmingham as part of a tour of the United
States.

For someone who never inhabited the segregated universe, the scene is baf-
fling. The first thing to understand is that Birmingham, in the late 1950s,
was a backwater, a provincial world in which the arrival of a foreigner—any
foreigner—was cause for amazement. And that amazement temporarily suspended the strict racial codes of the day. Disguised as black foreigners, who
didn't threaten the social order, the Davis sisters had a temporary pass to
participate in white society, at least in that particular shoe store. Class and
exoticism trumped race.

The make-believe ended just as in Angela's daydream, with ripping off
the mask, with social revenge. The gesture is so theatrical, so dramatic, it is
important to remember that the theater in question was real, and to appreciate their courage, for what Angela and Fania did next might have had dire
results. In Money, Mississippi, only a few years earlier, young Emmett Till
had been kidnapped and lynched for whistling at a white woman—and it's
not even clear that he whistled. What Angela and her sister did was much
more deliberate and more daring:

> We burst out laughing. He started to laugh with us, hesitantly, the way people
> laugh when they suspect themselves to be the butt of the joke. "Is something
> funny?" he whispered. Suddenly I knew English, and told him that he was
> what was so funny. "All Black people have to do is pretend they come from
> another country, and you treat us like dignitaries." My sister and I got up, still
> laughing, and left the store.[21]

The Summer of 1962

"All black people have to do is pretend they come from another country." Or
go to another country.

If so many American students in France became critics of their own
home in the 1960s and 1970s, it was in large part because France was point-
ing the way. Angela Davis's first experience of Paris took place in the summer
after her first year at Brandeis. She had worked on campus and in New York

to fund her trip to the World Festival of Youth and Students in Helsinki, Finland, and was meeting up with friends in Paris first.

By 1962, her own political education was advancing. A series of progressive organizations, institutions, and people, beginning with her parents' friends the Jacksons in Birmingham and the Southern Negro Youth Congress, gave her role models for the future and encouraged her travels. In high school, as a recipient of a Quaker scholarship, she stayed in the home of Reverend Melish, who was engaged in a long battle with his Episcopal diocese to retain his right to the pulpit after defending victims of McCarthyism and leading a Soviet-American Friendship organization. At Elisabeth Irwin, she joined a study group called Advance, which included Bettina Aptheker, daughter of Herbert Aptheker, the historian and intellectual dean of American communism. When it came time to choose a college, she picked Brandeis, known for a faculty in social theory that included the political philosopher Herbert Marcuse and the more conservative Philip Rieff, Susan Sontag's former husband. Nothing she had studied in her freshman year, including the writing by Sartre and Camus and Beauvoir that fascinated her, could have prepared Angela Davis for those first few weeks in a Paris of strikes and demonstrations and Algerian celebrations.

Transatlantic travel had begun to change since Jacqueline Bouvier and Susan Sontag crossed the Atlantic in their ocean liners, with a meditative week to absorb the transfer from New World to Old. Angela Davis first arrived in Europe on a charter aircraft; it was the era of Pan Am and the Caravelle, of millions of transistor radios sending news across the globe. Everything was faster, more direct.

But some things about Americans in Paris hadn't changed. Like Susan Sontag, Angela Davis found her first Paris lodgings in a hotel in the Latin Quarter. A strike at the Gare du Nord got in the way of her rendezvous with her friend Harriet Jackson, so they finally made contact through the American Express, the same American Express where Susan Sontag picked up angry letters from the husband she had left behind. It had been a mail drop for Americans abroad since before the First World War, and by now had blossomed into a kind of informal youth embassy. Harriet had a friend in Paris who rented a maid's room and was away for the summer, and they decamped there next. Their *chambre de bonne* was in the sixteenth arrondissement, six flights up, with a single windowpane set in the roof through which they could see the elevators on the Eiffel Tower, transporting tourists up and down. What was remarkable about the sociology of Paris was that you could be in the wealthiest district in the city, with monumental views, and still reside, in those high-up spaces, with the poorest sectors of urban society. Angela shared that tiny space with two roommates: Harriet Jackson, whose Jamaican-born father, James Jackson, had organized voting rights and workers' rights in Birmingham with the Southern Negro Youth Congress in the 1950s, and Florence Mason, a friend from Elisabeth Irwin and a member, with Angela, of the group of political activists called Advance.

Three eighteen-year-old girls, politically aware, with no official ties and no plans other than discovery.[22] Theirs was the same décor, the same endless walkup, the same mansard roofs that Susan Sontag had known. What Angela Davis felt, what she saw with Harriet and Florence from her sixth-floor window, was entirely different. Sontag later explained that her Parisian world, in 1958, was largely American, her everyday language English. She had not come to France, as had Angela Davis, with a built-in sense of her own lifelong exclusion from civil society, her own foreignness. She had come in search of sexual freedom and intellectual sophistication. What Angela Davis saw in France—what she had better eyes to see, what she understood better than white Americans traveling abroad in 1962—was a drama of migration, the pressure cooker of racial intolerance coupled with economic misery.

That summer was particularly intense: there was an influx of French soldiers returning from duty in Algeria; Algerians of European descent who had been fleeing the country for over a year at the rate of some five thousand a day; and, most meaningful for her, Algerian workers, arriving by the hundreds of thousands even as their country emerged from its war for independence, workers straining to eke out a living in the city. They were the fruit of France's loss; some hoped for full integration, others for an education or a nest egg to take home.

She was immediately aware of Algerians in the street, but the first immigrants she got to know were a family from Martinique—the country she'd claimed as her own in the Birmingham shoe store. Across the hall from Angela and Harriet and Florence, in a room of about the same size, was not the glamorous, fashionable Caribbean girl of Angela's shoe store make-believe, but a newly arrived single mother with four grown children.[23]

Unlike the Muslims living in Algeria, who had to petition for full French citizenship rights even when Algeria was still part of France, the people of

Martinique, Guadeloupe, and French Guiana were French citizens of three overseas *départements*.[24] A small, elite migration from the Caribbean was inseparable from France's intellectual and literary prestige in the first half of the twentieth century: it included novelist and colonial administrator René Maran (1887–1960), born in Martinique and schooled in Bordeaux, who won France's top literary prize, the Prix Goncourt, in 1921; the poet Aimé Césaire (1913–2008), born in Martinique and educated on scholarship in Paris's best schools, who founded the Negritude movement and became the leading critic of colonization in the French National Assembly; Gaston Monnerville (1897–1991) from French Guiana, who took his law and literature degrees in Toulouse, distinguished himself in the French Resistance, and went on to become president of the French Senate, first in line of succession for the French presidency; and, finally, the Martiniquan Frantz Fanon (1925–1961), a Resistance fighter trained in Lyon in psychiatry and philosophy, whose support of the Algerian revolution would play a major role in the revolutionary consciousness of a generation. A poorer sector of the population from Martinique and Guadeloupe migrated to France in the 1950s at a slow but steady rate, escaping the agricultural misery that came with mechanized plantations and the declining sugar industry. Their numbers jumped when the French government created an office to encourage migration from the overseas territories in order to provide metropolitan France with the workers needed to feed a booming postwar economy.[25]

The mother across the hall was part of that new social group: women from Martinique poised to take on the work that French women were abandoning, low-ranking jobs in the service sector as hospital and retirement-home attendants, mail sorters, messengers, and maids.[26] A year later, when Angela Davis returned to Paris for her junior year abroad, France signed labor agreements with Mali and Senegal and Mauritania. As workers from those countries made their way to the metropolis, giving it an unprecedented racial diversity, the architectural face of Paris was getting whiter. Malraux's decree ordering the regular cleaning of building facades in the capital dated from the summer of 1962, and the dark, sooty buildings that Jacqueline Bouvier and Susan Sontag had known would be gradually scraped down to a chalky surface.

It's often claimed, with a touch of wishful thinking, that the black Antillais living in France consider themselves entirely French, with no sense

: 153

of a racial identity—as if the fact of their citizenship itself were enough to protect them from discrimination. Citizenship is not a negligible privilege. But discrimination functions in complicated ways, modulated by class, context, social bonds, color itself, even with citizenship in place. In 1962, racism surely affected a Martiniquan woman in search of work, but nothing could match the violence directed toward the Arabs and Berbers from Algeria, who were identified with a long and bloody war for independence from France. So great was the sense, in Paris, that being Algerian meant living under dire threat that the Martiniquan women across the hall returned home at night with "horror stories of being mistaken for Algerian women."[27] The people of Martinique were African, Indian, European, and they had a vocabulary all their own for describing their skin color: *café au lait* for light brown; *chabin* for a person with light skin, red hair, and green eyes; *capre* for someone with one white parent and one parent born of a black-white marriage; *coulis* for a mix of black and Indian. Many Martiniquans had the light brown skin common to Algerians of Arab ancestry. And by 1962 the Algerian war had produced in France such a surplus of visceral hatred that "Algerian" was a default identity, a stubborn label of hate flung indiscriminately at any person of color.

On the surface, at least, the nightmare was supposed to be over. Algeria's official independence was celebrated on the streets of Paris on July 5, 1962, with free couscous in the cafés, parades on the street, and the green and white flag of the new Algerian nation flying everywhere. The government tried to ban the joyous demonstrations for fear of violence between Algerians and supporters of the secret army of the generals who had vowed to keep Algeria part of France—the Organisation de l'armée secrète, or OAS. Independence only goaded the OAS to continue to plot, and to plant bombs. In the weeks preceding Algeria's July 5th Independence Day, the *Herald Tribune* reported OAS machine gun raids on Muslim cafés in Paris, "cafés raked with pistol and machine gun fire from slow moving cars."[28] Not far from the *chambre de bonne*, a twenty-year-old man had stood at his window on the rue de Sontay the previous May dressed in full paratrooper camouflage, spattering the street with bullets.[29]

It was a far cry from the France evoked by Jacqueline Kennedy, who posed for photographers, that same summer, among the French furnishings of her newly restored White House.[30] Still, Angela and her friends had their pick of art exhibits: a Miro retrospective at the Musée d'art moderne, Debussy at the Opéra, next to the American Express office. The department store Le Printemps was reporting an influx of 150 tourists a day, of whom 75 percent were Americans. These American shoppers wanted "the Frenchiest items": snail holders, berets, garlic presses, dishcloths printed with French poetry, butter curlers, and camembert.[31] The ration tickets that the Smith juniors had needed in 1949—not even fifteen years earlier—were unthinkable now. You had to be French and at least thirty years old to remember a time when food wasn't plentiful.

It was a polarized society. On one side of the social equation were the tourists, enjoying luxury goods made in France; on the other, serving that society, the immigrants—the French citizens from Martinique and Guadeloupe and, beneath them in the social order, the Arab Algerians of Muslim faith.

The whole situation was a rude awakening to a young African American woman who, in her freshman year at Brandeis, had attended a lecture by James Baldwin, the expatriate African American writer known for finding his freedom in Paris. Indeed, to understand Angela Davis's relationship to France as a woman, a student, and later as a philosopher and theorist of revolution, it is important to recall the mythical power that France held for black Americans, through the course of two world wars and still today. After both wars, American soldiers stayed and remade their lives in a place they found far more open than home.[32] France held black writers and artists in special regard; and Paris, in the 1950s (as it had been in the 1930s) was home to the novelist Richard Wright, to James Baldwin, to Chester Himes and to Josephine Baker (who had become a French citizen in the 1930s and participated in the Resistance in World War II). It was Richard Wright who taught Simone de Beauvoir the basics of what W. E. B. Du Bois called "the double consciousness" of racial self-awareness, which became a reference point in *The Second Sex*.[33] Women lived with the consciousness that their world did not belong to them, that it was a man's world, in much the same way that African Americans were constantly negotiating white reality. Beauvoir talked about a screen—a sense of performing for men—the way Du Bois talked about the veil, or Fanon and the young Angela Davis, talked about the white mask.

Since the First World War, France had been a place where African Americans could take off the mask. France offered them relief from the racism at home, and African Americans offered France in turn a rich cultural legacy of music, literature, dance. Saint-Germain-des-Prés swung to the sound of bebop, and under the auspices of existentialist trumpet player and poet Boris Vian, jazzmen Miles Davis and Dizzy Gillespie starred in the basement clubs. Sidney Bechet, too, who liked to acknowledge his French name and origins, was an important figure throughout the 1950s.[34] Through jazz, which had wafted through Sartre's 1938 novel *Nausea* and made its appearance in any number of postwar books, both as setting and as an occasion for a kind of philosophical daring, the link between existentialism and African American culture was strong. For a young African American student like Angela Davis, being an existentialist on campus already amounted to a kind of mental expatriation. Still, there was something irritating to black artists in Paris about the French celebration of black American culture. Baldwin used to joke that he wanted to write a story for French readers called *Je ne joue pas la trompette*—"I don't play the trumpet."[35]

Richard Wright was well known for his faith in France, for his belief, as he put it, that "there is more freedom in one square block of Paris than there is in the entire United States of America."[36] Some African American writers in Paris considered him a sell-out, a darling of the French left who comforted French intellectuals with the belief that their country was less racist than the United States. But by 1957 even Richard Wright had begun to explore the underside of the country he loved.[37] For anyone who lived in France through the years of the Algerian War, it became clear that, as historian Tyler Stovall has argued, the Algerian War had "buried the myth of colorblind France for African American expatriates" and showed them that racism as a phenomenon reached well beyond American shores. *The Stone Face*, a nearly forgotten novel published in 1963 by the African American writer William Gardner Smith, provides a blueprint for this disillusion.[38] Its main character is Simeon, a black journalist from Philadelphia who has fled to France after a random beating by a white policeman. He joins Algerians in their demonstration of October 17, 1961, protesting a curfew. The episode is based closely on the real event, which ended in violence as unarmed demonstrators were beaten to death and thrown in the Seine. Others were taken to the Palais des Sports, all too reminiscent of the bicycle stadium where the Paris police had rounded up 13,000 Jews in 1942. In the novel, Simeon is arrested and taken to the stadium but quickly released, while the surviving Arabs who have demonstrated with him remain in custody. The police make it clear to him that he doesn't belong with them, that the Algerian trouble shouldn't concern him: "We like Negroes here, we don't practice racism in France, it's not like the United States. We can understand why you prefer to live here. We wouldn't like to have to expel you."[39] What the fictional Simeon experiences in *The Stone Face* was true in a larger sense for many African Americans in Paris in those years: exempt from the violence directed toward Algerians, American blacks were aware of their own privilege, their symbolic usefulness to the French, just as they were aware of the miserable conditions of Arabs. Wright, for one, worried that he would lose his asylum if he criticized French policy. The nagging guilt remained.[40]

"I lived mainly among *les misérables*," Baldwin wrote about his first expatriate years, "and in Paris *les misérables* were Algerian."[41] No one who knew both national contexts could ignore the obvious analogy: the Arab Algerians' struggle for independence from France, after generations of living under separate and unequal conditions, was comparable in myriad ways to the situation of black Americans struggling for their own liberation in the American South. Black American expatriates debated these issues in the same cafés where Burroughs, Sontag, and Harriet Sohmers had gathered a few years earlier: the Monaco, near Richard Wright's apartment on the rue Monsieur le Prince, and the Café Tournon, Baldwin's spot near the Luxembourg Gardens and the first port of call for African American intellectuals in Paris.[42] Angela Davis, on her first summer trip to Paris, had just finished her freshman year of college and her connections to this world were a decade away. But what these weighty writers and intellectuals saw, what disturbed them in the comfort of their Parisian exile, was as evident to the Brandeis sophomore as " the racist slogans scratched on the walls of the city threatening death to the Algerians."[43] About the pro-Algerian demonstration she attended on the place de la Sorbonne in July 1962, Angela Davis wrote, "When the *flics* broke it up with their high power water hoses, they were as vicious as the redneck cops in Birmingham who met the Freedom Riders with their dogs and hoses."[44]

Reading

Angela Davis's autobiography describes her undergraduate years as a time of reading and contemplation. The year before her first summer visit to

Paris and Helsinki, in addition to reading Sartre and Camus on her own, she took courses on Baudelaire and Rimbaud with the French poet Yves Bonnefoy. Bonnefoy was one of the foreign luminaries brought in to animate intellectual life in the humanities at Brandeis, a university that was only fifteen years old and still making its mark—a precocious, progressive Jewish cousin to Harvard and Boston University and Tufts. It's hard to imagine another school in Boston that would have assigned Ginsberg's *Howl* to the incoming class of 1965. Bonnefoy's own poetry was rich with philosophical resonance, drawing meaning from Hegel and Heidegger. As an art historian and a translator of Shakespeare, he brought his own vast culture to the classroom. He never forgot the strongest student in the class, her passion for philosophy, and the respect she earned from his friend Marcuse, who expected great things of her in the field of philosophy.[45]

Then there was Proust. *In Search of Lost Time* was taught in Angela Davis's sophomore year at Brandeis by Milton Hindus, a professor of comparative literature known for having conducted one of the rare interviews with the anti-Semitic writer Céline in his postwar exile in Denmark. In 1963, Hindus had just published his *Reader's Guide to Marcel Proust.*[46] French professors tend to worry about whether their twenty-year-old undergraduate students are equipped to get anything out of Proust, their theory being that you can't appreciate him unless you've felt, yourself, the passing of time, the way people can weave in and out of your life, the way faces grow to resemble character traits, the way a mystery at age eighteen can finally be resolved at age eighty. But it is intriguing to imagine the Proust that Angela Davis discovered on the nearly all-white, progressive, and Jewish campus of Brandeis, one adept reader of signs immersed in the pages of another. She spent her days in the library or in what she later called "hidden places" with her books.[47] "The idea of my work," explains the narrator of *Time Regained*, "was inside my head, always the same, perpetually in the process of becoming."[48]

What Proust had to offer Angela Davis in her understanding of her own society included his corrosive humor in analyzing the foibles of class structure in turn-of-the-century Paris, his portrait of exclusion and bigotry against Jews and "orientals" in the Parisian milieu he frequented, and his rendering of violence at home and on the front during the First World War. For a young woman of her intellectual intensity, her life experiences, he must have been a ruminative companion with his long, consoling sentences and his mastery of surfaces.

Orientation

The independent People's Democratic Republic of Algeria was a year old in the fall of 1963, when Angela Davis embarked on the Hamilton College Junior Year in France. The group took the *France*—study abroad programs still favored the traditional steamship crossing over charter flights. After what she had learned about French racism in the summer of 1962, it might come as a surprise that she elected to go back to France for a full academic year. Perhaps the shattered myth of France as the definitive escape from American racism had given way in her mind to a sense of France as a defeated empire, a place where new battles for liberation could take place, where she would have access to the work of thinkers analyzing the phenomenon of decolonization from an international perspective. Sartre, her favorite author, had been writing about Algeria's right to autonomy, about torture, and about colonialism as a system in regular articles in *Les temps modernes* since 1956. In 1961 he had written a foreword to Fanon's *Wretched of the Earth*. His apartment on the rue Bonaparte was bombed by the ultranationalist OAS in one of its last desperate attempts to keep Algeria French. To live in France was to be in Sartre's country.

There was another reason, even more basic. Angela Davis, at twenty, had just declared her French major. She was a reader of philosophy and literature, quiet, self-sufficient, disciplined in her studies. It was not the politically engaged Sartre who drew her at this stage of her education as much as Sartre the novelist and playwright, and especially the philosopher. On her own, she had worked her way through *Being and Nothingness,* in addition to the plays and novels. At Brandeis she'd met a German exchange student, Manfred Clemenz, who had introduced her to more philosophy. They had become engaged, and now he was back in Germany. Some of the girls on the program remember that she had traveled to France to be near him.[49]

As for her own political education, it was still in process—she was, as yet, on the theory side of praxis. To her friend Howard Bloch, an Amherst student on the Hamilton program, she was an intellectual model—a serious student who didn't wear her learning heavily. He decided that her extreme outward reserve was tied to how much was going on in her head: "I assumed she was thinking some great thought: she was ahead of everyone."[50]

Christie Stagg, a Wells College student from a small town in Vermont, wrote to her parents about the roommate who had been assigned to her, after a member of the Hamilton staff asked if she would object rooming with a Negro:

> She is an extremely exceptional girl—speaks French better than I can ever begin to, reads "vociferously," is learning German because her fiancé is German, and carries a most interesting conversation. She is much more mature than the rest of us, probably because she went two years in New York to school before going to Brandeis, and this is her second trip to Europe.[51]

Vivian Goldberg remembers her "shy, melodious laugh" and her striking beauty: "When she pulled out a cigarette in the cafeteria, young men would jump to offer her a light." She remembers, too, Angela Davis's disciplined study habits, her mastery of the material, and the quantity of index cards she kept.[52]

The woman admired from a distance by so many of her peers had a fine-honed wit and an affectionate warmth within her inner circle of friends. In the early 1960s, the study-abroad girls were still wearing skirts and sweater sets, girdles and hose, or tights in really cold weather. So when she packed to go skiing in Germany with Manfred, she had to borrow a pair of jeans from Howard, who became, from then on, "Howard the pants."[53]

This was the same young woman whose photo had appeared in the *Birmingham World* the spring before her first trip abroad—a picture of elegance, her bouffant hair smooth and lightened, her hands clasped under her chin, looking older than her twenty years, the way young women in those years looked older when they were dressed up. She had made the dean's list:

> Miss Angela Davis, daughter of Mr. and Mrs. B. Frank Davis of 11th Court North has been placed on the "Dean's List II" at Brandeis University, Waltham, Mass. . . . Miss Davis did a summer of study in Paris, France as part of the Brandeis program. Upon return to Birmingham, she gave a talk to members of the Birmingham Club of Frontiers International, of which her father is a member.[54]

The guest speaker at the Birmingham chapter of Frontiers International, the only national service organization for Negro entrepreneurs and community leaders,[55] was not yet the political radical who would make her mark on the world, though she was already a warrior against bureaucracies. It had taken some doing to transfer her Brandeis scholarship to the Hamilton program, and she had won that fight.[56]

By the time Angela Davis returned with the 1963–64 Hamilton College Junior Year in France, study in Paris had become a growing feature of American college life. Delaware offered its first program as early as 1923, Smith in 1925, Sweet Briar in 1948, Sarah Lawrence in 1953, and a conglomerate called the Academic Year Abroad Program in 1960. A number of these Paris programs, including Hamilton, were housed in Reid Hall.[57] The Hamilton program was founded in 1957, the year Susan Sontag arrived in Paris.

Hamilton was still an all-male school in 1963, one of the oldest colleges in the state of New York, with a small student body and a tradition of academic excellence. Like Smith, it had its Parisian headquarters at Reid Hall, but unlike Smith, the Hamilton Junior Year in France included both men and women, and accepted many more students from schools beyond its own campus than Smith did. That year there were only eight Hamilton students in the group of forty-six.[58] Jim Davis, a recent PhD who had just defended his thesis on "Autonomy and Relativism in the Contemporary French Novel" at the University of Pennsylvania, was the resident director, living in the college's Paris apartment with his French wife, Françoise, and making sure that the system functioned—that the students had the right classes at Sciences Po, the Sorbonne, and the Institut britannique; that the housing assigments in various families were working; that the students were profiting from their stay.

While Smith juniors went to Grenoble before settling in Paris, the Hamilton students always began their year with six weeks in Biarritz, the resort town on the Atlantic coast, site of a lavish casino and home to the luxurious Hôtel du Palais. Biarritz, in the era of Napoleon III, had been a favorite watering hole where wealthy English and Russian families spent their summers. In Colette's novel *Chéri*, Colette's courtisan Leah goes to Biarritz to console herself after her young lover Chéri gets married. Now, with the wild popularity of the Côte d'Azur, Biarritz was out of fashion, a stop for tourists en route to Spain. For the Hamilton group, Biarritz meant home stays and grammar review. Christie Stagg and Angela lived with a warm-hearted widow, Madame Salerni, who drove them to Spain for a shopping expedi-

: 161

18. Angela Davis (*right*), on her Hamilton College Junior Year in France, during orientation in Biarritz (fall 1963). *Left:* Diana Sumner; *center:* Howard Bloch. Photograph courtesy Jane Jordan.

. . .

tion and fed them multicourse meals twice a day. Before dinner, she liked to bring the soup tureen into their room for them to taste and approve.[59]

That September, Biarritz was experiencing a massive invasion of fleas. The souvenir shops were empty, abandoned by the departed tourists, and the students scratched day and night, until their skin was sore. The young Brandeis existentialist must have been reminded of Sartre's *Les mouches,* in which the gods send an invasion of flies, not fleas, to the city of Argos, to punish the people for the murder of Agamemnon. The fleas, her philosophical imagination, and the tragic news from home that was about to reach her there all meant she could never think of the coastal town in a happy or innocent way.

Chapter Five

Reading the Newspaper in Biarritz

Reconstructing the lives of young women in France has been in part an exercise in mapping their specific French spaces and habits—the halls of the Sorbonne, the Latin Quarter cafés, the "graph-paper cahiers" for class notes that Jacqueline Kennedy remembered with nostalgia. One habit, so obvious as to be almost invisible, may be the most important key of all to the revolution in perspective that a year abroad in France offered, and still offers, to Americans: the simple act of reading the newspaper.

It's a cliché transmitted regularly to American students in their French civilization courses that the French press is characterized by a politically committed and often passionate editorial tone ("advocacy journalism"), in contrast to the American press with its purported standards of balanced objectivity. The discovery that awaits American students abroad is that objectivity is always *someone's* objectivity—that behind the neutrality of a descriptive news report lies a point of view: the presence or absence of facts and figures, the salient detail placed just so, the order in the telling.

On September 16, 1963, in Biarritz, Angela Davis picked up a copy of the *Herald Tribune*. Susan Sontag's companion Harriet Sohmers had worked there; Jean Seberg, in the role of Patricia Franchini, had hawked its pages in Jean-Luc Godard's *Breathless*. The *Herald Tribune* was as American an institution in France as was the American Express office or the English-language Shakespeare & Co. bookstore. Reading the *Trib* was a way of going home without being home. What Angela Davis read that day, in the headlines and the wire service story that followed, was branded on her consciousness forever. Four fourteen-year-old Birmingham girls, friends and neighbors, died instantly in the bombing of the 16th Street Baptist Church. Of the four— Denise McNair, Cynthia Wesley, Addie Mae Collins, and Carole Robertson—Carole was Fania's close friend, and Cynthia lived in the house just behind the Davises.[60]

The first *Herald Tribune* article, a United Press wire service article dated September 16, 1963, begins with the fact of the bombing and the death of four girls and continues, in a second paragraph:

Thousands of enraged Negroes poured from their homes into the area around the shattered 16th Street Baptist Church. Police fought for two hours, firing rifles into the air, to control them.

The reader learned next that city officials feared trouble at night and called for help, that Governor Wallace rushed state policemen to the city and ordered the National Guard to stand by, that it took the police "two hours to disperse the screaming surging crowd of 200 Negroes who ran to the church at the sound of the blast," and that the incident sent fear through the city, which had known forty bombings in recent years—but the article does not specify that the targets of those earlier bombings were always black people (the Gaston motel, or the home of Martin Luther King's father). Not until the fourth paragraph are the four dead girls mentioned by name. And not until the very last column of the four-column front-page article is there any discussion of possible perpetrators. Finally, a police officer is quoted: "A call went out on the police radio for a 1960 model car occupied by two men. The officer said the men were dark skinned and could be either white men or Negroes." The article seems idiotic in hindsight—were they really suggesting that the Birmingham church bombing could have been perpetrated by black men? A man is quoted whose granddaughter is among the victims; he says he would like to burn down the town. There is a description of the preacher wandering through the crowd, asking them to go home. For Angela Davis, this hostile subtext and fear of black rage was surely one more sign to add to a lifetime of hostile signs. When she wrote her autobiography a decade later, she recalled the very moment she picked up that issue of the *Herald Tribune*, recalled her devastation and her feeling that her white friends on the Hamilton program were incapable of understanding, remembered, the way you remember a bad dream, that she had walked away from them to be alone with her grief. She doesn't quote the newspaper accounts, but reading them today gives a visceral sense of how deep white incomprehension went, even and especially in the mainstream press.

French newspapers were more sensitive than the *Herald Tribune* to what had happened. *L'Humanité*, the newspaper of the French Communist Party, set a frame on its front page that September 16: "Racist terror still reigns in Alabama," and its headline focused on the criminals. The article described men and women running out of the church covered with blood and collapsing on the sidewalk, and pointed out that the church had served as a meeting place for civil rights groups. They noted that two Whites had fled the scene. The French newspaper capitalized the word White just as it did Black, giving the sense that both white and black were constructed identities.[61] Governor

Wallace, it concluded, had the area encircled by soldiers after the bombing to prevent demonstrations.[62]

The popular illustrated weekly *Paris Match*—a favorite of American teachers of French because of its accessible language, its gossip and big black and white photos—sent a reporter to Birmingham in the wake of the bombing. Its lead article presented George Wallace as a menacing figure who had quipped at a Baltimore press conference on racial problems that "everyone was talking about attacks but there had been no deaths." *Paris Match* ventured a reaction: "Our correspondents who heard Wallace, governor of Alabama, pronounce these words on television had the feeling he was practically deploring the terrorists' lack of efficiency." The Birmingham deaths, they added, "occurred only seventy-two hours later . . . ." This was interpretation; it was political writing, imputing motives from facts, and it appeared in the most middle-of-the-road, pro-American, mass-market publication in France. Like the *Herald Tribune, Paris Match* emphasized the danger of escalating violence, with a huge photograph of a burly white policeman, blood running down his face. But in the story it told, the perpetrators of the violence were not in the black community; they were on the side of the forces of order: "les chiens policiers, les aiguillons électriques et les bombes" (police dogs, electric prods, and bombs).

An extended byline at the top of the *Paris Match* report conveyed the extent to which the French were making sense of the violence in the American south, in part by projection of their own situation: "Our own special correspondents in the States . . . where an Algerian War seems to be starting."[63] The irony is that so many mainstream French newspapers and magazines, under French government pressure, had whitewashed the massacre of Algerian demonstrators by the Paris police on October 17 and 18, 1961—the event William Gardner Smith had described in his novel *The Stone Face*. The French press—and the *Herald Tribune* as well—reported only two or three deaths in the Algerian demonstration and was silent about the rest. It wasn't only that it was less painful for the French press to locate racism in the exotic American South than it was to name it down the street. It was a question of literal repression—French newspapers had to worry about censorship or even seizure if they reported police or army violence against Algerians. But there was nothing to prevent the French press from reacting critically to American racial violence. More disturbing still is the fact that there was no censor preventing the American wire services from reporting the Birmingham bombings: The bias was so deeply engrained that a distorted version of the events was self-imposed.

What did this mean for Angela Davis and the American students who went to France before her and after her? Throughout the politically charged 1960s, reading the press, both French and American, became a critical exercise. American students had more to learn from the French press about race hatred in the American South than about state violence in Paris. From the civil rights movement through the Vietnam War and beyond, they learned to see the conflicts in their country through French eyes and through the lens of French history, so that history became for them, not the univocal limited sphere, but an echo chamber, where one national experience could inform another, and a country could be better understood from outside than from within. That was what mattered, recalls John Simon, one of the 1963–64 Hamilton group: not what they did in class, but what the street taught them, what the papers taught them. A way out of their protective campuses and a way to look back.[64]

In Biarritz, then in Paris, Angela Davis was thrust into the tightly knit group of forty-six American students, studying together day after day, sharing living space with their French hosts. The Hamilton students were tracked according to their expertise in French; Angela was in the most advanced group, taking her courses directly at the Sorbonne, along with other international students.[65] Only the theater course, which took advantage of the huge variety of plays available in Paris, was open to different levels, so that Angela, Christie, and Jane Chaplin, who lodged in the same Paris apartment, could go together. This was a course of the kind that is still offered in most study-abroad programs for Americans who have mastered French, consisting of weekly outings to the theater and reports on each play.

Their guide to the theater was Madame Colette Stourdzé, a pillar of the Hamilton program, one of those chic and brilliant pedagogical spirits in the tradition of Jacqueline Bouvier's Mademoiselle Jeanne Saleil. Patsy Martin remembers her entering the Sorbonne amphitheater from the back, clad in her cape and hat and gloves, making her way briskly down the aisle as she shed each garment in time to mount the dais.[66] Even her grammar lessons were unforgettable. For the theater course, Stourdzé sent them to the Théâtre de la Huchette to see Ionesco's Bald Soprano and The Lesson, which were still running at the same theater when the group had their Paris reunion in 2007. Diderot's *Le neveu de Rameau* was so boring that Paula Durbin remembers only the offstage performance: an elderly gentleman who dozed off and, when his neighbor woke him up, turned to her, outraged, and said "Je dors, madame." There was the Peking opera and a weak performance of a Garcia Lorca play on a Saturday afternoon. The schoolchildren in the audience were so rowdy that the lead actor stopped the performance to scold them.[67] Every week, Angela and her roommates dressed up for their theater outings. She had a beautiful red velvet dress that her host family remembers to this day, and a suede outfit she had bought on her outing to Spain during the Biarritz stay. Angela taught Jane to use eyeliner; Christie helped Angela apply the hair product she'd brought from home. The theater outings were performances in their own right, cultural rituals for the young women as important as what happened on stage.

Angela Davis was one of only six students out of the forty-six in her group who were advanced enough for the most difficult program of all—an intensive course in contemporary literature at a special Sorbonne institute. Twelve years later, during a television interview, she could still recite the institute's full name—"L'Ecole de préparation et de perfectionnement des professeurs de français à l'étranger"—and smiled to herself as she let the familiar phrase roll off her tongue again.[68] The mission of the Institute, which was affiliated with the literature departments at the Sorbonne, was to train the educators who would be teaching French abroad, whether they were themselves French or had learned French as a second language. Along with the six Hamilton students, there were about sixty students in the lecture course, who came from Europe, Asia, Africa, and Latin America. They attended two hours of lecture each week on poetry, novels, and theater, for a total of six hours. John Simon, a member of the class, remembers reading Saint-John Perse (a pseudonym for Alexis Leger), a Washington diplomat and Nobel laureate who was a guest, with Jeanne Saleil, at Jacqueline Kennedy's 1962 state dinner for Malraux. The son of a Guadeloupe planter, Leger was born into the white creole elite of the same islands that had sparked Angela Davis's imagination. Today there is a keen interest in his origins, but at the Sorbonne in 1963, the approach to his poem "Seamarks" was strictly formal.[69] He didn't make much of an impression on young John Simon, who was eager to grasp the social and political significance of art. Barbara Zurer was another of the students who braved the literature class. She wrote to her family about the number of hours she had to study, and the terrifying oral examination at the end of the semester.[70]

Angela Davis's Paris housemate Jane Chaplin, whose French was fluent because of an intensive French immersion track at Hunter School that went from elementary through grade twelve, opted instead for a class at the Institut d'études politiques, where the young Jacqueline Bouvier had studied international relations with Pierre Renouvin. Jane took the course in contemporary ideas, but she skipped the lecture, inaudible in the big amphitheater. Instead, she concentrated her work in the sections, taught by thirty-year-old Pierre Joxe, future minister of the interior, and Alain de Sédouy, who in 1969 produced Marcel Ophüls's documentary *The Sorrow and the Pity* about a French town during the Nazi occupation—the film often credited with undoing the myth of global French resistance to the Nazis. Joxe and de Sédouy were the bright young Frenchmen, the best that Sciences Po had to offer, and in 1963, the questioning of France's wartime behavior was just beyond the horizon, as were the student revolutions that would sweep up the youth of both countries.[71]

A Host Family

Angela Davis, Christie Stagg, and Jane Chaplin lodged with the Lamotte family on a quiet street in the sixteenth arrondissement, just off the Place de l'Etoile. The Lamottes occupied three floors of the building; Angela was in the mother-in-law's apartment on the first floor, sharing a room with Christie, and several floors up, in the Lamotte family apartment, was Jane Chaplin.

Micheline Lamotte, their host mother, was born in 1919 in Auteuil, a wealthy district on the western edge of Paris. I interviewed her in the winter of 2010, when she was ninety.[72] Though she complained that she had slowed down, she seemed little diminished by age. She told me that she had always been a spirited woman who, along with her future husband, had been drawn in her youth to the anti-parliamentarian movements of the 1930s, to the nationalist movement of World War I veterans founded by Colonel de La Rocque—the Croix-de-Feu. On February 6, 1934, a date that has become synonymous with right-wing revolt, veterans' groups and right-wing militias demonstrated against the National Assembly on the Place de la Concorde, and a riot broke out. Monsieur Lamotte was there, she told me proudly.[73]

19. Angela Davis and roommate Christie Stagg (Paris 1964).
Photograph courtesy Jane Jordan.

. . .

Micheline was a restless student who was thrown out of the Lycée
Molière the year before the baccalauréat exams. She considered herself
an athlete and an activist, and her hero was the French aviator Mermoz, a
Croix-de-Feu leader. "All my children had a rebellious spirit," she explained,
in the presence of her son, "and all of them were dunces."

Right-wing, with a strong dose of anarchism and a biting sense of humor,
Madame Lamotte was drawn to the Resistance as soon as France was occupied by the Nazis. Her granddaughter Camille grew up hearing the tale of

her grandmother's arrest at the Brasserie la Lorraine for independent acts of resistance, and how she was imprisoned for four months at La Santé, until she was released to make room for communists.[74] Angela, Christie, and Jane never heard about her arrest for resistance, but they did hear often about the war and about the German enemy—a concept that by 1963 must have seemed somewhat abstract to them. Angela hesitated to tell Madame Lamotte that her fiancé was German, and tried for the most part to keep him under wraps.

To the American observer, Madame Lamotte presents a dizzying set of ideological paradoxes, though she was not unusual for her era. There were other right-wing nationalists in the Resistance—including Jacqueline Bouvier's host mother, the comtesse de Renty. But how do you reconcile her fierce anti-communism with her esteem—then and now—for her most famous foreign boarder, whose political views were always clearly on the left?

Jane, who lived in a small room off the kitchen of the Lamotte apartment but who escaped to Angela and Christie's room downstairs as often as she could, paints a very different picture of life at the Lamottes than Madame Lamotte does, and from the clash of their two memories comes a kind of sociological understanding of study-abroad subcultures. The Lamottes had hosted students, three at a time, for several years. By Madame Lamotte's account, they hoped her five children—Patrick, Pierre-Yves, Martin, Sophie, and Adeline, who ranged in age from six to fifteen—would benefit. Jane remembers differently, and her memory is auditory, not visual: "C'est embêtant d'avoir des étrangers chez nous, mais après tout, vous payez nos vacances" (It's annoying to have foreigners in the house, but after all, you're paying for our vacations). Lest one forget the economic reality of study abroad, it's important to remember that the majority of families have always taken in foreign students not out of love for Americans or for educational experiences for their children but for income. But not many hosts make a habit of saying so.

Madame, to this day, is proud of her house rules for dinner: no English allowed. You came to the table on time. You couldn't come to the table with rollers in your hair.

The American students, she explained, were so unaccustomed to the multicourse sit-down dinners that she had always considered a regular feature of everyday life that they often took out their brownie cameras to capture a blanquette de veau, a strawberry tart, or an assortment of cheeses. Jane and

Christie remember that the Lamottes' traditional midday meal was copious, but it wasn't included in their room and board. The meal they did share with the family was the minimalist French supper—leftovers from the family's grand lunch, a salad and an occasional egg or portion of cheese. Afterwards, they relied on the jars of yogurt they kept in their rooms to appease their hunger.

Conversational rules included no discussion of the inappropriate topics: religion, politics, and money. Jane remembers Madame's barbs against the North Africans (*"les Nordasses"*), against Germans, against workers: a stream of bitter diatribe. One phrase was pronounced again and again: *pendant la guerre* (during the war). She wonders now if the year at the Lamottes was the beginning of her senior thesis at Barnard, "Traitor or Patriot: The Case for Marshal Pétain," in which she tried to understand a view of the world that was entirely different from her own.[75]

Jane Chaplin was born Jane Kaplan. She was a year old, in 1945, when her parents changed their family name, as several of their Jewish friends did, to something less recognizably Jewish. She had blue eyes and blond hair, so, as she tells me, "she could pass." But she wanted to know what Madame Lamotte's attitude would be once she knew her boarder was Jewish—she wanted to be authentic. At Hannukah, she decided to buy a cake and tell the family she wanted to celebrate her people's holiday and share it with them. From then on, she remembers, her relations with them got worse and worse. "It was an important discovery for me that being Jewish meant something in the world, and that I was experiencing being Jewish through the reactions of other people." She began spending more and more time with Christie and Angela in their large downstairs room.

When Angela was present, she remembers, there weren't any racial slurs. There was, instead, a show of respect she attributes to "Angela's exquisite French, her magnificent fluency." "Angela a toujours le mot juste" (Angela always finds just the right word). Chaplin remembers the compliment, and indeed, in my 2010 interview, Madame Lamotte uttered the very same sentence. A commonplace notion about French racism has it that Jews and Arabs were more distasteful to the French than Africans, and African Americans, who were aesthetically pleasing, and more exotic. Referring to the old Action française tradition, the critic Jeffrey Mehlman once quipped that Hitler had given anti-Semitism, formerly a respectable and perfectly French attitude, a bad name.[76] By a similar logic, if Madame Lamotte remembered

Angela as having a French grandparent, it could well have been a nationalist fantasy: if Angela had such a perfect mastery of the language, didn't she have to be, at least in part of her being, one of them?

Interviewing the women from the 1963–64 season today reveals a sea change in attitudes toward authority, in ways of understanding the world and their place in it. Barbara Zurer, who changed families at the start of her Parisian stay after upsetting the widow to whom she had been assigned (all it took was a young man from the Pyrenees knocking at her door); Patsy Martin, whose relationship with her host mother in the fifteenth arrondissement grew worse and worse with time; and Jane Chaplin, crowded in her tiny room behind the kitchen, with her auditory memory of the prejudices of her host family: these were not women who were accepting the world as it was. They did not, like so many of Jackie Bouvier's classmates, take their idealism to the CIA, to save France from communism. They were heading in the other direction, toward an era of contestation, and with an awareness of their racial and ethnic identity, their gender (though the word barely existed), through which they measured the world's reaction to them.

The terrible events in Birmingham on September 15, 1963, had marked the beginning of Angela Davis's junior year abroad. There was one detail of that day that her mother recalled years later, a truly exceptional event: Angela telephoned home.[77] Letter writing was still the normal way for her to communicate with her family in Alabama, but for the first part of September her parents hadn't even known her Biarritz address.[78]

Letters mattered. For all the 1963 students, phone calls were almost as rare, and expensive, as they had been for Jacqueline Bouvier's group in 1949. Barbara Zurer lived with the head administrator of France's national library, the Bibliothèque nationale, but the phone in his home—a single phone—was off limits, and besides she wouldn't have known how to use it. When they wanted to get together with their friends in Paris, the students dropped notes at each other's houses. Everyone wrote home. Many of the students had their favorite correspondents: Angela Davis and her Brandeis friend Lannie Goldberg wrote back and forth, creating their own epistolary novel.[79] The sense she had, since she had left Birmingham for high school in New York, of being away from the struggle, must have been nearly intolerable at such a distance in that violent autumn.

For her, the Birmingham church bombing set a tone of sorrow for the year. Then in November, a few weeks after the Hamilton group moved to Paris, Kennedy was assassinated in Texas.

A reception with hors d'oeuvres and dancing for all the study-abroad groups—Smith, Sweet Briar, and Hamilton—was scheduled at the American Embassy for November 23. With the news of the assassination, the dancing was canceled but the reception went on. Angela, Jane, and Christie joined the crowds of weeping students at the American Embassy, and Angela thought about her murdered friends. Who among these white kids had wept for them?[80]

Equally vivid are the girls' memories of their host family's reaction to the assassination. Jane Chaplin remembers one of the boys coming into her room—"un attentat—votre président." She has a bitter memory of Madame saying, "Madame Johnson est moins bien que Jackie"—that is, she's not as attractive as Mrs. Kennedy. Christie Stagg wrote home on November 24:

> Indeed, when we discussed the news with the Lamottes as we listened over the radio last night, their reaction was, well, it's too bad, but it's one of those things. De Gaulle was shot at twice, too, but he escaped. When Mme Lamotte said, "But after all, she's not the first woman who's ever lost her husband," I nearly hit her. Maybe it's because it's not their country involved that they're insensible, or maybe it's they've seen so much death (people here are still living the Second World War). But most of the French papers are very pro-Kennedy and seem to be relishing this chance to outdo each other in eulogies.

In her letters home, Christie tries to make sense of French reactions to news, measures its strangeness. At the same time, she has already changed. Living in a French-speaking environment, speaking nothing but French with her American friends, including Angela and even in the privacy of their room, has affected her language. She uses the word she's learned in French, "insensible," instead of "insensitive." Like generations of dedicated students before and after her, she would return home from her year abroad with her English imbued with French, her number 7 written with a little cross through it to distinguish it from number 1, and other, deeper habits of writing and habits of mind.[81]

In her autobiography, Angela Davis writes not an unkind word about the family who lodged her on the rue Duret. She recalls steaming bowls of café au lait, croissants and chunks of butter in the morning. But Jane Chaplin's more critical descriptions of life in the Lamotte household, and Christie Stagg's letters home, point to signs of the condescension and resentment that are just as likely to rear their heads in host families as cultural curiosity. From the French point of view, there are many exasperated tales of American students destroying property, going home pregnant (as was the case at the Lamottes in a previous year), coming to dinner with rollers in their hair, stealing food from the refrigerator, or just making too much noise—the other side of the Americans' accusations of cruel, reactionary, or severe hosts, weird food, even dysfunctional washing machines that boil and shrink favorite sweaters.

It's helpful to keep in mind that memory is a novelist. Madame Lamotte remembered Angela sitting down with her to explain segregation in the Jim Crow South. She told me the story of Angela and her sister in the shoe store and described the unfair sentencing of African Americans in California—two details from the autobiography that her son brought to our interview and placed on the coffee table, along with several other Angela Davis books in French translation. She was captivated by the story of the Marin county shoot-out that led to Angela Davis's arrest in 1970, by what she considered the true originality of Jonathan Jackson's crime. Her support for his daring matched her enthusiasm for the exploits of the aviator Mermoz. And so I wonder how much of what she remembered Angela Davis having taught her was learned later, reading about her life. On the other hand, it is easy to imagine the young Angela Davis, a born teacher, patiently explaining the life she had left behind in Alabama, and her family's outlook.

Testimony

"I did not want to contribute to the already widespread tendency to personalize and individualize history," Angela wrote in the preface to her 1975 autobiography and only added, in a later edition, that "the dialectics of the personal and the political" were missing from her original text, which she had conceived in the great tradition of the revolutionary *testimonia*, the story of a movement with herself as the occasion for recounting that movement—hence its subtitle, "An Autobiography," signifying that she is one of many.

An intensely private person thrust into public life, a political thinker and an analyst of society, Angela Davis considered her individual adventure important only in the way it might illuminate society.

In a 2009 speech at the Odéon Theater in Paris, she had this to say about Jean Genet, the French writer and playwright whose name was on every contemporary theater syllabus during the year she spent in France, and who became her friend and her champion. Her speech contains an admonition and a challenge:

> He even goes so far as to advocate the development of a "tactfulness of the heart" when dealing with Black folks. He also says that Blacks had silently been observing Whites for centuries and had learned a lot about them and their cultural background. And Whites did not even realize they were being observed. What we develop nowadays in our lectures means the same: White folks have got to go to Black school; they have to learn something from them.[82]

Angela Davis was not yet twenty-one when she left Paris. There was tragedy ahead of her, and struggle of the most basic kind. The time for taking lessons was soon to end, and the time for giving lessons about to begin.

Angela Davis: 1963–1964

SIX

Angela Davis

The Return

The Senior Essay

Angela Davis's return to Brandeis for her senior year was a turning point in her intellectual life. She had discovered Herbert Marcuse's *Eros and Civilization* when she was a sophomore, the year Marcuse took a sabbatical from Brandeis. Now he was back, and under his guidance Davis worked on the equivalent of a second specialization in philosophy, beginning with an independent study of the pre-Socratics and moving steadily forward through Plato and Aristotle.[1] She audited Marcuse's undergraduate course on European political thought and his graduate seminar on Kant's *Critique of Pure Reason*. But she maintained her official specialization in French and completed the senior essay, which was one of the requirements for the major. Hers was entitled "The Novels of Robbe-Grillet: A Study of Method and Meaning."[2]

In Alain Robbe-Grillet, Davis had chosen the writer most closely associated, in 1964, with the avant-garde of contemporary French fiction, the artistic cutting edge that Susan Sontag was cultivating. Robbe-Grillet was published by the Editions de Minuit, the press that had emerged from its underground beginnings in the Resistance and was now known for a commitment to experimental writing. Robbe-Grillet's fiction, lacking in traditional plot or characters, bore little resemblance to Sartre's, or Beauvoir's, or even to Camus's at his most absurd. By 1965, Robbe-Grillet had published six novels as well as a collection of critical essays in which he contested every received idea about fiction since *La princesse de Clèves*.[3] To triumph as an avant-garde you have to show that the last avant-garde is the arrière-garde: Robbe-Grillet went after the generation of writers who had reached their pinnacle of glory at the Liberation—the message-bound existentialists who believed that literature was the result of a situation and a struggle. Literature, Robbe-Grillet argued, was a world apart, and the revolution that interested him took place in the writing itself.

In the fall of 1964, when Angela Davis began her thesis, Robbe-Grillet toured fifty American universities to spread the word about his New Novel—more than doubling the number of schools Beauvoir had visited on her own whirlwind American tour in 1947. One of his stops was Brandeis.

Angela was better prepared than her peers for his lecture, having read both Robbe-Grillet and his first critic, the American Bruce Morrissette, in her contemporary literature class at the Sorbonne.[4] The year 1964 marked Robbe-Grillet's conquest of the American world, begun a decade earlier, when Morrissette, a professor at Washington University, happened to hear the French writer on his car radio on a trip through France. He began to work on Robbe-Grillet in earnest, publishing his *Alain Robbe-Grillet* in 1965 in both French and English editions. By the 1970s, Robbe-Grillet had become a regular visitor at New York University, a familiar figure on Washington Square with his salt-and-pepper beard and his pipe, but in Angela's student days he was a young Turk with a skinny mustache and sharp features, a man with a mission to revolutionize the novel. As a writer who was also a theorist of his own fiction, he was a perfect author for the American classroom. Stimulated by the games in his work and by plots that demanded acrobatic interpretation, professors and students took to him. In the Hamilton group alone, both Angela Davis and Howard Bloch, who had returned from Paris to Amherst, chose Robbe-Grillet as the subject of their senior essays for the French major.

If there were any need to confirm what Angela's fellow students said about her intellectual powers, and how far she seemed to fly ahead of them, her Robbe-Grillet thesis would suffice. At twenty-one, Angela Davis already possessed the analytic rigor, the sense of the urgency of critique and understanding that would characterize all her future work. She emerges in the thesis not merely as an attentive reader of Robbe-Grillet but as a fierce advocate of a cause: the New Novel and its revolutionary potential for understanding contemporary reality. By "reality," she understood the reality of the atom bomb, the growing anonymity of contemporary man—for it was always "man" in those years, rather than human or humankind—defined by a registration number in a vast bureaucracy and by the machines that fragmented his existence. This reality, she argued, meant that the traditional novel with its willful characters and straightforward plot no longer corresponded to the world as it existed. There were no more heroes. Alain Robbe-Grillet, she argued, was the only true New Novelist—Michel Butor tried to recuperate the values of Western Civilization, Claude Simon was nostalgic, so that their commitment to a new kind of fiction remained theoretical. [5] What she valued about Robbe-Grillet was what she called his "phenomenological attitude," a quality she defined in reference to Sartre and Merleau-Ponty, who had come to philosophy through Husserl and Heidegger, just as she was doing.

What did France matter in all of this? The other students on the Hamilton program had been up to their ears in French lessons, straining to understand, to get the grammar right. Angela's friend Jane never forgot how, in Biarritz, Mme Salerni would say something and Angela would answer, "Ah bon!" in such a natural way that Jane marveled at her ease. "That's what that year was about," she reminisced, "learning the little things like 'ah bon' that people really said."[6] Somehow, Angela already knew.

She knew, and she was already onto the next hurdle during her months in Biarritz and Paris, perfecting her German in order to read German philosophy in the original. Manfred Clemenz, the German boyfriend she had met at Brandeis in her sophomore year, who was now in Frankfurt, had something to do with it; he was attuned to the philosophers associated with the Frankfurt School and their concept of a Critical Theory. Intellectual passion is a kind of love, and the love she might have felt for Manfred Clemenz would be hard to separate from her discovery of philosophy. During her time in

France, and again in her senior year, she had become familiar enough with the phenomenological tradition to understand that it might be applied fruitfully to her literary studies. She made Robbe-Grillet's fiction a demonstration of what phenomenology could reveal about man and the object world.

In terms of strict literary history, a phenomenology of the New Novel was somewhat incongruous. The "phenomenological attitude" that Angela Davis was bringing to her study of Robbe-Grillet harked back to the literature of the existentialists. Sartre had studied phenomenology in Germany in the 1930s, and when he returned to France, he combined the phenomenological method, with its focus on the patterns that our thought imposes on the world, with his own political emphasis on responsibility and human agency, on liberty and choice in a godless world. By 1963, the phenomenological viewpoint was being challenged by a new school of thought, inspired by Claude Lévi-Strauss's structural anthropology and Ferdinand de Saussure's analysis of linguistic signs. The structuralists focused on structures in the world that were independent of the human mind and on systems of signs abstracted from the world. History, so important to the existentialists, was, for the structuralists, really just one byproduct of those signs and structures.

Roland Barthes, by far the most creative representative of the new structuralism in literary studies, had welcomed Robbe-Grillet onto the literary scene with open arms—and one of the things he valued most in Robbe-Grillet's fiction was its attention to the surface, its refusal to strain for depth. Angela Davis included Barthes's essays on Robbe-Grillet in her bibliography; she was aware of structuralism before it had time to reach the American classroom, before it had influenced the scholarship of most of her literature professors. Barthes had put Robbe-Grillet on the intellectual map, but Sartre found him elitist in his themes and attitudes and declared, in a 1964 interview: "You can't read Robbe-Grillet in an underdeveloped country."[7] By combining Sartrean phenomenology with Robbe-Grillet's fiction, Angela Davis was reconciling rivals for her own purposes, for in addition to her attentiveness to structures and signs, she maintained a deep commitment to the idea of human freedom.

It's also worth noting that the philosophical approach she applied to literature, with its emphasis on consciousness and concept, was a full analytic step beyond the legions of aesthetic studies that had characterized so much literary criticism at the undergraduate level until the 1960s. Here Merleau-

Ponty was her guide: "True philosophy," he had written, "means learning to see the world anew, and in that sense telling a story can signify as 'deeply' as a philosophical treaty."[8] In her thesis, Davis quoted Merleau-Ponty in support of her claim that Robbe-Grillet had indeed "conferred upon the novel a truly philosophical and existential purpose." Undistracted by partisan quarrels among schools of writers, she set serious philosophical standards for the novel. Its purpose was not to entertain; it was to help people clarify their relationship to the world. The novel was a school for consciousness.

She would later articulate her own consciousness through the analytic categories of race and gender, but it would be another two decades at least before the radical thought of Fanon, or even Sartre's decolonization essays from the 1960s, took center stage in the world of literary study. Today, in the era of postcolonial studies, it is impossible to read a novel like Robbe-Grillet's *La jalousie* without being struck by everything it owes to the colonial situation: the plantation setting, the banana trees, the native workers, the tropical centipede crushed on the wall, not to mention the title—"Jealousy," which in French means not just the psychological state of mind but also the plantation shutters that modulate the sunlight entering a room in the tropics. Robbe-Grillet himself was trained as an agronomist; he had worked in colonial settings, and his imagination had real roots in a distinct environment.[9] It wasn't until 1973 that the Marxist literary critic Jacques Leenhardt published a political reading of the novel around the issue of colonialism. Susan Sontag's great friend Richard Howard, who translated *La jalousie* in 1959 under the title *Jealousy*, considers it a terrible title for the English translation. He wanted to call it *The Blind*, but his publisher disagreed.[10]

Though there was no overt mention of political issues in her senior essay, Angela Davis reached a conclusion that expresses her own struggle to balance the life of the mind with political action. She pointed out that Robbe-Grillet's novels, due to their revolutionary character, were inaccessible. If Robbe-Grillet had published no novel since *In the Labyrinth* (1959) and had turned instead to film scenarios, she surmised, it was because film had replaced the novel "in its capacity to create and to destroy myths of society." Film, she suggested, had become "the most widespread means of communication with the masses of men today." She had great hopes for the future of this novelist turned filmmaker: "Perhaps it is by the intermediary of the film that [Robbe-Grillet] will firmly launch a movement dedicated to the purpose of teaching man to *see* the world and to *see* himself with eyes liberated from the constraints of outmoded and ineffective myths."[11] "Masses," "movement," and "liberation": the important concepts for her in evaluating this literature were already political.

In 1965, Robbe-Grillet did seem to have abandoned the novel for film-making. His 1961 screenplay for *Last Year at Marienbad,* directed by Alain Resnais, may not have reached the masses but was certainly known to the international world of Francophiles and cinephiles, from Jacqueline Kennedy at the White House to Susan Sontag, writing for *Film Quarterly.* The movie was set in a château, and its grounds were straight out of one of Atget's garden photographs, where the well-trimmed bushes look like chess pieces.[12] The actors wandered about in clothes designed by Chanel. It was a far cry from Resnais's previous films, *Night and Fog* on the Nazi camps, and *Hiroshima mon amour,* rooted in war trauma. Susan Sontag admired *Marienbad* for its "sluggish stateliness . . . . its outlandish, beautiful, barren setting."[13] Jackie Kennedy adored the Chanel chiffon. However experimental *Last Year at Marienbad* may have been, it went a long way toward giving Robbe-Grillet his reputation as an elitist.

Though he considered himself a man of the left and an opponent of the Algerian War (he co-signed the famous 1960 petition of 121 intellectuals against the draft), Robbe-Grillet was famous for his disquisition on the true commitment for the writer. "Instead of being of a political nature, commitment is, for the writer, the full awareness of the present problems of his own language, the conviction of their extreme importance, the desire to solve them *from within.* Here, for him, is the only chance of remaining an artist and, doubtless too, by means of an obscure and remote consequence, of someday serving something—perhaps even the Revolution."[14] Susan Sontag would take his credo to an extreme with her *Against Interpretation,* in a stubborn defense of form.[15] Angela Davis, eleven years younger than Sontag, was part of another generation, another sensibility, and for her the revolution was in the world, not on paper. Sontag's enthusiasm for Robbe-Grillet anticipated Angela Davis's, but soon it was Sontag who was taking her cues from Davis's political critique.

From Critical Theory to Prison

There's barely a book or article written about Angela Davis that doesn't mention, somewhere along the way, that she majored in French and studied at the Sorbonne. But those facts are always in the background, shoved aside by the dramas to come.

Even before becoming a public figure, Davis had left the field of French literature behind. Her teachers, especially Marcuse, expected her to make an important contribution to philosophy.[16] While she never abandoned French thought, her relationship to France expanded to accommodate her growing curiosities and passions. What no one knew in 1965 was that she would also, in her person and through hard-won experience, become identified with an international political cause in which France was to play a major role.

It is easy to imagine how it might have gone differently, how she might have lived a rather private intellectual life as a political philosopher. In 1965 she moved to Germany to study with Theodor Adorno, the most difficult and revered surviving member of the Frankfurt school. By now her engagement to Manfred Clemenz was off; German philosophy remained. She took up residence in Frankfurt in a communal living space called "The Factory" with like-minded left-wing German students, most of them sociologists. The closer she got to the community of German radicals, the more they wanted to hear from her about the various African American liberation movements that were taking shape in the late '60s. She saw photos from Oakland of the men in the new Black Panther Party in black berets, displaying their weapons and claiming their right to defend themselves against police brutality. As she read from her German university about the political developments on the American left, and especially among African American activists, she felt the same tug she had felt in Biarritz when she read about the church bombing in Birmingham. After two years in Frankfurt, she returned to the United States to finish her PhD with Marcuse, who had moved from Brandeis to the University of California, San Diego.[17] Her dissertation topic was Immanuel Kant's theory of violence. Kant's concept was based in large part on his reaction to the French Revolution, which he had followed closely. (His excitement at news of the taking of the Bastille, the story goes, was the rare event in his life that prevented this creature of habit from taking his customary afternoon walk!)

It was useful for understanding Kant, and violence, to think about other, more recent revolutions: the Russian Revolution of 1917, the Algerian insurrection of 1954. So many of the key readings in those years of intense interest in revolutionary thought were French: Frantz Fanon and Albert Memmi and Jean-Paul Sartre on colonialism and postcolonialism; Pierre

Vidal-Naquet and Henri Alleg on torture; Henri Lefebvre and Louis Althusser on Marxist theory; Daniel Guérin on anarchism. Because of her training in French and German, Davis had access to political and cultural analyses that didn't yet exist in English: her sense of radical politics was informed by French and German political philosophers, and her understanding of their thought was in turn informed by the political climate around her.[18]

Like many graduate students of her generation, she began working as an instructor after completing her oral exams. She had job offers from Yale and Swarthmore, but decided to accept a lectureship at UCLA that would give her time to finish the dissertation.[19] Her trajectory toward the PhD was swift, and it looked like she would finally be able to combine political work in her community with academic work at her university in a meaningful way.

Political groups that looked beyond American boundaries and approached the struggle against racism as an international issue were rare in those years. Traditional Marxists hadn't thought enough about race; the Black Power movements were taking a nationalist turn. It took Angela Davis several years to find an organization that corresponded to her intellectual affinities, but in 1968 she joined the Che Lumumba Club in Los Angeles. This group of African Americans affiliated with the Communist Party had named themselves after Che Guevara and Patrice Lumumba, the fallen revolutionaries of Cuba and the Belgian Congo. Their political work and their analysis focused on race, and they were sympathetic to the work of the Black Panthers, though skeptical about black power without socialism. Their working models for society were postrevolutionary Algeria and Cuba.

In 1969, she was invited with other members of the Che Lumumba Club to spend a month in Cuba with a delegation of American communists, including a group from Puerto Rico. During her Cuban month, she cut sugar cane, integrated into the life of a village, and worked on her Spanish by talking with young children. (She was, by now, a well-practiced language learner who understood she could learn more at the beginner stage from children than from adults.) It was a dreamlike interlude: it seemed to her as if socialism had effected a swift response to the problems of race that had plagued capitalist Cuba.

Angela Davis never stopped reading in French, but at the end of this trip an unexpected and seemingly minor event put her spoken French to the test. The delegation boarded a Cuban freighter bound for the French

Antilles. From Guadeloupe, they planned to fly home, to Puerto Rico and to the mainland. The Puerto Rican delegates were carrying cartons of Spanish language books from Cuba for a bookstore in San Juan. Then in Guadeloupe there was an incident: French customs seized the books, along with the passports of the Puerto Rican delegates, calling the travelers communist propaganda mongers. Angela Davis, the only one on the trip who knew French, was called in to interpret with a French customs official. Her sense of humor, her knowledge of her own didactic excesses, shine through in the way she sets the scene in her autobiography:

> I knew that I was carrying on a dialogue with a raving lunatic. But despite the bizarre circumstances, in this dingy cellar on the terrain of French imperialism, I felt called upon to defend my party, Cuba, the Socialist Countries, the World Communist Movement and the cause of oppressed people across the globe. "*Oui Monsieur, je suis communiste et je le considère un des plus grands honneurs humains, parce que nous luttons pour la libération totale de la race humaine.* Yes, I am a Communist and I consider it one of the greatest honors, because we are struggling for the total liberation of the human race."[20]

As it turned out, the moral high ground was not the best spot from which to negotiate; the French official became furious. Facing the loss of their passports and detention, the group approached Guadeloupean lawyer Gertie Archimède for assistance. A communist, a feminist, a member of the French National Assembly, and president of the Guadeloupe Bar, "Maître Archimède," to whom Angela Davis refers in her autobiography using the standard French form of address for barristers, was indeed master of the situation. She took charge of a complicated set of negotiations among the police, the judges, and the delegates. She found the delegates a place to stay, made sure their passports were returned to them, and promised to try and retrieve the books, which they were obligated, as a result of the negotiations, to leave behind in Guadeloupe. In Archimède, Angela Davis had found a rare role model, a communist woman who commanded respect, even from her ideological enemies. "If I had surrendered to my desires," she writes, "I would have remained on the island to learn from this woman." Their chance encounter would become a legend in Guadeloupe.

After this half annoying, half comic triumph over adversity, a more serious problem arose. While she was in Cuba, the student newspaper at UCLA reported that a member of the philosophy department was a communist.[21] A week later, the *San Francisco Chronicle* picked up on the story and published her name. Soon afterward, the regents of the University of California announced their intention to fire her.

Enough time has passed since the dramatic events of the 1970s that what happened to Angela Davis next is no longer common knowledge. That season, she was a household name, a recurring story on the evening news. Fifteen years after the heyday of McCarthyism, she became a target of lingering anticommunism and a cause célèbre. And here is where Angela Davis showed a strength that would become characteristic. Instead of taking the Fifth Amendment, as intellectuals called to testify before the House Un-American Activities Committee had done before her, she announced her party membership with pride, just as she had to the French customs official.[22] Instead of backing down, she went to court, seeking an injunction that would prevent the regents from firing her for political reasons.

She received hundreds of letters, mostly hateful, and so many death threats and bomb threats that she had to be accompanied to campus by a bodyguard. As she negotiated the challenges of a working environment in which she was constantly being watched, a French film student at UCLA approached her. Yolande du Luart—a cousin of the du Luarts whom Jacqueline Bouvier had visited near Saint-Tropez in the summer of 1950—was raised during the German Occupation by an American grandmother on the family estate, the Château du Luart. Her English was perfect. Perhaps it was that grandmother, perhaps it was the war itself that encouraged her to diverge from the prescribed itinerary of an aristocratic woman schooled by the Sisters of Notre Dame de Sion. In her twenties, Yolande met one of the leading figures of the Lettrist movement, Marc'O, with whom she wrote a manifesto for revolutionary cinema.[23] At age thirty-nine she was at UCLA, studying film and taking Angela Davis's philosophy class. It was Yolande du Luart's idea to gather a group of film students to follow Angela Davis for several months with a camera, commemorating her lectures and speeches. *Angela Davis: Portrait of a Revolutionary* is the first documentary about Angela Davis, and provides a rare glimpse of her life between the crisis of the UCLA controversy and the bigger crisis to come.[24] The camera moves from scenes of giant demonstrations and deadly police raids on Black Panther headquarters to lingering views of Angela Davis in deepest concentration, reading and writing. Focusing her camera on Davis's desk in her office at UCLA, the

French director captured a still life: a package of Gauloise cigarettes and a single book, Albert Camus's *Myth of Sisyphus*.

In those crucial months of 1969 and 1970, Davis was entering a hostile world that had become familiar to the Black Panthers in Oakland and Chicago, who were reeling from attempts by the FBI to sabotage their organization from within through misinformation, and through assassination of leaders.[25] Prominent supporters of the Panthers were targeted along with party members. *Newsweek* published the false rumor—fed to them by the FBI—that Jean Seberg, pregnant in 1970, was carrying the child of a Black Panther.[26] Seberg, who had been living in France since she played Joan of Arc in 1957, was part of a Franco-American contingent of Panther supporters, along with Jane Fonda, who was married to French filmmaker Roger Vadim and living in Los Angeles. Fonda joined Angela Davis in demonstrating for political prisoners' rights—you can see her in Yolande du Luart's film. Among the French, the most vocal and passionate of all the Panther supporters was the writer Jean Genet, who had turned his energies and desires to radical politics and for whom the Panthers were engaged in a liberation movement of poetic proportions.

Davis held her ground while the courts considered her case, and with the support of her colleagues in the Philosophy Department, she continued to give lectures to huge crowds of students under the intense scrutiny of her enemies. What brilliant lectures! The best known are her lectures on liberation, from her course "Recurring Philosophical Themes in Black Literature."[27] She began by considering slavery in the context of an existential debate on freedom, citing an oft-quoted statement by the thinker who started her on the path to philosophy, Jean-Paul Sartre: "Even the man in chains remains free, and for this reason: he is always at liberty to eliminate his condition of slavery even if this means his death." Sartre claimed that freedom meant freedom to choose death, she continued, but does the slave really preserve a vestige of freedom in choosing to die? By the time the lecture was over, she had demonstrated the insufficiency of the existentialist philosophy of her undergraduate years, and dismantled the Sartrean understanding of slavery. The fifteen hundred students who filled Royce Hall gave her a standing ovation.[28]

Angela Davis's fight to save her job came to a temporary halt when the California Supreme Court reinstated her on the ground that dismissal for political affiliation was unconstitutional. She was still lecturing at UCLA in

1970, when the Panthers asked her to serve as a translator for Jean Genet. He had entered the country illegally through Canada and was touring college campuses to raise white awareness about the Panthers' struggle.

Six hundred people turned out to hear Genet speak in the great UCLA Ballroom, expecting him to talk about literature. As he began by praising the Panthers, many in the audience walked out.[29] Angela Davis's contact with him that evening was a seam in her life, binding her French past, her university career, and her intellectual and political future. Eventually, the regents found an effective loophole: they refused to renew her contract because her dissertation wasn't finished. By then, her political energy had shifted from the university to those other institutions that Genet knew so well and that she came to understand as the legacy of slavery: the prisons.[30]

Prison Work

In January 1969, a case emerged from Soledad Prison in southern California that would capture the attention of people around the world. A guard had fired from the watchtower and killed three inmates. Two days later, a prison guard was found beaten to death. The three prisoners blamed for the retaliatory murder were among the most vocal black militants in the institution: George Jackson, Fleeta Drumgo, and John Clutchette. They now faced a murder trial and, if convicted, the death penalty. Angela Davis joined with the Che Lumumba Club to create the Soledad Brothers Defense Committee, for she believed that the men had been targeted for their political beliefs and unjustly accused. She realized she could use her notoriety from the UCLA incident to publicize their cause.

Depending upon what source you read, the leading Soledad Brother, George Jackson, was either a thug and a sociopath who had seen an opportunity in political grandstanding, or a seminal revolutionary thinker.[31] What is certain is that he became a rallying point, an inspiration to thousands of black prisoners and revolutionaries. He had educated himself in prison, reading Fanon and Mao and Che Guevera, and he made noise. Every year, when he came up for parole, it was denied. But now he was indicted for the murder of a guard—a far more serious crime than the one for which he was currently serving—and his indictment and the surrounding publicity brought his story to public attention.

George Jackson had been convicted at age eighteen as an accessory in a seventy-dollar holdup at a gas station; he was driving the getaway car. With a record of previous convictions for petty crimes, he was given a sentence of one year to life. This so-called indeterminate sentencing was once nearly universal, based on the belief that prison functions as rehabilitation, with success or failure determined by the annual decision of a parole board. By the time the Soledad murder case came up for trial, Jackson had spent a decade in a series of California correctional facilities. In jail, he had become a writer.

Fay Stender, one of Berkeley's most active prisoners' advocates and a former English major, was especially interested in prison writing; her own correspondence with Jackson convinced her that his letters might serve his defense by making his case, and his persona, public. She made contact with a publisher from Random House, who was as convinced as she that they had an extraordinary document in their hands. It was Stender's idea to contact Jean Genet, by then a well-known Panther supporter, for a foreword to the work.

Genet himself had been discovered as a writer in the 1940s while behind bars, and he was released on the strength of petitions from prominent writers who believed in his talent; he had written himself to freedom. His violent sense of power relations and his taste for homoerotic scandal gave him a special aura in the world of French letters. By the 1960s, his theater was world renowned. His 1958 play *The Blacks: A Clown Show* was performed in New York during Angela Davis's senior year in high school by an all-black cast of future stars, and it created a sensation, with its Fanon-like black actors wearing white masks. In 1964, Genet decided, with characteristic drama, never to write again—not even to hold a pen, and he burned the manuscript of the play he was working on. A few occasional pieces followed, but nothing literary. He turned his energies to politics.

Genet first visited the United States in 1968 to cover the Democratic National Convention for *Esquire*. In 1970, two representatives from the Black Panther Party, who had gone to Paris to garner support, asked for his signature on a petition. Instead of signing, he proposed to travel once again to the States on a support tour. It was an unlikely coalition consisting of Genet, who couldn't communicate without a translator, and his Panther hosts and their supporters. On the California leg of his tour, Genet learned about the

20. Angela Davis in conversation with Jean Genet at Dalton Trumbo's Panther Benefit (March 20, 1970).
Photograph © Robert Carl Cohen.

...

Soledad Brothers through the extended Panther network: Angela Davis, his translator for the UCLA lecture; Fay Stender, George Jackson's lawyer; and Dalton Trumbo, the blacklisted communist screenwriter, who threw him a party. A photograph of Genet and Davis at Dalton Trumbo's house commemorates the beginning of an important friendship.

Stender's original request to Genet to contribute a foreword to *Soledad Brother,* sent immediately after his return from California to Paris, survives in a file at Editions Gallimard, Genet's publisher and, not coincidentally, the French publisher of *Soledad Brother.* Her letter is handwritten in careful script, in a French that rings with idealism:

> I think that the community that exists between Jackson, isolated for ten years but now communicating his thoughts and his feelings with the outside world, and you, coming from another culture with another language, yet coming from the world of prisons . . . gives us the necessary inspiration to create

Chapter Six

moments of humanity that transcend the acts of the struggle. Huey Newton has read your books but not Jackson. I'm sending *The Blacks* to the three defendants, to start up communication. I hope one day we can all meet in the freedom we will have created.[32]

Through this invitation from a left-wing lawyer on Telegraph Avenue to a famous French writer in Paris, literature crossed a new boundary, encountered a new community of readers. French literature entered Soledad, and Soledad entered French literature.

Ellen Wright, Richard Wright's widow and a literary agent in Paris, negotiated the French language rights. *Soledad Brother: The Prison Letters of George Jackson* was published in the United States in 1970; the French edition appeared in 1971, while Angela Davis's trial was underway. Both editions carried Genet's foreword. On the eve of the French publication, a long excerpt from the foreword appeared on a full page of the newspaper *Le Monde* with a note linking George Jackson to Angela Davis.[33] Genet's publishers were thrilled with the foreword, for the writer who had burned his manuscripts in 1964 and taken a vow of literary silence had returned to the scene with a masterful statement.

The foreword presents George Jackson to the world both as an important revolutionary and as a writer who has renewed a literary genre. Jean Genet read *Soledad Brother* as an epistolary autobiography, a political coming-of-age through letters, and his text is a perfect synthesis of his own political and literary affinities. His close identification with Jackson as a common criminal, a thug who was writing himself to freedom, empowers every sentence:

> And from the first letter to the last, nothing was willed, written or composed for the purpose of putting together a book; and yet there is a book, hard and sure, and, I repeat, both a weapon in a struggle for liberation and a love poem. I see no miracle in this, except the miracle of truth itself, the naked truth completely exposed.[34]

Angela Davis had supported George Jackson since the Soledad Brothers Defense Committee was founded in February 1970, and in the spring of that year she and George Jackson began to exchange letters. Through her work with the Soledad Brothers Defense committee, she grew close to the Jackson family, especially to Jonathan, a high school boy who worshiped his older brother George. Jonathan attended Blair High School in Pasadena and lived for his brother's letters. "I work on words," George Jackson wrote him, as he grew strong with theory, with Che and Mao and Frantz Fanon. He wrote in another letter that he wanted to hurl their father through Fanon's revolutionary catharsis, to serve what he called "the historical obligation."[35] "I hope you are involved in the academic program at your school," he advised Jonathan. "They have not tried to ascertain what fits your character and disposition and to direct you accordingly. So you must do this *yourself*. Decide now what you would like to specialize in, *one thing* that you will drive at. Do you get it? *Decide now*."[36] So Jonathan, too, began to write: he was the political editor of an underground newspaper named, after Lenin's paper, *Iskra* (Russian for "spark").[37] In a demonstration for the Soledad Brothers captured in Yolande du Luart's documentary, you can see Jonathan Jackson shadowing Angela Davis. He is a quiet young man in a black T-shirt whose whole being speaks of an immense sorrow. He never strays far from Angela Davis's side, and when she picks up a microphone to plead for his brother, he appears to be hanging on her every word.

It was through *Les Frères de Soledad* that French readers first met Angela Davis, as the addressee of several of George Jackson's letters and as one of the recipients of the book's dedication: "to Angela Y. Davis, my tender experience."

"Should you run into Yvonne . . . ," George Jackson wrote in one of the most tender moments of his correspondence, as if Yvonne were Angela's alter ego, "make her understand that I want to hold her (chains and all) and run my tongue in that little gap between her two front teeth. (That should make her smile.)" This was in May 1970. She was still on the outside, George Jackson was still awaiting trial for the murder of the prison guard, and his little brother Jonathan, the one he called the "man child," was still alive.

The Shoot-Out

Tragedy came in waves. On August 7, 1970, young Jonathan Jackson entered a Marin County courtroom, armed. A prisoner from San Quentin named James McClain was appearing before a white judge. Jonathan threw guns to McClain and to several other prisoners, who were serving as witnesses. He took five hostages, including the prosecutor in the case and the judge. He threw McClain a roll of tape and McClain taped a sawed-off shotgun to the judge's neck. Jackson hustled them into a van and drove off under gunfire. Minutes later, four of the men in the van were dead—the judge, two prisoners, and Jonathan Jackson himself. Four of the guns involved, including the sawed-off shotgun, had been purchased by Angela Davis over several years, beginning in 1968; they were registered openly in her name.[38] Whether she had given those guns to Jonathan Jackson knowingly and for what purpose, whether he had stolen them from her, and what exact role each gun had played in the murders of the four men in the van would become central questions in the coming months. She had spent time with Jonathan Jackson before the shoot-out; they had become companions in the struggle for George Jackson. She had bought the last gun shortly before the shoot-out. Once the link to her guns was found, she was considered an accessory to kidnapping and murder, a conspirator in a plan.

A warrant was issued for Davis's arrest. On August 9 she went into hiding, and in the coming weeks, the FBI plastered her face on post offices all over the country, one of three women ever to have appeared on its "ten most wanted list." If you listened to the radio that August, you could hear her description: "five feet eight inches tall, 145 pounds, slim, with light brown skin; she may be armed and dangerous."[39]

One of the first things the authorities found significant about Angela Davis was that she had spent a year in France. The FBI contacted the French Ministry of the Interior, which sent out a bulletin forbidding her entry into the country; "Angela Davis, American communist, member of the Black Panthers, now wanted in the United States for accessory to murder, might have found refuge in France, according to the American press. . . . We are keeping a lookout for her name in hotel and boardinghouse ledgers."[40] Meanwhile, French police were conducting their own preliminary investigation, gathering the only documents they could find on French territory—files from the Hamilton College Junior Year in France, including Frank Davis's letter of permission for his daughter to attend the program; her official letter of acceptance; and her application for a *carte de séjour*, the residency permit for foreigners in Paris that is a headache to procure and the bane of existence to many a study-abroad office and many a student abroad. It wasn't the contraband they were looking for.

It had been six years since that junior year, and Angela's fellow students on the Hamilton program were no longer in touch with her. The FBI visited them all: Howard Bloch and his parents in Scarsdale, Vivian Goldberg, Patsy

Martin, Jane Chaplin and Christie Stagg from the Lamotte apartment, John Simon, and the thirty-nine other students whose names appeared on an administrative list of the 1963–64 group. It is touching and funny to imagine Jane, a vigilant person, suspicious of authority, and protective of her college friend, telling the agent, with all the conviction she could muster, that the FBI ought to focus their search on Algeria. Because, really, where else would she have gone?[41]

A white student on the 1963–64 Hamilton program barely knew Angela Davis, but his own story is parallel to hers in a number of ways and tells something important about the spirit shared by many young people who studied in France in the 1960s. John Simon was in New York when the FBI came calling. Like Angela Davis, he had devoted his twenties to social justice. During the year in Paris, he'd studied mime and music and had taken the rigorous contemporary literature course, where he was struck by the lack of any discussion, the atmosphere so unlike classes at home. He joined demonstrations in the streets of Paris against de Gaulle and nuclear weapons. He was arrested in a general sweep of protesters, and taken to the CRS barracks in the Parc de Monceau, then to a gymnasium, where he watched the police beating Africans—breaking arms and legs while other police watched from a balcony, aiming their machine guns downward.

He'd been so independent during his junior year in Paris, so eager to escape the American student world, that he wonders now if he didn't come off as a snob. With his two American best friends, Robert and David, he spoke only French. Unlike Christie and Jane and Angela, the young men all had the army to face, and Vietnam. Student status would exempt them, at least for a while.

Simon was a rolling stone. First, as he put it, "he talked his way into Cambridge," pursuing his literary studies for a master's degree. In 1967 he enrolled in a doctoral program at the University of York to work on Beckett, dividing his time among England, Dublin, Rome, and Paris. In 1968 he was in Paris, where he participated in the events of May from the streets and did research on his author at the Editions de Minuit. In 1969, the year Angela Davis joined the Che Lumumba Club in Los Angeles, John Simon joined up with a group of British Trotskyists and managed a parliamentary political campaign, in the form of street theater. Instead of completing his PhD he channeled his intellectual energies into a public lecture series at York called "Black Voices in White America"—from slave narratives to Malcolm X. Like Angela Davis, Simon had moved from an art-for-art's-sake interest in Robbe-Grillet and Claude Simon to political theory through writers like Frantz Fanon.

In 1970, when Angela Davis was fighting the regents of the University of California, John Simon was back in New York. Reading George Jackson and Eldridge Cleaver had convinced him that it was essential to help keep young people on the margins of society out of prison. With this goal, he worked first with a black-run organization called the West Side Community Alliance, then founded a group called the Dome, which still works with some of the most disadvantaged students in the New York school system.

When the FBI called him, he thought he was the one in trouble. "How well do you know Angela Davis?" the agent asked. "Not at all!" he answered. When the agent pointed out to John Simon that Angela Davis had been with him in Paris, on the Hamilton program, he was astonished. It was only then that he put together the public Angela Davis, the icon of a thousand posters whose cause he supported so fiercely, with the conservatively dressed young woman in his contemporary literature class.[42] "She was a shy person and I was goofy," he remembered. He had dressed in nothing but suits that year.

One Big Prison Yard

John Simon and Angela Davis both studied radical philosophy in Europe. Since their junior year on the Hamilton program, and with no connection whatsoever to one another, they had each deepened their commitment to political action. For John Simon, as for so many others, George Jackson and Angela Davis had come to embody that commitment. Month after month, news of their struggles reached the front pages of the international news. Their cause célèbre involved an escalating series of dramas: the capture of Angela Davis by the FBI in New York on October 13, 1970; her imprisonment at a Manhattan detention center; her extradition to California, to jails in Marin County, then in San José, Santa Clara County, after a change of jurisdiction. Her trial began in San José on March 28, 1971.

Meanwhile, George Jackson had been moved from Soledad to San Quentin to await his own trial, with Fleeta Drumgo and John Clutchette, for the murder of the Soledad guard. That trial was about to begin in August 1971, when Jackson was gunned down at San Quentin. A crazy escape attempt, a setup, or a combination of both? Some accounts claim he was unarmed, others that he was carrying a nine-millimeter automatic pistol. Whether the gun was smuggled to him in prison by a friend who wanted him free or by an enemy who wanted him dead isn't clear either. Claudine La Haye, writing for *L'Express*, told the official story: "George Jackson, the guards insist, tried to escape. He brandished a gun, threatened the jailers. Shots rang out."[43] To millions of readers of *Soledad Brother*, his death was tantamount to a political assassination.

Jackson's two Soledad brothers, Clutchette and Drumgo, were acquitted of the murder of the guard, but George Jackson never had his day in court. Bob Dylan's ballad hit the charts in January 1972. "Sometimes I think this whole world is one big prison yard," he sang. "Some of us are prisoners, the rest of us are guards. Lord, Lord, they cut George Jackson down."

From the spring of 1970 until the summer of 1971, Angela Davis and George Jackson had written feverishly to one another. They had argued about feminist theory, about the role of black women; they had flirted; they had fallen in love. In all that time they had met only once, with their lawyers, a month before Jonathan Jackson's violent shoot-out sent Angela Davis running and eventually put her behind bars for eighteen months. In that sorrowful August of 1971, what remained for Angela Davis of her love for George Jackson was alive in her letters, and even they were seized by the court.

France Mobilizes

Angela Davis's American drama touched the souls of French intellectuals. Djamila Bouhired's and Djamila Boupacha's torture at the hands of the French military in Algeria, the disappearance of mathematician Maurice Audin, had sensitized them to the crimes committed by their own state during the Algerian conflict. The student and worker revolutions of May 1968 had given them an experience and a taste for political action that the Jackson and Davis cases reawakened. So an African American woman fighting the state of California for her freedom became a rallying point for the French left. It mattered that she was a woman, that she was charismatic and beautiful; it mattered that she was a philosopher and that she lived in the world of books and ideas; and finally, it mattered that she was no stranger to France.

In March 1971, as her trial was about to begin, the French Communist Party organized a "committee in solidarity with the young, black communist university professor." Their initial list of signatures, published in the party newspaper *L'Humanité,* included Jacqueline Bouvier's literature professor Max-Pol Fouchet; Louis Aragon, the dean of communist poets; Picasso; Marie-Claude Vaillant-Couturier, survivor of Auschwitz-Birkenau and Ravensbrück and symbol of the communist resistance; and many professors, writers, actors, filmmakers, and party members and nonmembers.[44]

The Party took the lead, which in itself explains a major difference from the American political situation. Though there had always been strong anticommunist sentiments in France, there had been no French McCarthy in the 1950s, no committee on "un-French activities." Instead, communists had held cabinet posts on and off since the early postwar period. In the previous elections of 1968 they had captured four and a half million votes (20 percent in the first round of the presidential elections) and won thirty-four seats in the National Assembly. In 1973 they won even more votes. Until the Mitterrand era, the French Communist Party had more votes than any party on the left, and wielded more political clout than the Socialists. Despite the scandal of the Hitler-Stalin pact of 1939, French communists were proud of their contribution to the Resistance movement in occupied France, proud of their martyred comrades—whose numbers had been inflated through party propaganda and myth to 75,000.[45] Nothing could offer a sharper contrast than the American Communist Party of the early 1970s, whose members were practically a secret society. As an American communist, Angela Davis was part of a tiny, disavowed political minority with no representation in Washington. In France she was instantly recognized as a comrade by several million voters on the left.

Independently of the communists, Jean Genet headed a second hub of activity; he made a dozen or more interventions on behalf of George Jackson from July 1970 to December 1971, and just as many for Angela Davis.[46] Through her cause, Genet joined forces with a group of French intellectuals called the GIP, the Groupe d'Information sur les Prisons.

The GIP was the brainchild of Michel Foucault. One of the key figures in the poststructuralist revolution, Foucault worked at the crossroads of sociology, history, and philosophy. He had challenged Sartre's existential humanism, his sense of individual responsibility, with the idea that knowledge was already constructed by institutions before it was experienced. With *Discipline and Punish,* his seminal work on the modern prison, he suggested that imprisonment was not only a physical state but a technological strategy, a means of control that extended to all areas of society. His concept of the "panopticon," a state of surveillance whose central metaphor was the relationship of the individual prisoner to the watchtower, was reflected in the dramas between prison guards and prisoners at Soledad. And although he was writing about the nineteenth century in *Discipline and Punish*, he had been thinking about George Jackson and about Angela Davis since his encounter with Genet in the summer of 1970, just as Genet was returning from his American tour in support of the Panthers. The person who brought them together that summer was Katharina von Bülow in the foreign rights department at the Editions Gallimard, who shepherded the French edition of *Les Frères de Soledad: Lettres de prison de George Jackson*. She would make two trips to California, one to visit Angela Davis and George Jackson in prison in June 1971, and a second for George Jackson's memorial service in Oakland, organized and orchestrated by the Black Panthers. She remembers San Quentin as a place made even more hellish by the beautiful view of San Francisco Bay, a reminder of impossible freedoms just beyond its walls. George Jackson showed her the enormous calluses on his hands, and told her that he hit his fists against a wall every day to keep them hard for the struggles inside.[47]

The Groupe d'Information sur les Prisons gave another, more theoretical inflection to Genet's passionate enthusiasm for the Panthers. They had already published two pamphlets under the title *Intolérable*, devoted to letters from prisoners and analyses of prison suicides and conditions in specific French prisons. After Jackson's death sparked prison revolts all over the world, the GIP published a third and final volume, entitled "The Assassination of George Jackson." Genet wrote the preface, and Foucault had the last word, echoing Jackson's own rhetoric: "the struggle in the prisons has become a new revolutionary front."[48] One American philosopher has gone so far as to suggest that Foucault owes the gist of his theoretical insights on incarceration to Jackson's writings.[49]

The Trial

A month after a fugitive Angela Davis was captured by the FBI, James Baldwin sent "An Open Letter to my Sister, Angela Y. Davis" from France.[50] When he was interviewed on American radio about his letter, the first question he was asked was about the reaction to the Angela Davis case in France.

Twenty years after the Marshall Plan, he began, speaking in the resonant former preacher's voice for which he was famous, "the dream is over." The dream was over, he explained, because the current administration was out to destroy the world. And in a Europe that had shed so much blood during the Second World War, where people had been through things that most Americans had not been through, no one really believed anything the American government had to say: "To believe this girl is guilty . . . well nobody believes it for a minute."

Baldwin made the following argument: Angela Davis was being tried for complicity in a murder committed by Jonathan Jackson, when in fact it was law enforcement officers who had fired the guns that killed Jonathan Jackson. Indeed, from the earliest news reports about the shoot-out to Davis's trial itself, the question of who had pulled the trigger on the shotgun taped to Judge Haley's neck was never satisfactorily resolved. Although Jackson created the situation, took the hostages, and distributed the weapons, it was conceivable that he had never fired a shot. For some people there was an infinitesimal difference between having a shotgun taped to the judge's neck and actually killing him; for others, responsibility for the four deaths lay in part with the prosecutor—also a hostage inside the van—and the guards in the parking lot, because they had opened fire. Baldwin made the most of what he considered an outrage: "They pulled the trigger and they committed the murder and they should be on trial."[51]

The heart of a good defense is to reframe the story, so that the accused is no longer the person on trial. What the defense attorneys needed to do was to replicate Baldwin's argument, but in an even fuller sense: they needed to show that the case against Angela Davis was not about her conspiracy with Jonathan Jackson; it was about the state's conspiracy against her as a black woman and a communist activist.[52]

Angela Davis was charged with murder, conspiracy, and kidnapping. The main evidence against her was the fact that the guns used by Jonathan Jackson in the courtroom shoot-out belonged to her, and that she had been seen with him in early August. The question was whether Jonathan Jackson had stolen her guns, or taken them with her blessing. The prosecution would have to rely on circumstantial evidence, on conjecture.

What may look like a weak case today looked entirely different in the context of 1970. President Nixon had already convicted her rhetorically as he was signing a new bill for the control of organized crime. He congratulated the FBI on the capture of a woman "engaged in terrorist acts."[53] The killing of four Kent State students by the National Guard, the murder of Panther Fred Hampton, the formation of the Weather Underground, the trial of Bobby Seale and Ericka Huggins in New Haven were so many signs of an ideological state of emergency. Susan Sontag had entered the fray as early as May 1968, writing to the *New York Times* with James Baldwin and Norman Mailer to protest the killing of an eighteen-year-old member of the Panthers, Bobby Hutton, and the wounding of Eldridge Cleaver. The Oakland shoot-out, they wrote, was an attempt to destroy black leadership, "another act of racism against persons who take a militant stand on the rights of black people to determine the conditions of their lives."

Bettina Aptheker, whose San José home served as a rallying point for Angela Davis's defense, put it succinctly when she evoked the atmosphere of 1970: "Where groups like the Panthers were concerned there wasn't a semblance of constitutional law."[54] And with the death penalty still in effect in California during trial preparation, Angela Davis's life was at stake as surely as Bobby Hutton's had been.

In the history of American criminal law, *The People of the State of California v. Angela Y. Davis* is regularly cited for three reasons: first, for setting a new standard for voir-dire (the jury selection process) in ferreting out racism among potential jurors. Second, for the brilliant strategies of a defense that included Angela Davis herself as co-counsel, working with a team of African American lawyers—Doris Walker, Leo Branton, Jr., and Howard Moore. Third, for demonstrating the weakness of eyewitness testimony by revealing the racial stereotypes used by whites in identifying African Americans. More subtle, but rarely discussed, is the way in which Angela Davis's own education, and even her love of French literature, surfaced in a trial that became a debate about language.

The *People v. Angela Y. Davis* was not televised. Instead, over 450 newspapers from all over the world had requested credentials to cover the trial; over two hundred journalists who couldn't get into the courthouse crowded into a basement, where a video feed connected them to the courtroom. In the audience during those first fifteen days of juror questioning was Jules (Antoine) Borker, legal counsel to the French Communist Party and representative of the French Committee in Support of Angela Davis, which had sent him to San José as an observer. He was a veteran of tough legal battles, having spent three years in Algeria defending FLN militants. When the young communist Maurice Audin was "disappeared" by the French army in 1957, it was Borker who represented the Audin family. This prominent attorney, closely identified with the party, was granted a visa by the American consulate on the condition that he say nothing to the press.[55] He explained as much to the first American journalist who approached him for his opinion on jury selection. Once he'd told his story, he was ushered to the basement to meet the press corps. The reporter jumped onto a chair and explained the situation, shouting out to Borker: "From now on you are under the protection of the American press corps!" The assembled reporters applauded the French communist.[56]

Another European was there, who has to this day a vivid memory of the courthouse. Simon Pleasance had begun to work with Fay Stender in her Prison Law Project and had gotten a press card through the London *Times*. Every day he sat in court, admiring the members of the Che Lumumba Club, stalwart in the front rows. The security measures were so draconian, the pressure so acute, that the courthouse itself began to feel like a prison, an example of everything that was wrong with the U.S. In a private, playful form of protest, Pleasance and a reporter from the American newspaper of record planted marijuana seeds in a little patch of soil in the foyer of the San José courthouse.[57]

A trial is always about two competing stories. If the defense needs to reframe the story, shifting the identity of the guilty party away from the defendant, the prosecution needs to make its story fit the frame. Every detail counts.

For the prosecution, it mattered that Jonathan Jackson had stormed the Marin courtroom with a satchel. Every object in that satchel mattered—the tape, the wallet, the guns registered to Angela Davis, and six paperback books, some with her name on them, others with her fingerprints. Three of them were in French: Daniel Guérin's *L'anarchisme* (1965); Claude Estier's *Pour l'Algérie*, an account of life in postrevolutionary Algeria (Editions Maspéro, 1964); and an issue of *L'homme et la société*, a Marxist journal of sociology.[58]

The titles were entered into the record by the sheriff who had found them. He spelled the French words for the court letter by letter, lending to the proceedings an exaggerated sense of their foreignness—something like what John Kennedy was referring to when he said the U.S. Congressmen found Jacqueline Kennedy's White House menus "too Frenchy."

There was no analysis of the contents of the books; the prosecution assumed they would have been of no use to Jonathan Jackson.[59] They may have been wrong, since French would have been the most likely language for him to be taking at Blair High School in Pasadena, where he was a junior.[60] He had edited an underground newspaper; he took honors and advanced classes. The prosecution argued instead that carrying Angela Davis's books was a flag—a signal that he was carrying out her violent mission, and that she had approved. More than one analyst of the trial has murmured a theory that can never be proved: If Angela Davis's French books hadn't been in the satchel, could someone have gone to her apartment, taken them, and placed them there? In the war against the Panthers, says this theory, dirty tricks were business as usual.

Angela Davis met with her defense team regularly and lent her philosophic mind to the trial strategies, first from her prison cell, then on the outside, after she was released on bail, in regular meetings at Bettina Aptheker's house in San José. In February 1972, a year after it began, the nature of the trial changed. First, the state of California declared the death penalty unconstitutional. Angela Davis was no longer threatened with a death sentence.[61] Bail came soon after, and it was a turning point for the defense, for it allowed Angela Davis to appear before the jurors as a free woman. Already, as a defendant, she did not have to appear on the witness stand in the role of suspect, or submit to cross-examination—those were her rights. But as co-counsel, she was the authority. She had delivered the opening argument, lecturing, as a professor would do, and instructing the members of the jury on the key issues in the case from the point of view of the defense.[62] Why had she owned four guns? She began with her childhood, with dynamite hill in Birmingham: "Because of the constant threats and actual incidents of violence, my father had to keep guns in the house. . . . You will understand that for a black person who had grown up in the South—and particularly during that period—guns had to be a normal fact of life." The hate mail and death threats she received after the controversy at UCLA only confirmed her need for weapons. And in the Che Lumumba club, she and her comrades collected guns, which they kept on a gun rack in a closet. From a form of protection, guns became a sport, and the members of the club used to go to target practice. "As we all shared whatever we had, it was often I who paid for weapons used by others—as I often paid rent, medical costs, and other necessary expenses for my comrades."[63] She was measured and patient, and she was unapologetic.

The prosecution, for its part, was trying to undo the image of a brilliant and thoughtful defendant, and to substitute the image of a woman crazed by love. Albert Harris, the prosecutor, opened:

> Angela Davis's own words will reveal that beneath the cool academic veneer is a woman fully capable of being moved to violence by passion. The evidence will show that her basic motive was not to free political prisoners, but to free the one prisoner that she loved. The basic motive for the crime was the same motive underlying hundreds of criminal cases across the United States every day. That motive was not abstract. It was not founded basically on any need, real or imagined, for prison reform. It was not founded on a desire for social justice. It was founded simply on the passion that she felt for George Jackson, and the evidence of that motive will not be circumstantial. You won't have to make any inferences. It will rest on the Defendant's own words.[64]

This last line was the gauntlet: the case would not just be about evidence, but about language as evidence. Only Angela Davis's correspondence with George Jackson, her desire to see him free, could point to a motive for conspiring with Jonathan Jackson. And only on the assumption that Jonathan Jackson had taken his hostages, not in some act of desperate rebellion, but as a part of a plan to force authorities to free his brother, could the conspiracy have any logic. As the prosecutor put it, "The charge in this case is that the defendant conspired with other people to bring about the freedom of George Jackson through violent means."[65]

It was the best argument the prosecution had, since it was next to impossible to prove that guns purchased by Angela Davis over several years were intended for the express purpose of helping Jonathan Jackson take hostages. In the course of the trial, a member of the Che Lumumba club testified about target practice with her at Jack Rabbit Pass; another described how she and Angela discovered the empty spaces on the gun rack the day after the shoot-out and realized with horror that Jonathan Jackson had been alone in the house a few days earlier. No one had looked at the gun rack since.[66]

With a plausible scenario of stolen guns, Angela Davis's purchase of those guns receded from the heart of the case, and a vigorous legal battle devel-

Angela Davis: The Return

oped around the admissibility of her letters to George Jackson.[67] The prosecution wanted to enter into evidence three letters written by her in June 1970, at the start of their correspondence, as well as an eighteen-page typed document, part diary and part love letter, finished a year after the courtroom shoot-out and taken from George Jackson's cell by a sheriff after his death. In one of the most moving passages in that journal intended for George Jackson alone, she describes what it was like to wait for him in the glassed-in cubicle at San Quentin, the prison to which he had been transferred in July 1971 to await his trial. She had been able to visit him once, a day-long visit in the company of his lawyers. She wrote the letter in the aftermath of their only meeting, their only physical contact.

What is bound to strike any reader familiar with Angela Davis's public, political voice is the vulnerable and passionate young woman who emerges in this private communication, a woman so different from the analyst of Robbe-Grillet, the professor of political philosophy, or the activist, and yet still the analyst, the philosopher, the activist, through her passion. This Angela Davis is twenty-six years old, and she is in love with a man she can only reach through her words:

A scene frozen in my mind: I am standing in the little glass cubicle downstairs, standing, waiting, loving, desiring, and then hot cold rage when the chains begin to rattle as you slowly descend the stairs surrounded by the small army of mindless but armed automatons. I, your wife, your comrade who is supposed to love you, fight with you, fight for you, I'm supposed to rip off the chains. I'm supposed to fight your enemies with my body, but I am helpless, powerless. I contain the rage inside. I do nothing. I stand there watching, forced to assume the posture of a disinterested spectator, the whole scene perceived through glass, laboratory-like, mad at them for thrusting this upon me, mad at myself for doing nothing.[68]

As a student of Camus, Angela Davis knew the scene in *The Myth of Sisyphus*: "A man is talking on the telephone, enclosed in a glass booth. You can't hear him, but you see his gestures, which are meaningless. You wonder why he is alive."[69] Only in her world, the world of the imprisoned and the chained, the scene she viewed from behind glass, forced to watch without being able to act, produces something very different from the alienation and stupor of the scene in *The Myth of Sisyphus*. She looked within and without, she saw herself passive behind the glass, and she saw George Jackson in chains, descending the staircase. She felt love, desire, then impotence and rage.

In objecting to the prosecution's use of her client's personal diary, defense attorney Doris Walker used a phrase Angela Davis herself had used in one of her letters to Jackson to explain the way she was writing: stream of consciousness.[70] You can't edit a stream of consciousness without destroying it, Walker argued: "verbal utterances must be taken as a whole, not by fragments or summary." From a fight over the meaning of the letters, the case became a fight over the meaning of words and their relationship to each other and to reality. Harris, for the prosecution, argued that allusions to revolutionary violence in letters written before the shoot-out—to "fighting instincts," "going all the way," "beautiful plans ahead"—represented Angela Davis's true intention: to use violence to free George Jackson. Leo Branton, for the defense, suggested that the notion of Angela Davis's love for George Jackson being a basis for a crime of passion was strange, if not preposterous. Crimes of passion were motivated by negative feelings of jealousy, or betrayal, but never by love.[71]

The defense team had a problem of literary criticism on their hands. They needed to prove, in general, that the language used in letters represented something very different from the literal meanings imputed by the prosecution. They sought the advice of Leonard Michaels, a professor of English at Berkeley, and a creative writer. As lawyers do, they were looking for precedents, only in this instance the precedents had to be in literary, rather than legal history.

Professor Michaels sent them a passionate memo about Alexander Pope's poem "Eloise and Abelard":

Imagining the state of mind of Eloise, imprisoned in a convent, produced the most flamboyant, extravagantly passionate poem of [Pope's] career. At one place in the poem he comments, through Eloise, on the character of what his poem is trying to imitate—that is a letter, exactly the kind of letter it would be natural for an imprisoned woman to write to the man who represented the highest spiritual ideals to her. And he defines letters, particularly letters written in such circumstances by an imprisoned woman, as being taught, virtually *dictated* to the writer of the letter by Heaven itself. Such a letter, then, is to be understood—however passionate, however physical it may seem—as sanctified, divinely inspired address from one soul to another.[72]

A research assistant for the defense, Kathy Kalil, sent a description of Elizabeth Barrett Browning's diary and described the writer's unexpected and transformative love for Robert Browning.[73] Elizabeth Barrett Browning made a brief appearance in Branton's closing argument as an intellectual woman who wrote about love.[74] But the example that was used in the thick of the trial was neither Eloise nor Barrett Browning, and the defense owed it, not to literary experts, but to Angela Davis's own French literary culture:

> Howard Moore: I just want to make an inquiry if the Court had read Proust's novel, "In Remembrance of Things Past," which was written . . . from a self-inflicted padded cell. The novel is about 5,000 pages and, in the novel, he goes back in his life and sees things before his eyes which have been entirely transformed, things which were once viewed by him and have become passionate, and he sees the events from a vantage point of a self-inflicted padded cell where he tries to recapture, through some 5,000 pages, his life in the Remembrance of Things Past.[75]

The asthmatic Proust had indeed lined his room on the rue Hamelin with cork to keep out dust and noise, and it was there that he lay dying in the fall of 1922, struggling to make his last corrections on *In Search of Lost Time*. He would have made an excellent witness for Angela Davis's defense—he who, as a young man, had joined his mother in supporting Alfred Dreyfus against trumped-up charges of espionage.[76]

In response to Moore's question, the judge answered, "I must confess that this is one of many things I haven't read." You can almost hear him smile. Moore's analogy sounded far-fetched, and certainly prosecutor Harris received it that way, protesting that this was not an academic discussion or a debate, but a criminal trial. There was nonetheless a real legal issue at stake: whether Angela Davis's private communications with George Jackson could count as evidence for the prosecution, proof of her "wild passion and will to conspire"; whether they were inadmissible by virtue of her constitutional right to privacy; or, even if deemed admissible as evidence, whether they could be considered promises of violent behavior or a touching example of Proustian memory work behind bars.

The defense won their battle, but only partially. The judge admitted eight pages of the eighteen-page diary, and three letters. The argument then moved to a debate over what Sontag's Oxford teacher J. L. Austin might have characterized as the performative force of language. What exactly does speech (or writing) have to do with acts? Angela Davis had written, "My love for you reinforces my fighting instinct and makes me want to go to war," about which the defense had this to say:

> Mr. Harris would have the jury believe that "makes me want to go to war" means "makes me want to go out and organize a group of people and take guns and go in and liberate somebody in a courtroom." . . . She is not a nation; she doesn't declare war. It is rhetoric. It says "makes me want to go to war, makes me want to fight, makes me want to defend my honor, my country, my people, myself, you." It could mean that.

The prosecution was trying to prove that she had lost all reason over her love for George Jackson. Meanwhile, behind the scenes, she was advising her defense on literary hermeneutics.

Albert Harris entered the admissible parts of the letters into evidence by reading them aloud in a monotone.[77] He wasn't able to make the letters sound like the words of a violent, irrational person, and perhaps he knew it as soon as he started to speak them and dulled his tone accordingly. In the closing, the defense returned to the so-called damning epistolary evidence, seizing it for its own purpose, which was to represent Angela Davis as a caring and loving person. To prepare their coup de théâtre, the defense team called on screenwriter Dalton Trumbo. Trumbo, a communist intellectual, had been blacklisted by McCarthy. He had met Angela Davis at the reception he gave for Jean Genet in Los Angeles in the summer of 1970. He took the text of her letters to Jackson and edited them, not for content but for form, streamlining the cadence of the long sentences to create a prose poem. Leo Branton's rich voice conveyed the simple lyrical beauty of the lines. Words were all that Angela Davis and George Jackson had had to offer one another from inside their prison cells. In sharing those words with the jurors, Branton was sharing the body of their love.

Down to the closing argument, Angela Davis's defense took on the very deepest questions raised by her case: what it means to be black in a racist society; what it means for passion to be personal and political; what it means to write, and to act. In his closing argument, Leo Branton, the most theatrical of the three defense lawyers, asked the jurors to commit an act of imagination:

> I'm going to ask you, if you will, for the next few minutes to think black with me—to BE black. Don't worry. When the case is over I am going to let you revert back to the safety of being what you are. You only have to be black and think black for the minutes that it will take for me to express to you what it means to be black in this country.[78]

This rhetorical device allowed him to take the jurors through three hundred years of African American history, and to sensitize them to the politics of color. Angela Davis, "a product of some of the finest schools of this country and of the world," was not content to rest with her own achievements; she

21. Angela Davis at a press conference following her release on bail (February 1972). Courtesy of Department of Special Collections and University Archives, Stanford University Libraries. Photograph © Michelle Vignes.

Chapter Six

dedicated her life to freeing the men in chains, the modern slaves. He read from vile hate mail that Davis had received over the UCLA firing; he pointed out that no black person would wonder why she went underground—since the only reasonable assumption, which was proved correct by the way she was treated in jail, was that she would be treated unfairly. And if she had really planned the courthouse shoot-out, would she have been foolish enough to sign her own name to the gun registrations and have Jonathan Jackson put books with her name on them in his knapsack?

After thirteen hours of deliberation over a period of three days, the jury announced its verdict of not guilty on all three counts. Angela Davis was free.

Roses for Angela

Until the summer of her acquittal, Angela Davis had appeared regularly not just in court, but in the court of public opinion. A committee for her defense sent out mimeographed analyses of the trial almost daily. Committees were formed all over the world; funds were raised, including income from reprints of George Jackson's letters, which had sold half a million copies in their first year of publication.

There were plenty of demonizing news stories about her in the U.S. press, where she was portrayed as a wild radical, a danger to society. *Ebony,* the mainstream African American magazine, which had never been radical, published the most sympathetic American portrait, lingering on the experience of the junior-year-abroad student smoking gauloises in the café-tabacs with dark-skinned Algerian students on the boulevard Saint-Michel. Charles Sanders, who had been the *Jet* correspondent in Paris during the Algerian war, argued that the young Angela Davis had seen in the Algerian situation a mirror of her own Birmingham, Alabama.[79]

Ebony's interest in Davis's Paris experience was matched only by the French press itself. A long article by Claudine La Haye in *L'Express,* based on an interview, described Angela Davis's year abroad as an encounter with Algerian students and with the writings of Karl Marx: "She loves ideas. Her lucid spirit is at ease with them. She might as well have invented the dialectic." La Haye described her as the larger-than-life black girl who was once protected by the teenager with the tragic expression (Jonathan Jackson), and who was now alone, a prisoner speaking in her calm, low voice behind the bullet-proof glass partition of the visitors' parlor.[80] These were early days, before bail, and La Haye retained a skepticism about the innocence of the Soledad Brothers that would disappear from later French coverage. She gave the prison authorities the benefit of the doubt: "A guard is assassinated by inmates. Within a week the authorities have identified the guilty parties: Jackson, Clutchette and Drumgo," she wrote. There was no speculation in her article that George Jackson had been set up for murder at San Quentin, only a quote from the guards about his armed escape attempt.

Four months later, Edmonde Charles-Roux's editorial in *L'Humanité,* coinciding with Angela Davis's release on bail, was, by comparison, an ode: "Uncompromising Angela," she intoned; Angela who owed her freedom to people of all political beliefs. Charles-Roux described the campaign in Davis's support as "unprecedented in the world." She may have been right.[81]

It's useful to step back from the beautiful language of the editorial and think about what it represented politically. Edmonde Charles-Roux brought to *L'Humanité* the cachet of a former Resistance fighter and a former editor of Paris *Vogue.* Legend had it that she had been fired from the magazine in 1966 when she chose a black mannequin for its cover. She was the companion and soon-to-be wife of Gaston Deferre, a leading French socialist. Her byline in the party newspaper was a sign that French support for Angela Davis could encompass, perhaps not all, but certainly a range of political beliefs. It was also a sign of the French Communist Party's plan to participate in a union of the left with the socialists, to forge a common program. The campaign to save Angela Davis needs to be understood in the context of this opening, of the party's sleek new headquarters on the Place du Colonel Fabien and the transition to a new, resolute leader, Georges Marchais—all signs of a last moment of effervescence before its long decline.

French support for Angela Davis was left-wing and it was also intellectual. What happened to her relationship to literature through this movement was as dramatic as all the rest. The same writers she had read and written about as a twenty-year-old student abroad in 1963–64 and as a French major at Brandeis—men and women she would never have expected to meet— were now fighting for her cause. While she was still in prison in New York after her capture by the FBI, four hundred French intellectuals sent an appeal to Governor Rockefeller, protesting her inhuman treatment and demanding her release. Among them was Daniel Guérin, who didn't yet know that his book on anarchism had been found in Jonathan Jackson's knapsack and would figure in Angela Davis's trial; the poet Jacques Prévert, who wrote a poem for her; and the editorial board of *Cahiers du Cinéma*.[82] In March 1971, Jean Genet circulated a petition calling for a committee in support of black political prisoners; his statement quoted Angela Davis, arguing that "repression will only cease if a mass movement intervenes to make the enemy back off." Signing for the cause were two of the New Novelists she had studied, Sarraute and Duras. Juliette Greco, darling of the postwar Saint-Germain-des-Prés jazz scene and the former lover of Miles Davis, signed. Actress Maria Casarès, Camus's great love, and the daughter of the last prime minister of doomed republican Spain, signed as well. Among the literary avant-garde signing were Maurice Blanchot, Jacques Derrida, Philippe Sollers, Julia Kristeva, and Roland Barthes—all writers in Angela Davis's intellectual constellation.[83] It must have seemed as though her own education were parading before her, reaching out in solidarity.

Alain Robbe-Grillet, the subject of her senior essay and the man who believed that his total commitment to literature had only an "obscure and remote" connection to the revolution, signed a letter to Governor Ronald Reagan with Foucault, Aragon, and Picasso, among others. It was a demand for bail, written in English in a single sentence whose intricate syntax was a rare sight in the California governor's office:

> So that there may be at least a minimum certainty that Angela Davis's fight for life will take place in an open court and not in the obscure depth of some prison cell block beyond the scrutiny of those for whom her fate is inevitably linked with the fate of dissent in the United States, we the undersigned urge that Angela Davis be set free on bail at once.[84]

Support for Davis was not confined to intellectuals. Rank-and-file communists along with thousands of others on the left, who, since the revolutionary events of May '68, were accustomed to gathering in the streets around social issues, wrote to her and marched. *L'Humanité* estimated at sixty thousand the number of supporters who followed the two-and-a-half mile path from the new Communist Party headquarters on the Place du Colonel Fabien to the Place de la Bastille, the revolutionary heart of the city. The *Herald Tribune*, covering the same event, reduced the number to twenty thousand. At the head of the procession that October day were the communist poet and former *résistant* Louis Aragon, arm-in-arm with Fania Davis Jordan, who

22. Fania Davis (*center*), marching for her sister Angela in Paris, with writer Louis Aragon (*right*) (October 4, 1971). Photograph © Agence France-Presse.

. . .

was touring Europe in Angela's defense. She evoked France's revolutionary traditions and expressed her gratitude for a show of support that was like no other she had seen on her world tour—she couldn't wait to share the news of the demonstration with her sister. She called for Angela's liberation, for a halt to prison assassinations, for the unconditional return of American troops from Vietnam. Her speech was broadcast on French national radio. She spoke in what the radio announcer described as "more than correct French." Fania, like her big sister, was a French major.[85]

Thousands of French people wrote to Angela Davis. They wrote as if to someone very close, as if to a sister. People of color from Africa and the Antilles wrote to her; office workers wrote; schoolchildren wrote, sending drawings of their pets or bouquets. Fania was quoted in *L'Humanité* saying that roses were her sister's favorite flower. Hundreds of rose postcards, rose notecards, rose watercolors, popup roses arrived at the prison and at the office of the committee in support of Davis's liberation. Olivier, ten years old, sent a drawing of a panther, a flower, and a peace sign: "My name is Olivier.

23. Card with a drawing of a black panther and a note on the back from "Olivier," sent to Angela Davis in prison (November 14, 1970). Courtesy of Department of Special Collections and University Archives, Stanford University Libraries.

I live in France, in Paris. I'm ten. I hope you will get out of prison soon."[86] A young man from Martinique, doing his military service in a hospital, told her that he was writing because he had heard her French was perfect; that he was afflicted by her detention, by her misfortune, as if it had happened to him, "since you must know that my own skin is black." He asked, "Please let me know the state of your health when you can," wishing, with all his heart, for a just trial, and apologizing for any French mistakes he might have made.

A woman began her letter by saying she wasn't a member of any group: "Angela, I wish, despite my sorrow, despite your life in prison and the torturous machinations of all those moneyed, powerful roaches, I wish for you the courage, the force, and the pride to hold your beautiful head up High. And may the force of the World be with You. My three sons and I embrace you, our beloved sister." Her letter was signed "37 years old, secretary, divorced with three children."

The Beret

A free woman but no longer a private citizen, Angela Davis had become the best-known communist intellectual in the world. The party had rallied the masses to her cause, and in her travels in the months following her acquittal

MARTINIQUE *Petite Antilles*
1000 km²
300.000 habitants.
EN AVANT!

Sauvons

Angéla DAVIS

Le 27 Septembre aux Etats-Unis, commence le pocès d'Angela DAVIS, jeune professeur d'Université.

Son crime ? Etre noire et communiste. Avoir lutté pour les droits de ses frères de race. Angela est menacée de mort.

Les racistes et les réactionnaires des Etats-Unis veulent la supprimer pour terroriser les combattants de la liberté, comme ils ont assassiné bien des militants noirs et récemment dans sa prison le jeune Georges JACKSON.

Il ne faut pas que se renouvellent les **parodies de justice** qui ont conduit à la chaise électrique SACCO et VANZETTI en 1927, les époux ROSENBERG en 1953, et bien d'autres.

Dans le monde entier, les honnêtes gens réclament la libération d'Angela DAVIS.

Martiniquais, élevons notre voix !
Solidarité avec les Noirs Américains !

A bas les racistes américains !

Liberté pour Angela DAVIS !

Venez nombreux au

Meeting de Protestation
Mercredi 29 Sept. à 18 h.
Salle ALIKER
(2e étage) de l'Imprimerie Populaire — Angle des rues André Aliker et Emile Zola (Terres Sainville).

Entrée libre.

Union de la jeunesse Communiste Martiniquaise
Sections de Fort-de-France du Parti Communiste Martiniquais

Imp. Populaire

24. "Let Us Save Angela Davis": announcement of a protest meeting in Fort-de-France, sponsored by the Communist Youth of Martinique (September 1971). Courtesy of Department of Special Collections and University Archives, Stanford University Libraries.

she paid homage to her supporters and strengthened her ties to an international communist movement. In 1972 she visited Karl Marx University in Leipzig, where she received an honorary doctorate in philosophy. On a second trip to East Germany in 1973 she hosted the International Youth Festival in East Berlin—the same festival she had attended as an undergraduate student the summer she first saw Paris. She returned to Cuba, where, with the support of Castro and the Communist Party, she worked on her political autobiography.

When she returned to France in May 1975, it was to publicize the French translation of her book, *Angela Davis: Autobiographie.*[87] On France-Inter radio, she found herself at odds with a hostile interviewer, who wanted to know when she was going to stop going to political meetings and start enjoying Paris.[88] To his questions about her personal feelings and desires, she countered him at every turn: "I don't separate political life and personal life," and "What is more important? Our subjective desires or the struggle of our people?" It was what the French call a dialogue of the deaf (*dialogue de sourds*). With every journalist who interviewed her, there was always the same struggle to keep the political issues front and center and to insist that her personal story was not the point. This was hard to do because of her beauty, her charm, her mastery of French. An interpreter sat discreetly behind her in all of her interviews, but she didn't need an interpreter. Though it had been ten years since she had lived in France, the language hadn't deserted her.

By contrast with the France-Inter radio interview, her conversation about racism with Bernard Pivot and his guests on the popular literary talk show, *Apostrophes*, was a consecration into the French literary world. She began her interview by thanking the people of France for their decisive support throughout her imprisonment and trial.[89] Angela Davis was seated across from Gaston Monnerville, who had just published his own autobiography.[90] For the French television audience, that pairing was heavy with symbolism and gave the broadcast a special energy. Monnerville, a Resistance fighter in World War II, president of the French Senate until 1968, was one of the pillars of postwar French politics. He claimed both his Guianan and Martiniquan ancestry and his French citizenship with pride—Guiana had been French, he noted, since the seventeenth century. He was of the generation who learned in school that the Gauls were his ancestors; he wasn't troubled in the least by the fact that the Gauls were white, and not his racial ancestors.

25. Angela Davis with Bernard Pivot, before her appearance on *Apostrophes* for a discussion on racism (May 16, 1975). The French translation of her autobiography had just been published. Photograph © AFP / Getty Images.

. . .

After Angela Davis had described the terrorist bombings in her neighborhood in Birmingham, Pivot turned to Monnerville and asked if he had ever experienced racism in France. His answer was no. No white man had ever called him a "dirty negro" (*un sale noir*)? "Yes, they must have, I can't remember" he replied, "but I don't call that racism; I call that idiocy." As president of the Senate, Monnerville had been seated next to Jacqueline Kennedy at the Elysée dinner in 1961; de Gaulle sat on her other side. Here he was, thirteen years later, discussing race with another American woman, whose point of view was starkly opposed to his. As he talked about the universal values of the French Republic, Angela Davis looked at him with an absolute interest and curiosity, with respect. She listened as a teacher listens.

Angela Davis returned to France a year later to gather support for Ben Cha-

26. Angela Davis, Gaston Monnerville, and Bernard Pivot on the set of *Apostrophes* (May 16, 1975). Photograph © Richard Melloul / Sygma / CORBIS.

. . .

vis, sentenced to thirty-four years in prison for arson in connection with the desegregation of the Wilmington schools in North Carolina. The journey coincided with the second French documentary devoted to her story, by Jean-Daniel Simon, a communist intellectual known for his leadership among independent film producers.[91] Simon called his film *L'enchaînement,* referring both to prisoners in chains and to the process of transition, of linking one political struggle to another. Accompanied by his crew, Simon traveled with Angela Davis across the United States, stopping at her family home in Birmingham, at McCain prison in North Carolina, and at Soledad Prison and San Quentin in California. With its own rhythms and forms, *L'enchaînement* uses an assortment of dramatic clips—the FBI radio announcement of the fugitive Angela Davis, a chase scene from *Starsky and Hutch,* Ku Klux Klan photographs, and a scene with Angela Davis in Smithfield, North Carolina, standing in front of the town's "welcome" billboard on highway 70: "Help Fight Communism and Integration. Join and Support United Klans of America. KKK Welcomes You to Smithfield." The film's jazz soundtrack, its

Angela Davis: The Return

visions of American highways lit by night, and the voice of the Haitian singer Toto Bissainthe reading from the French translation of Angela Davis's autobiography—all give *L'enchaînement* the feel of the New Wave, of Saint-Germain cupping its ear to hear the sound of revolution from across the ocean. The last segment of the film is a long traveling shot of Angela Davis walking along the corridors of an airport. She is wearing a chic, hounds-tooth jacket and the same black beret she wore throughout the filming of *L'enchaînement*. She needed a bodyguard everywhere she went, and the beret, which hid her Afro, made it less likely that she would be recognized, or targeted by an extremist. Looking French still offered a respite from American racism, just as it had so many years before in a Birmingham shoe store.

Her work with Jean-Daniel Simon on *L'enchaînement* led to a life-long friendship between the American academic and the French filmmaker and political activist. In 1983, when Angela Davis visited him on one of her lecture tours, she was still under the protection of the full-time bodyguard supplied by the French Communist Party. Simon remembers how they headed to the Champs-Elysées one afternoon to see Euzhan Palcy's film *Rue Cases-Nègres* at the Lincoln cinema, and how the irritated bodyguard tracked them down. Palcy's story of a Martiniquan grandmother who struggles so that her grandson can avoid a life of hard labor in the sugarcane fields took Angela Davis back to scenes of Martinique, to the family she had met in the summer of 1962 in a Paris *chambre de bonne,* and to her own dreams of the past.

Influence

After her acquittal in 1972, Angela Davis continued her academic career. Before she retired as Distinguished Professor at the University of California at Santa Cruz, she taught many courses on what she called the Prison Industrial Complex. Her syllabus included Michel Foucault's *Discipline and Punish*—the book Foucault conceived while working for her cause, and for George Jackson's cause, with the Groupe d'Information sur les Prisons. You could say that their intellectual connection had come full circle. Whatever she owed to his thought, in her ongoing work on prison abolition, he had owed to her struggle.

Beyond Foucault, beyond Genet, and beyond the French Communist Party, there is yet another angle by which to understand Angela Davis's relationship to France, and that is through the works of art she has inspired in the aftermath of the 1970s. Taken as a whole, this artistic production suggests that Angela Davis means something very different in the French-speaking world than in the United States.

One of the most emblematic French perspectives on her trial is contained in a remark in a 1973 interview of Gilles Deleuze and Félix Guattari. Objecting to psychoanalytic clichés that ignore political reality, Deleuze explained: "It's at the same level of repressive work as the prosecutor in the Angela Davis case who affirmed: 'Her behavior can only be explained by her being in love.' What if, on the contrary, Angela Davis's libido was a social revolutionary libido? What if she were in love because she was a revolutionary?"[92]

France has a long history of female icons who represent revolt and revolution, for whom, in Deleuze and Guattari's sense, passion *is* revolutionary passion: Jeanne d'Arc the Catholic martyr and voyante; Madame Roland the revolutionary; Louise Michel, heroine of the Commune; Marianne, symbol of the French Republic; Djamila Boupacha, successor to Djamila Bouhired, painted by Picasso; and, finally, in her own way, Angela Davis, who for a time in 1971 became simply "Angela." The girl who read the anti-Algerian graffiti on Paris walls in 1962, who befriended a family of Martiniquan immigrants in a Paris *chambre de bonne*, continues to haunt the imagination of French artists, in novels and songs and films that occupy completely different registers of culture, from experimental fiction to mass market pop.

Daniel Maximin, the Guadeloupean novelist, has constructed a national epic, *L'isolé soleil*, around three characters—Angela, George, and Jonathan—who reappear in two incarnations. Maximin uses the 1970s story of Angela Davis to echo the slave rebellion that took place on the island in 1802 by giving the characters the same names. For his contemporary story, Maximin takes pieces of language whole cloth from the French translation of Angela Davis's 1975 autobiography, including the letters she quoted from George Jackson. Jonathan, the "man-child," the boy who had to grow up before his time, becomes, in creole, *ti-mâle*. And, of course, Maximin retells the story of Davis's 1969 encounter with the communist lawyer Gertie Archimède in Basse-Terre, making the two women emblems of a revolutionary spirit—as if Angela Davis's few accidental days in Guadeloupe, en route from Cuba back to the U.S., gave the Guadeloupean people a kind of revolutionary blessing.[93]

The title *L'isolé soleil* is a play on the name of Soledad Prison. The Spanish word *soledad* means "solitary," but in Maximin's understanding it also contains a germ of hope in the syllable *sol*, Spanish for "sun." The French title means "isolated sun" or, more poetically, "lone sun." "Dans Soledad il y a Soleil et l'isolé," Maximin has said. From slavery to prison, from the United States to Guadeloupe, from isolation to sun, the figure of Angela allows him to cross centuries and oceans.[94]

In the United States she has been a sympathetic character in Anna Deveare Smith's monologue *The Fires Within*, and an inspiration in her niece Elsa Davis's play *Angela's Mixtape*, but only in Philip Roth's *American Pastoral* does she have anything approaching the fantastical power Maximin gives her. *American Pastoral* is a despairing novel, and an epic in its own way about the American 1960s. The narrator, a father who has lost his daughter to the revolutionary cause (she is wanted for a terrorist bombing) has nightly fantasies of kitchen table dialogues with an imagined Angela Davis, philosophy professor and revolutionary: "Her hair is extraordinary. She peers defiantly out of it like a porcupine. The hair says, 'Do not approach if you don't like pain.'"[95] Roth's Angela Davis spouts hard revolutionary prose, writes revolutionary pamphlets, is unforgiving and dangerous. She has a seat at the table and the force of her convictions, but she represents the tragedy of violent revolutionary aspirations, not their utopian dreams.

As recently as 2010, Yannick Noah has brought Angela Davis into the realm of French pop culture. Noah was a tennis champion in the 1980s and remains one of the most beloved athletes in French history. He has remade himself as a pop artist, and his songs often reflect his African origins—his father was from Cameroon and his mother was French. He lives in New York. In 2010, Noah released an album called *Angela*, whose title song brings together Martin Luther King, Barack Obama, and the Mexico City black athletes of 1968, all under the rubric of Angela, the angel who protests. In the music video, Noah, dressed as a gentleman, sits in a café with a décor that looks like 1950s or '60s Harlem. He is reading Davis's autobiography with her photo on the cover, and her familiar poster appears on the wall behind him. The words of the song are reassuring and vague: "your name resounds in our lives"; "my home is your home." I talked about the album with a thirty-year-old taxi driver from Cameroon in the summer of 2010, in Paris; he had learned of the existence of Angela Davis for the first time through Noah's song. However confusing, however jumbled its references, the song's spirit had touched him and Angela Davis had entered his pantheon: "She's important for our history."

After Yolande du Luart's 1972 *Portrait of a Revolutionary* and Jean-Daniel Simon's 1976 *L'enchaînement*, plans for a third French film about Angela Davis have made the news—a feature film this time. Rachid Bouchareb, the Franco-Algerian filmmaker known for his films about racism in the French army (*Indigènes*) and the massacre of Algerians at Sétif (*Hors la loi*), has announced his intention to make a *bio-pic* about Angela Davis.[96] In an interview in the Algerian paper *El Watan*, he said that as a student abroad, she used to hang out with Algerians in Barbès. That detail attracted his attention.[97]

Her French myth has traveled, from the boulevard Saint-Michel, where an *Ebony* reporter imagined her in deep conversation with Algerian students, to Barbès-Rochechouart, in the northern part of the city, a neighborhood of African and North African immigrants. For a contemporary film about a beautiful young black revolutionary sitting in cafés and smoking Gauloises with Algerian youth, Barbès is a better location than the boulevard Saint-Michel, where budget shoe stores now outnumber the cafés and bars of the 1950s and '60s.

When she was a child, Angela Davis found a way to be free by speaking French. Today, French speakers turn to her for their own myth of freedom. A myth, said Claude Lévi-Strauss, is a story made up of a few essential elements: African American girl studying in France acquires revolutionary wisdom from the decolonization struggles and returns home to challenge the powers that be and triumph over her enemies. A story told by Jean Genet; by Michel Foucault and Gilles Deleuze; by Yolande du Luart and Edmonde Charles-Roux; by Daniel Maximin, Yannick Noah, and Rachid Bouchareb; by taxi drivers and secretaries and thousands of ordinary French citizens. The details change; their power remains.

Conclusion

France *secured* them. For Jacqueline Bouvier, for Susan Sontag, and for Angela Davis, the year in Paris changed their relationship to their bodies, to their words, and strengthened their sense of being in the world. This other country brought them new friends in a new language. And in the end, for completely different reasons, France gave each of these women a deep and lasting confidence, confirmed their spirit of adventure, and guaranteed their freedom from home constraints.

What happened to them during their Paris years was an alchemy made of discipline and distraction. The deep history of their transformation involved smells and tastes and visions—fleeting sensual experiences not easy to capture in a conventional life story. You have to imagine Jacqueline Bouvier in her red traveling skirt, joking with her women friends about the hat-pin device she'd perfected for protection on the trains; Susan Sontag in a tiny Paris movie house, or in her favorite café, recording the slang she was hearing in one of her journals; Angela Davis taking pleasure in a new suede coat, in the taste of couscous in the Latin Quarter, even in something as simple as taking notes on index cards printed with squares rather than lines. You have to imagine too the way the French saw these young women, for if there is anything common to all three, it was beauty, a theatrical way of presenting themselves in public that was both a performance and a protection. To use an old-fashioned expression, they cut quite a picture: Sontag, literally, in her walk-on part in *Le bel âge*; Davis in the student restaurant where young men jumped up for a chance to light her cigarette; Bouvier dancing, or sitting in the Brasserie Balzar after class. Where else but Paris is there so much space that is designed simply for being seen, and how different from the isolating private spaces of American highways and suburbs.

What they made of those Parisian spaces was unique. In an interview in the 1960s, Susan Sontag said about her time in Paris that although she was surrounded by English speakers, "J'ai senti la ville." The verb *sentir* can mean either "to feel" in the most sensual, tactile way, or "to know" as in sentience, perception. Each of the three American women in Paris has her own feel for the city—from Jacqueline Bouvier's painterly vision, to Sontag's lists of cafés, authors, and expressions, to Angela Davis's political reading of signs.

Their access to France was different in each case. For Jacqueline Bouvier, it was a foregone conclusion that she would cross the ocean as a young woman, since European travel was part of the ordinary experience of her class. Angela Davis earned her trip through scholarships and work-study and through the sacrifices of her parents, who had valued their own educations and wanted even better for their children. Susan Sontag was the scrappiest of the three, the self-made student who couldn't afford a junior year abroad. Her trip to Paris after marriage and the birth of her child was belated, and she was isolated, for better or worse, from any institution.

For the rest of their lives, each woman maintained an ongoing relationship, an ongoing dialogue, with France. Jacqueline Bouvier, faithful to the arts, worked with Malraux to bring *Whistler's Mother* and the *Mona Lisa* to the U.S., and later, as an editor, helped her writers make the court of Louis XIV and the Paris of the 1950s come alive. Susan Sontag unlocked French avant-gardes for her American audience, and became the kind of writer normally found only in a Parisian universe of café arguments and street life. Here Angela Davis is the exception, for despite her mastery of French literature and French philosophy, despite the importance for her of Frantz Fanon or Michel Foucault, the force of attraction between France and herself worked mainly in the other direction. Sixty thousand people marched for her liberation in Paris in 1971, in a single demonstration. Thirty-six years later, a nursery school was named for her, the "Ecole Maternelle Angela Davis," in Aubervilliers in the northeastern suburbs of Paris, a multiracial community with its theaters and festivals, its creoles and slangs—a school for the France of tomorrow.[1] As far as I know, there is no school or street in France named after Susan Sontag or Jacqueline Kennedy Onassis, and no plaque commemorates their Paris sojourns.

As representatives of the aspirations of three generations, these women might be said to typify the aesthetes, the bohemians, the political activists. By following them in their travels, we can witness an entire intellectual and cultural history of France: the transition from the aesthetic values leading up to World War II, to the iconoclastic formalism of the avant-garde 1950s, to political revolt in the 1960s, when France was reestablishing its historical values, experimenting with the new, and striking out, at the height of its affluence, against oppressive authority. French writers and artists changed guard alongside the three Americans: Juliette Greco, Simone de Beauvoir, and Saint-Germain-des-Prés in Jacqueline Bouvier and Susan Sontag's generation gave way to Julia Kristeva, Roland Barthes, and Michel Foucault in Angela Davis's. Classical France yielded to swinging France, to the France of high concepts and of deconstruction.

In traveling to France, these three women were touched differently by the great political events of the postwar decades—the emergence from four years of German occupation; France's loss of her colonial empire; and, most dramatically, the long, bitter Algerian "war without a name" and the return of de Gaulle to power to handle the national emergency engendered by that war. You have only to read the *Salmagundi,* the student newspaper at Miss Porter's, to understand how fervent was the idealism, the sense of making a better world, that Jacqueline Bouvier took with her to Paris. Susan Sontag's radicalism, formal in the 1960s, political in the 1970s, was inspired by the bohemian circles that so excited her artistic and sexual imagination in Paris. Angela Davis's belief in equality and justice, rooted in her family's tradition of political activism, took on a new urgency the day she picked up a newspaper in Biarritz to read about the church bombing in her hometown. Distance brought clear vision and anger.

The French people encountered by Bouvier, Sontag, and Davis in their student years and beyond saw these women, at least in part, as expressions of an American national character. From the Liberation to Vietnam, the

United States was a cipher, positive or negative, for France's own aspirations. Writers like Sartre and Beauvoir could disdain American capitalism while adoring American music, American film, and the American rebels who sought freedom in France. Foucault, Genet, Agnès Varda rallied to the defense of the Panthers. If French intellectuals—from Gaullists in the International League against Racism and anti-Semitism to communists in the Youth League—marched for the liberation of Angela Davis, if Francophone writers were inspired by her story, it was because they felt on some level that her struggle against American empire was theirs. You might accuse them of romanticizing American radicals when in fact they were hitching them to their own wagon.

There was of course overlap in what the three women learned in France, if only because the French literary canon, the sense of what matters in arts and letters, has remained remarkably consistent throughout the twentieth century, and still today. Like all serious students of French before and after them, they read Marcel Proust. All three shared a love of this literary philosopher of memory and analyst of desire, jealousy, and social class. It says something about the versatility of his genius that he became meaningful to all three. Jacqueline Bouvier Kennedy read Proust on the campaign trail as a consolation for time lost and as a field guide to the underside of Camelot. Susan Sontag wrote about him in a diary from her senior year in college: "I have almost finished *Swann's Way* and there are moments during my reading, of exhilaration so painful that my head begins to ache, my hands tremble, and tears crowd in my eyes."[2] She was only eighteen at the time. She would return to Proust again and again, first through her friend Richard Howard, who was translating him; then through her lover Nicole Stéphane, who bought the film rights to *A la recherche du temps perdu*; and later still through her study of photography, one of Proust's abiding passions.[3] Angela Davis also came to Proust at the age of eighteen, in her freshman and sophomore years at Brandeis. He honed her sense of social reality and, later, strengthened her in her solitude. He even came to her defense in court.

Educated by modernists, receptive to avant-gardes, the three women were attuned to the New Wave and the New Novel that came of age in the 1950s and 1960s. Angela Davis read Robbe-Grillet in her advanced literature course at the Sorbonne. She returned to Brandeis and wrote about Robbe-Grillet's phenomenology just as Sontag began to celebrate the New Novel in her first critical essays in the *New York Review of Books*. Jacqueline Bouvier was in France too early to be exposed to either of these literary trends, but by 1961, Robbe-Grillet and Alain Resnais were well-enough known to have First Lady Jacqueline Kennedy screen their *Last Year at Marienbad* at the White House. In 1966, when Sontag was interviewed in France about the French translation of her novel *The Benefactor*, she had to insist that Robbe-Grillet hadn't influenced her. For any French journalist who wanted to evoke a cutting edge of fiction in 1965, his was the first name that leaped to mind.

Bouvier, Sontag, and Davis could admire the same writers or filmmakers, but for different reasons. For Jacqueline Bouvier, influenced by Malraux's aesthetic theories, artists and writers were in conversation with one another, across the generations, in a museum without walls. Susan Sontag's understanding of culture was much more combative. Translation was a struggle not to betray or be betrayed; art and politics were a matter of getting it or missing it. Angela Davis was a utopian. She wrote about liberation and revolution when she was still a student of literature—for her, art wasn't art without a humanitarian purpose, a revolutionary purpose.

Many of the best things that happened to them in France were independent of their teachers or their schools. Jeanne Saleil thought that Mademoiselle Bouvier wasn't serious and wondered if she would ever amount to anything; Angela Davis was the best student of the three, but by the time she enrolled in the Hamilton program she had already abandoned French for German, and literature for philosophy. Susan Sontag was the maverick, having dropped her Oxford fellowship to pursue a life in Paris; as Harriet Sohmers reminded me, "Susan was not doing anything academic in those years."[4] By the time they left Paris, each one of them had her own ideas of what counted.

This has been a story of three women and the city they discovered. Each was loyal to Paris in her own way, with many returns, many new discoveries. Paris itself changed as they came and went. Over the years, familiar streets acquired layered memories, or disappeared altogether. All three experienced the Sorbonne as a single place, a centuries-old building "exuding sacredness," as Angela Davis described it.[5] The reforms of May 1968 fragmented the great medieval university into a series of Paris campuses, though the original Sorbonne still stands, retaining some of its old aura as Paris IV, the Université Paris-Sorbonne, in the heart of the Latin Quarter. Les Halles, the central market that Zola called "the stomach of Paris," would have been familiar to all of them. When I visited Paris during my own junior year abroad in 1973–74, the market was under construction as a shopping mall, its full belly reduced to an enormous hole in the center of the city, with the tiny restaurants and cafés around it the only reminder of the bustling, smelly place it had been.

The meaning of study abroad, the temporary version of expatriation it offers students, has always been transmitted through these details of everyday life, political events and family traditions, neighborhoods and landscapes immutable or changing. Angela Davis connected the Algerian conflict with the civil rights struggles in the American south; Susan Sontag puzzled over Racine's *Britannicus*, as foreign to her as Kabuki theater; Jacqueline Bouvier gained an intimate understanding of the war in Europe through her friendship with a Ravensbrück survivor and her daughter. They learned by comparison, and by contrast with their lives at home.

In the United States, what is known of their French legacy? Jacqueline Kennedy remains the eternal First Lady, the unique American woman who set standards of beauty and grace for an era. So much so that the expert use she made, throughout her life, of her deep knowledge of French culture and history, especially in her work as an editor, has often been overlooked.[6] Susan Sontag is the ultimate New York intellectual, a handsome warrior of ideas. She is so identified with New York that her debt to France has been glossed over. Angela Davis is best known as an African American communist intellectual, for her visits to East Germany and Cuba, and for her connection with the Black Panthers. Her deep mark on French culture, on Francophone film and literature, has gone unnoticed.

Now, at a time when ambitions and landscapes are "global" and so much of the world's business is in English, I like to think about how joyfully all three of them took to a foreign language and an unfamiliar city, how much France gave them, and how much they've given back.

Conclusion

A Note on Sources

Three women, two languages, a city, and the institution of study abroad: behind this *pièce montée* are the nuts and bolts of many archives, books, and interviews, which in themselves made for a captivating journey.

When I began this project, I learned that Whitney Walton was writing a general history of study abroad in France, which has since been published as *Internationalism, National Identities and Study Abroad: France and the United States 1890–1970* (Stanford: Stanford University Press, 2010). Her book is full of information about the origins of study abroad and the various governmental institutions, such as the U.S. Fulbright Scholar Progam, that fostered educational exchanges to and from France. It's hard to tell much from the official reports that students have filed with these organizations, whereas Walton's portraits of individual French students in the United States and American students in France are much more revealing. There is also plenty to be gleaned from her analysis of generational differences among students, and different gendered experiences abroad. Within the growing critical literature on study abroad today, Anthony Ogden's "The View from the Veranda:

Understanding Today's Colonial Student," which appeared in *Frontiers: The Interdisciplinary Journal of Study Abroad* 15 (Fall–Winter 2007–8), is already a classic, challenging study-abroad administrators to get their students *involved* in the foreign culture rather than merely consuming it from on high.

Exploring these study-abroad experiences from the 1950s and '60s brought back many memories of my own junior year abroad in Bordeaux, in 1973–74, which I've recounted in *French Lessons: A Memoir* (Chicago: University of Chicago Press, 1993).

Jacqueline Bouvier Kennedy Onassis

For Jacqueline Bouvier, I faced a multitude of challenges in making my way through volumes of celebrity biographies. The scholarly apparatus for most of these books is minimal or unreliable. One biographer claimed that Jacqueline had written essays about the Enlightenment and the French Resistance for her student newspaper. Having now read the entire corpus of *Miss Porter's Salmagundi* during the period of Jacqueline's enrollment in the school, I can confirm the existence of a few cartoons thought to be in her hand, a short story, and an editorial about senior year nostalgia.

As for de Gaulle's legendary remark that Jacqueline Kennedy "gave the world an example of how to behave," my search for a source for these words that appear in nearly every book about Jacqueline Kennedy but in no French books about de Gaulle finally led me to the Duke of Edinburgh. He is supposed to have heard the phrase from de Gaulle in the Oval Office after John Kennedy's funeral, conveyed it to Jacqueline Kennedy, who conveyed it to Nancy Tuckerman, who conveyed it to Carl Sferrazza Anthony, author of *First Ladies: The Saga of the Presidents' Wives and Their Power, 1961–1990* (New York: Quill/Morrow, 1991). The Duke of Edinburgh, responding to my query through his archivist, replied that "His Royal Highness has no recollection of conversing with General de Gaulle after President Kennedy's funeral. He feels sure that, if he had, he would have remembered the occasion" (Annie Griffiths, archivist to H.R.H. the Duke of Edinburgh, to the author, May 17, 2011). Along the way, I turned to André Malraux, who wrote that de Gaulle, while admiring Jacqueline Kennedy's dignity and courage, had told him privately that he figured she'd end up on a yacht with an oil millionaire. When Malraux, according to his book *Les Chênes qu'on abat* (Paris: Gallimard, 1971), reminded de Gaulle in 1969 that his prediction had come to pass, the president replied, "Did I really say that? I actually thought she'd end up married to Sartre. Or to you!" Which sounds exactly like something de Gaulle might have said to remind his all-too-inventive minister of culture who was boss.

The best-documented biography of Jacqueline Kennedy is one of the most recent, Sarah Bradford's *America's Queen* (New York: Viking, 2000). Bradford has interviewed many of Jacqueline Kennedy's American friends, as well as her sister, and her sense of the Bouvier-Auchincloss-Kennedy family dynamics is complex. In general, the biographies repeat the same few facts about Paris and include nothing about the Smith program in France with its rigor and its riches. None describe the incomparable Jeanne Saleil, the study-abroad director to whom Jacqueline Kennedy remained loyal throughout her White House years. For that story and so many others, I am grateful to the students on the Smith 1949–50 program who have shared their memories and allowed me to reconstruct the intellectual and personal aspects of their journey. In Paris, Claude du Granrut (Claude de Renty in 1949–50), Jacqueline Bouvier's host sister, was an especially precious source of documents as well as memories and analysis. Claude taught me to read the *Bottin mondain*, the French society register, and encouraged me as I pursued countless contacts and suggestions. On the French aristocracy and upper classes, any of the books by the sociologists Michel Pinçon and Monique Pinçon-Charlot are enlightening.

My work on Jacqueline Bouvier Kennedy Onassis was limited by the fact that unlike Sontag and Davis she produced no extensive written oeuvre. From what sources are available, and especially from a few prefaces she wrote as an editor, her talent is clear. The John F. Kennedy Presidential Library and Museum in Boston houses Bouvier's application to *Vogue* for the Prix de Paris, one of the best records we have of her tastes and talents in 1951, and it is open to researchers. Claude de Renty uncovered the bilingual poem I have quoted, Florence Malraux the letter to André Malraux; and the French National Archives houses Jacqueline Kennedy's thank-you letter to de Gaulle after the presidential couple's June 1961 visit to Paris. A number of her letters and statements have been published in Carl S. Anthony's very rewarding *As We Remember Her* (New York: HarperCollins, 2003). In that volume, Letitia Baldrige recalls that Jacqueline Kennedy sent "handwritten letters that go on for pages and pages" to General de Gaulle. We may hope that more of her correspondence will come to light.

A long-awaited source became available just as my own book was going to press. Several months after Kennedy's death, Jacqueline Kennedy sat for a series of interviews with Arthur Schlesinger, Jr., as part of an oral history project for the future Kennedy Library. The interviews were released by her family in 2011 on the fiftieth anniversary of Kennedy's presidency.

In response to my questions about the availability of Jacqueline Kennedy's as-yet-unprocessed papers in the JFK Presidential Library and Museum, Chief Archivist Karen Adler Abramson wrote on February 16, 2011, with this explanation:

> Processing of the Jacqueline Kennedy personal papers will begin in 2011, with an initial focus on materials related to Mrs. Kennedy's years as First Lady. These White House–related materials will be made available in the fall of 2011 to coincide with the publication of Mrs. Kennedy's 1964 oral history interview with Arthur Schlesinger, Jr. Additional materials will become available as they are processed over the course of several years; these include scrapbooks created by and for Mrs. Kennedy before, during, and after her tenure as First Lady. Selected scrapbooks will be professionally conserved and digitized with grant funding from the National Trust for Historic Preservation.

Susan Sontag

For Susan Sontag, the challenges were of a different order. Discreet about her personal life, she sold her personal papers to the UCLA library, where they are now open to researchers. These archives include diaries and correspondence of the most intimate kind. All that's missing, from the point of view of my own research, are the letters she received from her husband and those she wrote home while she was in France.

One has the sense at UCLA of delving deep into her inner life—but as always with archives, a constructed inner life. I'm grateful to David Rieff for authorization to study Sontag's University of Chicago transcript, and to John W. Boyer at the University of Chicago for helping me understand the difference between courses, qualifying exams, and honors papers, such as the important paper on *Nightwood* that she completed during her junior year.

Given the extraordinary opportunities afforded by Sontag's papers and diaries, the challenge was to keep sight of what was happening around her, for example the Algerian War and the fall of the Fourth Republic, about which she remains silent in her notebooks. For her larger context, I turned to Allen Ginsberg's correspondence with his father; to the *Paris Herald Tribune* from December 1957 to September 1958; and, among her 1957–58 cohort, to Harriet Sohmers Zwerling, Annette Michelson, and Sydney Leach. (It was a smaller cohort than the large groups from Smith and Hamilton I was able to interview.) I've learned a great deal from my exchanges with film-maker Nancy Kates, who shared with me the French photographs and video interviews she unearthed while making her documentary *Regarding Susan Sontag*. Daniel Horowitz, whose study of consumer culture is forthcoming, has also been a valued interlocutor.

Angela Davis

For Angela Davis, the challenge has been to interpret the partisan accounts—for and against. I've relied on rich information in her own memoirs, *Angela Davis: An Autobiography* (New York: Random House, 1974), published three years after her acquittal; and on Bettina Aptheker's *The Morning Breaks: The Trial of Angela Davis* (Ithaca: Cornell University Press, 1999), a tour de force of legal analysis and thick description by an insider on the defense team at the trial who had also been one of Angela Davis's friends since their teenage years. Bettina Aptheker guided me through the Angela Davis trial material in her own papers at the University of California, Santa Cruz, and introduced me to the vast collection of correspondence Davis received in prison, which is housed at Stanford and is as yet uncatalogued. I'm grateful to her for her patience with a hundred questions. For an understanding of the unique combination of local and international influences on Davis, I recommend Cynthia A. Young's *Soul Power: Culture, Radicalism and the Making of a U.S. Third World Left* (Durham: Duke University Press, 2006), as well as Lisa Lowe's interview with Angela Davis, "Angela Davis: Reflections on Race, Class and Gender in the U.S.A.," in *The Politics of Culture in the Shadow of Capital*, edited by Lisa Lowe and David Lloyd (Durham: Duke University Press, 2006). For the French view of Davis's trial, I turned to coverage in *L'Humanité* and in the weekly news magazines *L'Express* and *Le Nouvel Observateur*. French police records at the Préfecture de Police archives in Paris gave me another kind of insight into French attitudes. Two documentary films, Yolande du Luart's *Angela Davis: Portrait of a Revolutionary*, made at

UCLA, and Jean-Daniel Simon's *L'enchaînement,* made after the publication of Davis's autobiography, provide affectionate and admiring portraits of the young philosopher; both filmmakers gave additional insight in conversations with me. I am grateful for the intellectual hospitality of Jean-Daniel Simon, who found me a rare copy of *L'enchaînement.*

Cheryl Morgan, professor of French at Hamilton College, was a precious source for the history of the Hamilton Study Abroad program. My contact with many of the students who were with Angela Davis in 1963–64 gave me a detailed sense of their studies and their social life. Jane Chaplin Jordan and Christie Stagg Austin shared letters home, photographs, and memories of life on the rue Duret. Angela Davis's sister Fania Davis was a rich source of family history and political memories. I was not able to interview Angela Davis, despite several attempts. Finally, for thinking about the French versus the American Communist Party from the late 1930s to the early 1970s, I relied on Robin D. G. Kelley's account of the Southern Negro Youth Congress and the Alabama Communist Party, *Hammer and Hoe: Alabama Communists During the Great Depression* (Chapel Hill: University of North Carolina Press, 1990), and on interviews with Jules Borker, legal counsel to the French Communist Party and an observer at Angela Davis's trial.

On the status of the French Antilles, and the meaning of Martinique in French intellectual life, I recommend Pierre Bouvier's *Aimé Césaire, Frantz Fanon: Portraits de décolonisés* (Paris: Belles Lettres, 2010), as well as Pap Ndiaye's *La condition noire* (Paris: Calmann-Lévy, 2008).

For a critical vision and analysis of the culture of the *trente glorieuses,* Kristin Ross's *Fast Cars, Clean Bodies: Decolonization and the Reordering of French Culture* (Cambridge, MA: MIT Press, 1995) is essential. Also essential on African-Americans in Paris is Tyler Stovall's richly synthetic *Paris Noir: African-Americans in the City of Light* (New York: Houghton Mifflin, 1996). For the social history of Americans in Paris from the mid-nineteenth century to World War II, my ongoing dialogue with Nancy Green concerning her forthcoming book, as yet untitled, was key. I also benefited greatly from Rosemary Wakeman's urban history, *The Heroic City: Paris 1945–1958* (Chicago: University of Chicago Press, 2009), and from two memoirs: André Schiffrin's *A Political Education: Coming of Age in Paris and New York* (Hoboken, NJ: Melville House, 2007) on literary Paris in the 1950s, and Paul Zweig's *Departures* (New York: HarperCollins, 1986, reprinted in 2011), by an American poet in left-wing Paris in the early 1960s. François

Cusset's *French Theory: How Foucault, Derrida, Deleuze & Co. Transformed the Intellectual Life of the United States* (Minneapolis: University of Minnesota Press, 2003) provides a brilliant history of structuralism and poststructuralism in the United States.

Finally, no other source is quite like the radio and television interviews conducted in French with Jacqueline Kennedy, Susan Sontag, and Angela Davis, housed at the Institut national audiovisuel at the Bibliothèque nationale de France.

Notes

Introduction

1. Associated Press Photo, "Smith Students are guests at a reception given by the French Government at the French Embassy, New York, August 23," Junior Year Abroad program files: France 1927–present, Class of 1951, Box 1132, Smith College Archives. Virginia Lyon Paige recalled Jackie Bouvier singing her own verse of "La vie en rose," on the *De Grasse* (interview with the author, March 26, 2009). On Jacqueline Bouvier as debutante see Cholly Knickerbocker, "Queen Deb of the Year is Jacqueline Bouvier," *New York Journal American*, September 2, 1947.

2. The institution of study abroad provides a structure for two out of the three women, and here Whitney Walton's *Internationalism, National Identities, and Study Abroad* (Palo Alto: Stanford University Press, 2009) provided valuable historical background from the 1920s to the 1970s.

3. Michel's dying words to Patricia (played by Jean Seberg), in the last scene of the 1960 film, are "*Tu es vraiment dégueulasse*"—which means, more or less, "you're disgusting." "*Qu-est-ce que c'est dégueulasse?*" she answers, running her finger over her lips to feel the foreign phrase: "What's *dégueulasse?*"

4. James Baldwin, "A Question of Identity," from *Notes of a Native Son*, in *Collected Essays* (New York: Library of America, 1998), 91–101. See also James Salter, *A Sport and a Pastime* (San Francisco: North Point Press, 1967).

5. Note from Jacqueline Onassis to George Plimpton, quoted in "The Paris Review Sketchbook," 25th anniversary issue, *The Paris Review* 79 (Spring 1981): 415–16.

6. Mary McCarthy, "Mlle Gulliver en Amérique," *The Reporter*, January 1952, reprinted in McCarthy, *On the Contrary: Articles of Belief, 1946–1961* (New York: Noonday Press, 1962), 24–31.

7. Simone de Beauvoir, *America Day by Day* (1954), trans. Carol Cosman (Berkeley: University of California Press, 1999), xvii–xviii.

Chapter One

1. The best source on the Bouvier-Vernou family history is John H. Davis, *The Bouviers: Portrait of an American Family* (New York: Farrar, Straus & Giroux, 1960).

2. Sarah Bradford, *America's Queen: A Life of Jacqueline Kennedy Onassis* (New York: Viking, 2000), 11. Gore Vidal sparked a controversy in his memoir *Palimpsest: A Memoir* (New York: Random House, 1995) by quoting an offhand remark of his mother's about Jacqueline Bouvier's mother Janet: "Janet, born Lee or, as my mother used to observe thoughtfully, Levy. Apparently Janet's father had changed his name in order to become the first Jew to be a vice president of the Morgan bank" (404). He seems to be making fun of his mother's anti-Semitism, but the "apparently" led many readers to take him at his (mother's) word. Carl S. Anthony's *As We Remember Her* (New York: HarperCollins, 2003), 12–13, explains that Janet Lee's grandfather was in fact an Irish Catholic immigrant who fled the potato famine in the 1840s. He became superintendent of the New York public schools and later put himself through medical school. His son—Janet's father—made his fortune in banking and real estate.

3. Donald Spoto, *Jacqueline Kennedy Onassis: A Life* (New York: St. Martin's Press, 2000), 8.

4. John Vernou Bouvier, Jr., *Our Forebears: From the Earliest Times to the End of the Year 1925* (New York: Privately published, 1925), 6, 33. (Facsimile, Orange Park, FL: Quintin Publications).

5. Davis, *The Bouviers*. On Joseph Bonaparte's Philadelphia exile and his Point Breeze estate, see page 21.

6. For information on Jacqueline Bouvier's travels in the summer of 1950, I have relied on interviews with Claude du Granrut (née de Renty) and Paul de Ganay, electronic correspondence with Roland du Luart, and a telephone interview with Rosamée Henrion.

7. Davis, *The Bouviers*, 338. For a history of the poisoned bread, the town, and mid-century France, see Steven L. Kaplan, *Le pain maudit: Retour sur la France des années oubliées 1945–1958* (Paris: Fayard, 2009).

8. On Pont-Saint-Espit, see Davis, *The Bouviers*, 6.

9. Davis, *The Bouviers*, 335. The incident is recounted in *Le Figaro, France-Soir*, and *Paris-Presse* for May 29, 30, and 31, 1961; the American press told the story in "Jacqueline Kennedy's French Cousins," *Look*, August 29, 1961.

10. Bradford, *America's Queen*, 5; Anthony, *As We Remember Her*, 18.

11. Jacqueline Kennedy to Peter Duchin, as quoted in Anthony, *As We Remember Her*, 27: "You know, Peter, we both live and do very well in this world of Wasps and old money

and society. It's all supposed to be so safe and continuous. But you and I are not really of it. Maybe because I'm Catholic and because my parents were divorced when I was young—a terribly radical thing at the time—I've always felt like an outsider in that world."

12. Davis, *The Bouviers*, 288.

13. Stéphane Groueff, untitled portrait of John F. Kennedy, *Paris-Match*, June 3, 1961, 77. JFK spent the summer of 1937 in France; in the spring of 1939 he lived in the American Embassy in Paris.

14. Spoto, *Jacqueline Kennedy Onassis*, 58–59. "And what she learned, she incorporated into short articles published in *Salmagundi*, the school newspaper: essays on American political philosophy's roots in the French Enlightenment and observations on the war, the scourge of Nazism, the survival of democracy and the heroism of resistance fighters." My thanks to Ann Befroy, archivist at Miss Porter's School in Farmington, Connecticut, for allowing me to consult Miss Porter's *Salmagundi* during Jacqueline Bouvier's years at the school.

15. Spoto, *Jacqueline Kennedy Onassis*, 62.

16. Nancy Tuckerman et al., auction catalogue, *The Estate of Jacqueline Kennedy Onassis* (New York: Sotheby's, 1996), 531.

17. Anthony, *As We Remember Her*, 38.

18. Beauvoir, *America Day by Day*, 48.

19. Anthony, *As We Remember Her*, 39. The Jacqueline Kennedy Onassis papers at the John F. Kennedy Presidential Library and Museum have not been processed; her letters to her stepbrother Yusha Auchincloss are also closed.

20. Marjorie Flory, interview with the author, April 8, 2009.

21. Martha Rusk Sutphen, interview with the author, February 4, 2010.

22. The Sacré-Cœur, a late-nineteenth-century addition to the hill of Montmartre, was made of a kind of travertine stone whose calcite surface kept it white.

23. Jacqueline Bouvier's *carte d'alimentation*, courtesy Claude du Granrut. Shortages remained intense, and rationing would continue through the 1949 season.

24. The history of toilets in France is as revealing about life in the apartments and pavilions of that nation as any sociological study. See Roger-Henri Guerrand, *Les lieux: Histoire des commodités* (Paris: La Découverte, 1997).

25. Mary Ann Freedman Hoberman, e-mail communication to the author, February 17, 2009.

26. Gertje Utley, *Picasso: The Communist Years* (New Haven: Yale University Press, 1999), 140 ff.

27. The diary was first published in the Netherlands in 1947. Two years after the French and German translations, the first American edition appeared, *Anne Frank: The Diary of a Young Girl* (New York: Doubleday, 1952).

28. Barbara Vagliano, née Allen, summered in Newport. Her daughter, Sonia Eloy, played an important role in de Gaulle's Free French and in postwar refugee work. Sonia was married to Philippe Eloy, the son of the comtesse de Renty's best friend (letter to the author from Claude du Granrut, November 4, 2010).

29. Stanley Geist, "Mémoires d'un touriste: Paris 1947," trans. René Guyonnet, *Les temps modernes* (1948): 536–47.

30. Jean Luchaire was tried for treason and executed in February 1946; by then Schlesinger had returned to the U.S.

31. Johanna Barasz, Institut d'études politiques, interview with the author, July 3, 2009. A book based on her doctoral thesis, "De Vichy à la Résistance: Les Vichysto-résistants," is forthcoming from Editions Payot.

32. Claude du Granrut, "Aux petits-enfants de Robert de Renty, matricule 77096," unpublished memoir of her father, October 1999. Courtesty Claude du Granrut. Further details on the deportation of the de Rentys and on life on the avenue Mozart come from a series of interviews with Claude du Granrut, 2007–10.

33. See Germaine Tillion, *Ravensbrück*, trans. Gerald Satterwhite (New York: Anchor Books, 1975). Tillion was an exceptional public figure, who later served as a mediator in the Algerian war. See Claire Andrieu, "Women in the French Resistance: Revisiting the Historical Record," *French Politics, Culture, and Society* 18, no.1 (2000): 13–27. She points out that neither the underground National Council of the Resistance nor de Gaulle's cabinet ever included a woman.

34. Until 1949, Munich and Dachau had been in the American zone; France occupied a southwestern portion of Germany, with its headquarters in Baden-Baden. The Allied High Commission remained in operation until 1955. When the Allies agreed to dissolve the High Commission, France added an addendum to the agreement, stipulating that Dachau and all other sites where remains of Nazi victims were discovered be conserved as memorial sanctuaries. For the history of the Dachau camp and its memorial, see Harold Marcuse, *Legacies of Dachau: The Uses and Abuses of a Concentration Camp, 1933–2001* (Cambridge: Cambridge University Press, 2001), 147.

35. See Marcuse, *Legacies of Dachau,* 142–51, on "the Leiten Affair." For the debate in the French parliament, see the *Débats parlementaires, Assemblé nationale*, December 13, 1949. On Munich after the war, see Anne Duménil, "L'expérience intime des ruines: Munich, 1945–1948," in Bruno Cabanes and Guillaume Piketty, *Retour à l'intime au sortir de la guerre* (Paris: Tallandier, 2009), 101–16.

36. André Siegfried, *L'âme des peuples* (Paris: Hachette, 1950), 162.

37. Beauvoir, *America Day by Day*, 310.

38. Courtesy Brenda Gilchrist, and with thanks to Cordelia Ruffin Richards for her correspondence. Blaikie Forsyth Worth was a Bryn Mawr student on the Smith Program.

39. Henriette Nizan, "Quand la jeunesse américaine vient respirer l'air de Paris," in *Rapports France-Etats-Unis* (Paris: Service d'information de la mission spéciale en France de l'ECA), September 1950, 42: 45–50. Among other useful information, Nizan gives precise figures for fellowships. The Fulbright scholars had 50,000 francs for the year, the GI bill students $75 a month, $105 if they were married, $120 if they had a child.

40. Madeleine Guilloton, Report on the Junior Group in Paris, April 16, 1948, President Herbert John Davis Files, Box 459, JYA-France, Smith College Archives.

41. From the diary of a happy student lodging on the avenue Mozart in 1951, in "Coming of Age in Paris: Smith Junior Year Abroad 1950–1951: Letters, Diaries and Recollections," ed. May Allison Kirschner, Reid Hall archives, Paris.

42. Jacqueline Bouvier, "The Paris Review Sketchbook," 25th Anniversary Issue,

The Paris Review 79 (Spring 1981): 415–16, quoting a letter from Jacqueline Onassis to George Plimpton.

43. Mary Ann Peyser Horenstein, interview with the author, December 19, 2007.

44. See Henriette Nizan and Marie-José Jaubert, *Libres mémoires* (Paris: Laffont, 1989), 396, on the 1949 scandal at the Tabou: women posing nude for the annual Miss Tabou contest.

45. Mlle Saleil to President Wright, December 9, 1949, Benjamin Wright Files, Box 476, JYA-France, Smith College Archives.

46. Horenstein, interview.

47. In the France of 2010, Claude du Granrut has worlds in common with the adult versions of the people in this photograph; she attends their weddings and their funerals; knows their children and grandchildren. But in 1949, she was not one of them, and how she got the photograph in the first place is a mystery to her. A second slightly different photograph appeared in *France-Soir* in 1960, on the eve of Jacqueline Kennedy's official visit to Paris.

48. "Paparazzi" comes from the name of the Italian news photographer portrayed in Fellini's *La dolce vita* (1960).

49. Mauriac's editorial in *Le Figaro*, November 19, 1949, and Roger Grenier, response, typescript courtesy Roger Grenier.

50. Gore Vidal tells the elevator story in his memoirs without mentioning Marquand by name (*Palimpsest*, 309); Edward Klein adds the name (*All Too Human: The Love Story of Jack and Jackie Kennedy* [Simon and Schuster, 1996], 19); Sarah Bradford (*America's Queen*, 58) describes a romantic relationship with Paul de Ganay; David Heymann (*A Woman Named Jackie* [New York: Lyle Stuart, 1989], 81) with Ormonde de Kay, Donald Spoto (*Jacqueline Kennedy Onassis*, 75) with the son of a French diplomat; and Bertrand Meyer-Stabley (*La véritable Jackie* [Paris: Editions Pygmalion, 1999], 52–53), with an aide to Georges Bidault.

51. Paul de Ganay was beginning his university studies with "la classe propédeutique," a preparatory year after the baccalaureate exam and before the first year of an undergraduate curriculum that led to the "licence"—the rough equivalent of a bachelor's degree.

52. For an ethnography of the French upper classes, see Eric Mension-Rigau, *Aristocrates et grands bourgeois: Education, traditions, valeurs* (Paris: Perrin, 1994); on athletic life as an extension of social life: "la beauté est confondue avec la vigueur" (beauty and physical prowess are of a piece), 443.

53. On Courances, recounting the history of the château through essays and illustrations, see *Courances*, ed. Valentine de Ganay and Laurent Le Bon (Paris: Flammarion, 2003).

54. Anthony, *As We Remember Her*, 40.

55. Jacqueline Bouvier Kennedy Onassis, Prix de Paris application materials, Papers 1951, John F. Kennedy Presidential Library and Museum, Boston, MA.

56. Jeanne Saleil, *A House in the Cevennes* (New York: Macmillan, 1949).

57. For information on Jeanne Saleil, I have drawn primarily from interviews with 1949–50 Smith-in-Paris juniors Martha Rusk Sutphen and Mary Ann Peyser Horenstein;

from a letter from Cordelia Ruffin Richards; and from Jeanne Saleil's faculty file in the Smith College Archives (Faculty Biography, Box 995, Jeanne Saleil, Prof. of French 1930–1963).

58. Jeanne Saleil to President Wright, December 9, 1949.

59. Martha Rusk Sutphen, interview with the author, February 4, 2010.

60. Jeanne Saleil to President Wright, December 9, 1949.

61. For negative responses by Mauriac and Camus, see Toril Moi, *Simone de Beauvoir: The Making of an Intellectual Woman* (Oxford: Oxford University Press, 2008), 180. Judith G. Coffin, in "Sex, Love and Letters: Writing Simone de Beauvoir 1949–1964," based on letters Beauvoir received in response to *The Second Sex*, reveals a positive and more private reception (*American Historical Review* 115, no. 6 [October 2010]: 1061–88).

62. Horenstein, interview.

63. Kirschner, ed., "Coming of Age in Paris."

64. *Fontaine* was published in Algiers from 1937 to 1944 and then moved to Paris, where it continued to appear until 1947.

65. On Max Pol-Fouchet, I have drawn on interviews with Virginia Lyon Paige and Martha Rusk Sutphen, as well as the portrait in "Coming of Age in Paris."

66. Rusk Sutphen, interview.

67. Jacqueline's course work is listed by subject matter, as follows: Literature—18th Century; Literature—19th Century; Literature—20th Century; History—International Relations since 1870; Philosophy and Art; Philosophy—Aesthetics (Course titles, without grades, communicated courtesy the Smith College Archives).

68. With thanks to Jacqueline Cerquiglini-Toulet for her vivid evocation of the old-style *cours magistral* at the Sorbonne.

69. Mary Ann Freedman Hoberman, e-mail communication to the author, July 23, 2010.

70. Du Granrut, interview. See Bouvier's letter to her stepbrother Yusha Auchincloss and her bilingual poetry, quoted above.

71. Paul Nizan, a classmate of Sartre's at the Lycee Henri IV and his roommate at the Ecole normale, a former communist, and cult novelist of Parisian student life, is best known for *La conspiration* (1938).

72. See Henriette Nizan, *Libres mémoires* (Paris: Robert Laffont, 1989).

73. Henriette Nizan, "Quand la jeunesse," 45–50.

74. In the summer of 1947, Claude attended the Wellesley Institute for Foreign Students, then spent the 1947–48 academic year at Mount Holyoke, teaching French.

Chapter Two

1. Jacqueline's courses that semester included special readings for the major in French, a sociology course called, in the spirit of the times, "Man in Modern Society," and a course on the development of European civilization.

2. Information on Jacqueline Bouvier's senior year course work is from the George Washington University Bulletin 49, no. 5 (1950), The George Washington Bulletin Records, Special Collections Research Center, Gelman Library, Washington,

DC, available online: http://encyclopedia.gwu.edu/gwencyclopedia/index. php?title=Kennedy%2C_Jacqueline_Lee_Bouvier (consulted November 5, 2010).

3. See Jacqueline's correspondence with *Vogue* magazine, below.

4. Virginia Lyon Paige, interview with the author, April 1, 2009.

5. Jacqueline Bouvier Kennedy Onassis, Prix de Paris application materials, Papers 1951, John F. Kennedy Presidential Library and Museum, Boston, MA.

6. Carol Feisenthal, *Citizen Newhouse: Portrait of a Media Merchant* (New York: Seven Stories Press, 1998); Gigi Mahon, "S.I. Newhouse and Condé Nast: Taking off the White Gloves," *New York Times Magazine,* September 10, 1989, www.nytimes.com/si-newhouse-and-conde-nast-taking-off-the-white-gloves.html (accessed November 6, 2010).

7. André Malraux, *Le musée imaginaire,* vol. 1 of *Psychologie de l'art* (Geneva: Skira, 1947), translated by Stuart Gilbert as "Museum without Walls," in *The Voices of Silence* (Princeton: Princeton University Press, 1978), 13–16.

8. CIA, written communication to the author, March 6, 2009; Paige, interview; Rusk Sutphen interview. Martha Rusk worked for the CIA from 1951 to 1953; Virginia Lyon Paige from 1951 to 1964.

9. Bradford, *America's Queen,* 68, opts for the theory that Jacqueline wanted a working atmosphere with eligible males; Klein, *All Too Human,* 72–73, attributes the decision entirely to Janet Auchincloss.

10. In 1974 the two sisters published their scrapbook: *One Special Summer,* written and illustrated by Jacqueline and Lee Bouvier (New York: Rizzoli, 1974).

11. Ibid., 20.

12. Arthur M. Schlesinger, Jr., *Journals, 1952–2000* (New York: Houghton Mifflin, 2000), 56.

13. John Kenneth Galbraith, *Name-Dropping: From F.D.R. On* (New York: Houghton Mifflin, 1999), 127 ff.

14. Duc de Saint-Simon, *The Age of Magnificence: The Memoirs of the Duc de Saint-Simon,* edited and translated by Sanche de Gramont (New York: Putnam, 1963), 155.

15. As portrayed by Bradford, *America's Queen,* 177–79.

16. Norman Mailer, "An Evening with Jackie Kennedy," *Esquire,* July 1962, 57–61, rpt. in *The Presidential Papers* (New York: Putnam, 1963), 84.

17. Arthur Schlesinger Jr., "Jacqueline Bouvier Kennedy in the White House," in Hamish Bowles, ed., *Jacqueline Kennedy: The White House Years* (Boston: Little, Brown; New York: The Metropolitan Museum of Art, 2001), 3–12.

18. Quoted by John Fairchild himself in his memoir *The Fashionable Savages* (New York: Doubleday, 1965), in a chapter on Jacqueline Kennedy entitled "Her Elegance," 118.

19. Ibid., 120.

20. Oleg Cassini, *A Thousand Days of Magic* (New York: Rizzoli, 1996), 18: "I had created a concept for her. I talked to her like a movie star and told her that she needed a story, a scenario as First Lady."

21. Jacqueline Kennedy to Oleg Cassini, December 13, 1960, in Cassini, *A Thousand Days of Magic,* 29–30.

22. Ibid.

23. Ibid.

24. For the early history of the cockade, see Richard Wrigley, "Cockades: Badge Culture and its Discontents," in *The Politics of Appearances: Representations of Dress in Revolutionary France* (Oxford: Berg, 2002), 97–134; and for an evolution of the cockade and its various colors and political meanings, see Caroline Weber, *Queen of Fashion: What Marie Antoinette Wore to the Revolution* (New York: Holt, 2006).

25. Jacqueline Kennedy to Charles de Gaulle, June 3, 1961, Voyage officiel en France de personnalités étrangères, 5AG1 579 1AGV, Archives nationales.

26. "Parisians Await Mrs. Kennedy: They Talk the Same Language. Television Interview Ends Doubts on Her Fluency—Curiosity Rises," *New York Times*, May 31, 1961.

27. Pierre Crenesse, interview with Jacqueline Kennedy in French, at the White House, for French television, May 29, 1961 (reported by the *New York Times* on May 31, see note above), broadcast June 30, 1961, ORTF, journal de 20h, première chaine, RTR002, French audiovisual archive (Inathèque), Bibliothèque de France. "Il ne relaxe [*sic*] pas dans une chaise à bascule—il ne se détend jamais," she told Crenesse. When he asked her if she talked about politics with her husband, she answered charmingly that she didn't like him to bring his work home: "Si je peux lui le faire oublier [*sic*] . . . Ce n'est pas un type qui aime se détendre."

28. From Stéphane Groueff's profile of the presidential couple in *Paris Match*, June 3, 1961, 77.

29. Madame Kennedy to General de Gaulle's attaché, April 10, 1961; Madame Kennedy, telegram with list of friends, May 10, 1961, Voyage officiel en France de person-nalités étrangères, 5AGI 579 / 1AGV, Archives nationales.

30. Smith College News Bulletin, Jeanne Saleil folder, Box 995, Smith College Archives: "Smith College will be represented at a dinner to be held at the White House May 11 by President and Mrs. John F. Kennedy. Mlle Jeanne Saleil, professor of French, has been asked to meet André Malraux, the famous novelist who is France's Minister of State in charge of cultural affairs, and his wife. Mlle Saleil has directed the Smith Junior Year in France so many times that she has lost count, and was its director when Mrs. Kennedy was spending her own junior year from Vassar with the Smith group in Paris."

31. Rusk Sutphen, interview.

32. Seating chart, AG/5(1)579, Archives nationales.

33. The scene was depicted in one of Jacqueline Duhême's charming watercolors in *Elle*, and reproduced in the children's book *Jacqueline Kennedy et Jacqueline Duhême partent en voyage*, preface by John Kenneth Galbraith (Paris: Gallimard Jeunesse, 1998), 27.

34. Olivier Todd, *Malraux: Une Vie* (Paris: Gallimard, 2001), 450. On her vast library: "Sale Set for Treasures Left by Jackie Onassis," *New York Times*, December 15, 1995. On her career as an editor, see Greg Lawrence, *Jackie as Editor: The Literary Life of Jacqueline Kennedy Onassis* (New York: St. Martin's Press, 2011), and William Kuhn, *Reading Jackie: Her Autobiography in Books* (New York: Doubleday, 2010).

35. See Herman Lebovics, *Mona Lisa's Escort: André Malraux and the Reinvention of*

French Culture (Ithaca: Cornell University Press, 1999), and Charles-Louis Foulon, *André Malraux: Ministre de l'irrationnel* (Paris: Gallimard, 2005). See also Marguerite Leslie Davis, *Mona Lisa in Camelot* (New York: da Capo Press, 2008), a narrative of Jacqueline Kennedy's adventure in bringing Leonardo da Vinci's *Mona Lisa* to Washington, DC.

36. More than 1,750,000 Americans visited the *Mona Lisa* between January and March 1963, in exhibits in Washington and New York. Kennedy, in his thank-you speech to Malraux for loaning the masterpiece, referred to France as "the first artistic power in the world." See Charles-Louis Foulon, *André Malraux et le rayonnement culturel de la France* (Brussels: Editions Complexe, 2004).

37. Many of Jacqueline Kennedy's biographers have implied that she fled the White House as often as possible because of her husband's philandering. There has been little speculation that she may have traveled abroad for her own, positive, reasons—independence, a need for solitude or for the company of friends, intellectual and artistic curiosity.

38. "Nation: Vacation Time," in *Time,* August 3, 1962. Jacqueline Kennedy and her daughter joined her sister Lee that August at the Villa Sangro above the Bay of Salano.

39. "Je suis un peu détachée de la vie actuelle ici—Les cosmonauts russes étaient dans l'air trois jour avant que j'ai découvert qu'ils étaient là—un état qui n'est pas sans charme—mais qui non plus est très propice pour arranger une chose aussi important que votre offre de Whistler's Mother à la musee d'Atlanta." Jacqueline Kennedy to André Malraux, August 26, 1963, on the letterhead of the bishopry of Ravello in the Province of Salerno, courtesy Florence Malraux (transcribed here with original spelling and syntax). Letitia Baldrige Hollensteiner, Jacqueline Kennedy's White House social secretary, marveled at the First Lady's habits of correspondence: "She would write letters to heads of state, friendly social, chatty letters when things were going wrong and, of course, we would go wild in the East Wing because we didn't have carbon copies and we didn't know what she was saying. She would write hand-written letters and go on for pages and pages to General de Gaulle and Prime Minister Nehru [Shri Jawaharlal Nehru] and all. . . . I am sure no other First Lady has ever done that, and I am sure no other president has dared let his wife do that, and I hope that history will some day unearth those famous letters." Letitia Baldrige Hollensteiner, interview for the John F. Kennedy Oral History Program, April 24, 1964, 70–71, John F. Kennedy Presidential Library and Museum, Boston, MA.

40. If Baldrige was right that there were no drafts or carbons of letters like this one, it is unlikely that many of them will surface on the American side. De Gaulle's personal papers after 1958 are still closed, and Jacqueline Kennedy's thank-you letter to him after the Paris trip is in a French national archive file of the Elysée Palace on visits of foreign heads of states. To find Jacqueline Kennedy's letters to de Gaulle will take hunting and waiting.

41. See Schlesinger's analysis of the conflicts among these advisers in "Jacqueline Kennedy in the White House" in Bowles, ed., *Jacqueline Kennedy*, 3–12.

42. In *The Bouviers,* 346, John Davis describes "a pier table that had belonged to Joseph Bonaparte at Breeze Point" and a gift from a Mr. and Mrs. Henry T. MacNeil of two maple chairs in Empire style made by Michel Bouvier in 1820, "purchased by them from a great grandson of Michel's, John Vernou Bouvier Patterson." The chairs were used in the presidential private living quarters.

43. Jackie Kennedy interviewed by Pierre Crenesse at the White House for French television, May 29, 1960, broadcast June 30, 1961, ORTF, journal de 20h, première chaine, RTR002, French Audiovisual Archives (Inathèque), Bibliothèque nationale de France.

44. Jacqueline and John F. Kennedy, "Cinq Colonnes chez les Kennedy," interview by Etienne Lalou and Igor Barrère, September 2, 1960. http://www.ina.fr/histoire-et-conflits/decolonisation/video/CAF89031102/exclusif-5-colonnes-chez-les-kennedy.fr.html (accessed May 11, 2011).

45. Baldrige Hollensteiner, interview.

46. Ibid.

47. Mailer, "An Evening with Jackie Kennedy," 97.

48. Ibid.

49. Schlesinger, "Jacqueline Bouvier Kennedy," 8.

50. I've tried to track down the origin of de Gaulle's much-quoted remark, "She gave an example to the whole world of how to behave," which appears without annotation in nearly all the American books on Jacqueline Kennedy, but in no French book about de Gaulle. I'm grateful to Carl Sferrazza Anthony, who confirmed that the sentence came from Jacqueline Onassis through Nancy Tuckerman in a letter of December 3, 1989. "Andromaque for a day" and the daisy story are from Jean Lacouture, *De Gaulle: Le Souverain*, vol. 3 (Paris: Editions du Seuil, 1986), 370. See my notes on sources, below, for more about tracking the runaway sentence, and for Malraux's imaginary dialogue with de Gaulle about Jacqueline Kennedy.

51. Jacqueline Kennedy, interviews with Arthur M. Schlesinger, Jr., *Jacqueline Kennedy: Historic Conversations on Life with John F. Kennedy* (New York: Hyperion, 2011), 199–200, 292–293.

52. Carolyn Heilbrun, *Writing a Woman's Life* (New York: Norton, 1989), 126.

53. Truman Capote, "La Côte Basque 1965," *Esquire,* November 1975, 113, referring to drag queens dressing up as Audrey Hepburn and Marilyn Monroe and Jackie Kennedy: "And in life, that is how she struck me—not as a bona fide woman, but as an artful female impersonator impersonating Mrs. Kennedy."

54. Gloria Steinem, *Outrageous Acts and Everyday Rebellions* (New York: Holt, 1983), 206.

55. Marly Rusoff, interview with the author, March 15, 2009, on working with Onassis at Doubleday.

56. Louis Auchincloss, in *Quest Magazine,* May 1997, quoted in Bradford, *America's Queen,* 549.

57. Louis Auchincloss, *Women in the Age of the Sun King* (New York: Doubleday, 1984), 142.

58. Jacqueline Onassis, "Introduction," in William Howard Adams, *Atget's Gardens* (New York: Doubleday, 1979), 7.

59. The diaries were edited and published a decade later by John Julian Norwich, Artemis Cooper's father, as *The Duff Cooper Diaries* (London: Weidenfeld and Nicolson, 2007).

60. Danuta Kean, "Antony Beevor, On the Joys of History," *The Independent,* May 21, 2006.

61. On November 27,1988, the *New York Times* reported that Jacqueline Onassis was one of the first twenty women proposed for membership of the Century Club, along with Beverly Sills and Brooke Astor.

62. Jean-Paul Sartre, *The Words: The Autobiography of Jean-Paul Sartre* (New York: Vintage, 1981), 203.

63. Jacqueline Onassis to Claude du Granrut, July 7, 1993, on the Concorde, courtesy Claude du Granrut.

64. *In Memoriam: Jacqueline Bouvier Kennedy Onassis,* Funeral Mass, Church of St. Ignatius Loyola, New York City (New York: Doubleday, 1995), 31.

65. Valéry Giscard d'Estaing, France Inter radio (May 20, 1994): "Et suivant l'usage le Général de Gaulle est entré avec à son bras Jackie Kennedy, et c'était l'un des plus beaux spectacles qu'on pouvait imaginer que de voir en même temps la jeunesse et la gloire." On Jacqueline Kennedy's criticisms of de Gaulle, see Kennedy, ed., *Jacqueline Kennedy: Historic Conversations.*

66. Bradford, *America's Queen,* 590, from an interview with Frederic Papert, president of the Municipal Art Society in 1994.

67. *Auction Catalogue,* 122. On the sale price, see "At Miss Porter's School, Miss Bouvier Is Just Not for Sale," *New York Times,* April 27, 1966.

Chapter Three

1. Susan Sontag, *Reborn: Journals and Notebooks, 1947–1963,* ed. David Rieff (New York: Farrar, Straus & Giroux, 2008), 136.

2. Djuna Barnes, *Nightwood,* preface by T. S. Eliot (New York: New Directions, 1936), 88.

3. Sontag, *Reborn,* 170–71.

4. Susan Sontag, "Vies plurielles: Les Années de Formation" interview with Chantal Thomas, "A voix nue: grands entretiens," part one, France Culture radio, January 1, 2001, Audio-Visual Archives, Bibliothèque nationale de France.

5. Valentina Polukhina, "He Landed among Us Like a Missile: An Interview with Susan Sontag," November 11, 2003, in *Brodsky through the Eyes of His Contemporaries,* vol. 2 (Lancaster, UK: Academic Studies Press, 2010), 324 ff.

6. Nancy Kates, interview with Harriet Sohmers for "Regarding Susan Sontag," documentary film in progress.

7. Sontag, *Reborn,* 48.

8. Ibid., 17.

9. Ibid.

10. See Molly McQuade, "A Gluttonous Reader: Susan Sontag," in McQuade, *An Unsentimental Education: Writers and Chicago* (Chicago: University of Chicago Press, 1995), 161–68.

11. Sontag, *Reborn,* 52.

12. Georges Perec, *An Attempt at Exhausting a Place in Paris,* trans. Marc Lowenthal (New York: Wakefield Press, 2010).

13. Sontag, *Reborn,* 43–44.

14. Sontag, *Reborn,* 56. The engagement and marriage both took place in December 1950, in the middle of her second year in Chicago.

15. Sontag, *Reborn,* 193.

16. Sontag, "The Letter Scene," *New Yorker,* August 18, 1986, 24–32.

17. Leslie Garis, "Susan Sontag Finds Romance," *New York Times,* August 2, 1992, 20–23, 31, 43.

18. Sontag, *Reborn,* 62.

19. Susan Sontag to "Merrill," embedded in journal entry March 23, 1950, Box 123, Folder 8, Susan Sontag Papers, Charles E. Young Library, UCLA. Daniel Horowitz, in a review of the diaries in the *Chronicle of Higher Education* ("I am alive . . . I am beautiful . . . what else is there?" December 19, 2008), first drew attention to this passage, and criticizes David Rieff for not including it in the *Journals,* for it might have allowed readers to understand the otherwise mysterious marriage as a consequence of financial pressure. But as the draft of a letter sent to her friend "Merrill," rather than a diary entry per se, it has an ambiguous status.

20. Susan Sontag, Journal, 1949–1950, Box 123, Folder 8, Susan Sontag Papers, Charles E. Young Library, UCLA.

21. New York Passenger Lists, 1820–1957, www.ancestry.com. Susan and Philip Rieff returned from Le Havre and Southampton on August 24, 1951 (accessed November 3, 2010).

22. Djuna Barnes, *Nightwood,* with marginal annotations by Susan Sontag and Philip Rieff, Susan Sontag Papers, Box 217, Folder 2, Charles E. Young Library, UCLA.

23. Susan Sontag, "The Dialectic of Decay," May 15, 1950, 1–2, paper on Djuna Barnes's *Nightwood,* Susan Sontag Papers, Box 147, Folder 5, Charles E. Young Library, UCLA. The paper is labeled "B.A. thesis." In fact it was an honors paper written in the spring of her first, junior year at Chicago, in lieu of the final exam for Burke's Humanities 3B, one of the general education requirements in the undergraduate college.

24. With thanks to Michael Denning for the epithet.

25. Carl Rollyson and Lisa Paddock, *Susan Sontag: The Making of an Icon* (New York: Norton, 2000), 32: McQuade, *An Unsentimental Education.*

26. Susan Sontag, analyses of Joseph Conrad's works, Susan Sontag Papers, Box 147, Folder 4, Charles E. Young Library, UCLA.

27. Sontag, "The Dialectic of Decay," 20.

28. For those who love it, *Nightwood* has retained its standing as a masterpiece of avant-garde queer fiction, yet Barnes's language is often pretentious and disorganized, and it is easy to quote her sentences out of context and miss their heady charm, for example: "You wash your brawl with every thought, with every gesture, with every conceivable emollient and *savon,* and expect to find your way again." While individual sentences seem garbled when taken out of context, the novel still does its work, putting the reader in a semi-hallucinatory state.

29. Sontag, *Reborn,* 69–70.

30. Wallace Fowlie, *The Clown's Grail: A Study in Love in Its Literary Expression* (London: Dobson, 1947).

31. Sontag, *Reborn*, 69–70.

32. Sontag had done a year of graduate work in English at the University of Connecticut at Storrs and audited literature classes at Harvard before beginning her doctoral work in philosophy.

33. Sontag, *Reborn*, 193.

34. Ibid, 171.

35. Oxford spiral notebook, England and France travel notes, Susan Sontag Papers, Box 152, Folder 3, Charles E. Young Library, UCLA.

36. Susan Sontag, "A voix nue," part 2, January 2, 2001.

37. Much more was to come under de Gaulle, who returned to power in 1958: the UNESCO building, the Maison de la Radio, and then, under Pompidou, a skyscraper, the Montparnasse tower—massive shapes on a grand scale that broke with tradition. That year saw ambitious new plans for urban renewal in "prioritized zones." But for now, the quiet dark Paris of the immediate postwar era remained in place.

38. Rosemary Wakeman, *The Heroic City: Paris 1945–1958* (Chicago: University of Chicago Press, 2009), 173.

39. Sontag, *Reborn*, 160.

40. Jean-Paul Sartre, *What Is Literature and Other Essays (1949)*, introduction by Steven Ungar (Cambridge: Harvard University Press, 1988), 143–44.

41. Harriet Sohmers Zwerling to the author, January 27, 2011.

42. Annette Michelson, interview with the author, October 19, 2009.

43. For a detailed history of the hotel on the rue Gît-le-Cœur and the writers who graced it, see Barry Miles, *The Beat Hotel: Ginsberg, Burroughs and Corso in Paris, 1957–1963* (New York: Grove Press, 2001).

44. Harriet Daimler (pseudonym), *The Woman Thing* (Paris: Olympia Press, 1958), 69. Sontag commented in her journals that Iris Owens was the "brightest girl of her class at Barnard, thought she would go to Columbia Graduate School and study with [Lionel] Trilling" (see Sontag, *Reborn*, 162). Instead Iris went to Paris in the early 1950s and wrote pornography for Girodias to make ends meet. *The Woman Thing* chronicles the erotic entanglement of an American woman and her Scottish lover, who may have been based on another of the beat pornographers, Alexander Trocchi, editor of the avant-garde journal *Merlin*, which supplied Girodias with any number of writers.

45. Miles, *The Beat Hotel*, 13.

46. University of Chicago Official Announcements of the College, 1950–1951, 25; Susan Sontag, University of Chicago, transcript, Office of the Registrar: entrance, September 1949; Degree of AB conferred December 1951. Between 1942 and 1954, undergraduate degrees were awarded on the basis of comprehensive exams and not on the basis of whatever course students might have taken to prepare for them. Sontag took French 1a in the fall of 1949; French 1b in the winter quarter of 1950, and French 1c in the spring quarter of 1950. She received an A in her French 1 comprehensive exam in June 1950, at the end of the spring quarter.

47. Sontag, transcript.

48. Allen Ginsberg, *Journals Mid Fifties*, ed. Gordon Ball (New York: Harper Collins, 1995), 340.

49. Tristan Renaud, interview with Susan Sontag on *Le bienfaiteur* (the translation of Sontag's 1963 novel *The Benefactor*), *Lettres françaises,* September 3, 1965.

50. Edward Field, *The Man Who Would Marry Susan Sontag, and Other Intimate Portraits of the Bohemian Era* (Madison: University of Wisconsin Press, 2005), 160. The man in question was a writer named Alfred Chester, who was close to Sontag and Sohmers and Irene Fornés in Paris and New York, an eccentric, larger-than-life character who succumbed to schizophrenia in 1971.

51. Susan saw *Breathless* twice at the Bleeker in 1961, April 26 and November 21 (Sontag Archives, UCLA, Box 124, Folder 9, film lists). Her first essay on Godard appeared in *Against Interpretation* (New York: Farrar, Straus & Giroux, 1966); a second essay in *Styles of Radical Will* (New York: Farrar, Straus/Picador, 1969). Among her papers housed at UCLA is a long fax from Jean-Luc Godard addressed to her in 2002 (Box 86, Folder 36). He asked if she would appear in the movie he was making, a political movie that would be set in a Palestinian apartment and in which she would have a major role. After she died in 2004, Godard made his movie without her—*Notre musique.* As life scripts go, this one has a beautiful and satisfying symmetry: At age twenty-four, Susan Sontag had a ten-second walk on in a minor New Wave film; at age sixty-nine, she entertained a request from the New Wave master, who wanted to cast her as herself, as the real Susan Sontag.

52. Marquis de Sade, *The Misfortunes of Virtue,* trans. Harriet Sohmers (Paris: Obelisk Press, 1953), 79.

53. Pieralessandro Casavini, *Justine, or Good Conduct Well Chastised* (Paris: Olympia Press, 1953).

54. Sade produced three versions of Justine: *Justine, ou les infortunes de la vertu* was published in 1787; *Justine, ou les malheurs de la vertu* in 1791; and *La nouvelle Justine, ou les malheurs de la vertu (suivie de Juliette, ou les prospérités du vice)* in 1797. The 1797 version, the lengthiest, has never been translated into English. I'm grateful to Anne Garréta for clarifying this complex literary history.

55. The revised translation, *Justine, or Good Conduct Well-Chastised,* was published in New York by Grove Press in 1965, the translation attributed to Austryn Wainhouse and Richard Seaver. Both men been involved with the expatriate literary magazine *Merlin,* many of whose writers had supplied Girodias with "db's." Along with the African American writers and the *Paris Review* crowd (who had their office at the Editions de la Table Ronde, around the block), their watering hole was the Café de Tournon.

56. Sohmers published three stories in the early 1950s in *New Story: The Monthly Magazine for the Short Story,* edited in Paris: "The Nearest Exit," *New Story* 2 (April, 1951): 82–87 (immediately preceded by James Baldwin, "The Outing," 52–81); "Snow White," *New Story* 8 (November 1951): 59–68; "Money in the Sun," *New Story* 12 (November, 1952): 27–34.

57. Joyce Johnson, *Minor Characters* (Boston: Houghton Mifflin, 1983), focuses on the period 1957–58 in New York.

58. Miles, *The Beat Hotel.*

59. Sontag, *Reborn,* 179.

60. Ibid., 183.

61. See Alice Kaplan, "On Language Memoir," in *Displacements: Cultural Identities in Question,* ed. Angelika Bammer (Bloomington: Indiana University Press, 1994). My own *French Lessons* (Chicago: University of Chicago Press, 1993) is a contribution to the genre.

62. Susan Sontag, France travel notes, Susan Sontag papers, Box 124, Folder 4, Charles E. Young Library, UCLA: Word lists in French, idiomatic expressions.

63. Sontag, *Reborn,* 182–83.

64. AAUW report on grant recipients, "Susan Sontag (1957, Philosophy)," courtesy AAUW.

65. Nancy Kates interview with Harriet Sohmers Zwerling, May 2010, New York. Interview transcript courtesy Nancy Kates.

66. *Artists, Intellectuals and World War II: The Pontigny Encounters at Mount Holyoke College, 1942–1944,* ed. Christopher Benfey and Karen Remmler (Amherst, MA: University of Massachusetts Press, 2006).

67. Sontag, *Reborn,* 195.

68. Susan Sontag, "A Century of Cinema," in *Where the Stress Falls* (New York: Farrar, Straus & Giroux, 2001), 118.

69. Sontag, *Reborn,* 181–182.

70. Pascal Baudry, *French and Americans: The Other Shore* (Berkeley: Les Frenchies, 2005).

71. Jean Guignebert, *Libération,* December 6, 1957, quoted in André Blanc, "Britannicus à la scène," *Revue d'histoire du théâtre* 4 (1999): 347–65. With thanks to Volker Schröder, who also reminded me that Barthes's famous "Dire Racine" (rpt. in *Sur Racine* [Paris: Editions du Seuil, 1963]) with its riff on "To say or not to say" was a response to Jean Vilar's Théâtre national populaire production of *Britannicus* in March 1958.

72. My thanks to Noël Burch for alerting me to the Sontag walk-on. The location for the shooting was Steph Simon's design gallery at 145 boulevard Saint Germain, opened in 1956—a center of the modern design movement.

73. De Gaulle made *Time*'s cover after his return to power (May 28, 1958); General Salan after his failed putsch and treason trial in 1962, with the heading "terrorist Salan" (January 26, 1962).

74. Ginsberg, *Journals,* 447.

75. "Kennedy: U.S. Should Sway Paris," *Herald Tribune,* April 1, 1958.

76. *Jacqueline Kennedy: Historic Conversations,* 65. She recalls translating and summarizing at least ten different books on Indochina, notably works by Ho Chi Minh and French High Commissioner Georges d'Argenlieu, whose hawkish maneuvers triggered the first Indochinese war. Michael O'Brien, *John F. Kennedy: A Biography* (New York: St. Martin's Press, 2005), quotes the sardonic letter Jacqueline wrote to her in-laws Joe and Rose Kennedy after JFK's criticism of French policy: "Who cares if you never go to another ball at the French Embassy, and if Dior has you bounced out of the fitting room. We can always go and eat sheep's eyes with the Arabs" (359).

77. "Memories of Sontag: From an Ex-Pat's Diary," *Brooklyn Rail* (November 2006),

www.brooklynrail.org/2006/11/express/memories-of-sontag (accessed March 5, 2009).

78. Sontag, *Reborn*, 206.

79. A particularly sensational element of *The Lovers* was its indirect yet near explicit representation of a female orgasm: a close-up of Jeanne's hand, trembling, draped over her bed. The censorship trial for *The Lovers* in the United States went all the way to the Supreme Court, and produced the now famous quip by Judge Potter Stewart, who, in his failed attempt to define pornography, said: "I know it when I see it."

80. On New Wave cinema, gender, and history, see Geneviève Sellier, "Images de femmes dans le cinéma de la Nouvelle Vague," *Clio* 10 (1999), http://clio.revues.org/index265.html (accessed November 6, 2010), and *Masculine Singular: French New Wave Cinema*, trans. Kristin Ross (Durham: Duke University Press, 2008).

Chapter Four

1. Sontag, "The Letter Scene," *New Yorker*, August 18, 1986: "I couldn't tell him I wanted a divorce, not by letter. My letters had to be loving. I had to wait till I returned. He met me at the airport, breaking out of the waiting area onto the tarmac as I stepped off the plane. We embraced, collected my suitcase, reached the parking lot. Once in our car, before he put his key in the ignition, I told him. We sat in the car, talking; we wept." The story is often read as a disguised version of their separation after her return to Europe. What rings true is the idea of the narrator having to disguise her feelings in her letters, a sentiment echoed in Sontag's 1957–58 diaries in Paris (for example, see *Reborn*, 193).

2. Sontag, *Reborn*, 221.

3. Field, *The Man Who Would Marry Susan Sontag*, 162; and Harriet Sohmers Zwerling, *Notes of a Nude Model* (New York: Spuyten Duyvil, 2003), 61.

4. Field, *The Man Who Would Marry Susan Sontag*, 162.

5. According to a story told by Alfred Chester (see ibid.).

6. Milan Kundera, *Encounter*, trans. Linda Asher (New York: Harper, 2010), 64.

7. Susan Sontag, "*Muriel, ou le temps d'un retour*," *Film Quarterly* 17, no. 2 (Winter 1963–1964): 23–27; rpt. as "Resnais' *Muriel*," in *Against Interpretation*, 237.

8. Sontag, "Nathalie Sarraute and the Novel," in ibid., 100–111.

9. See *Against Interpretation* (1966).

10. American Association of University Women, report on grant recipients, "Susan Sontag (1957, Philosophy)," courtesy AAUW.

11. Susan Sontag, Journals 1963–1965, Susan Sontag Papers, Box 124, Folder 11, Charles E. Young Library, UCLA. Sartre, in his essay on Camus's *The Stranger*, translated in 1962 by Sontag's friend Annette Michelson ("Explication de l'*Etranger*, *Situations I* [Paris: Gallimard, 1947] in *Literary and Philosophical Essays* [New York: Collier, 1962], 28–29), described Camus's novel in this tradition: "a short novel by a moralist . . . remains very close, in the end, to a tale by Voltaire."

12. Susan Sontag, *The Benefactor: A Novel* (New York: Farrar, Straus, 1963), 6–7.

13. Alain Robbe-Grillet, "On Several Obsolete Notions" (1957), rpt. in *For a New Novel*, trans. Richard Howard (New York: Grove Press, 1965), 41: "Instead of being of a political nature, commitment is, for the writer, the full awareness of the present problems

of his own language, the conviction of their extreme importance, the desire to solve them from within."

14. Stephen Koch, "Imagination in the Abstract," *Antioch Review* 17, no. 2 (1964): 257.

15. "Identifiable as Prose," *Time,* September 13, 1963.

16. Susan Sontag, Journals 1963–1965, April 20, 1965 entry, Box 124, Folder 11, Charles E. Young Library, UCLA.

17. Sontag's first publication, during her senior year at Chicago, was a review of expatriate Harold Kaplan's novel *The Plenipotentiaries* in *The Chicago Review* (Winter 1951). Kaplan was a Newark native, educated in French literature at the University of Chicago and close to the anti-Stalinist left in Paris.

18. Sontag, *Reborn,* 235–36. Nancy Miller puts her finger on a coincidence: Sontag likely had read Harvey Swados's much discussed "Good and Short," *Hudson Review* 12 (1959): 454–59, a pairing of Roth and Paley, characterized by their "muscular prose." See Nancy Miller, "Starting out in the Fifties: Grace Paley, Philip Roth and the Making of a Literary Career," *Contemporary Women's Writing* 3 (September 8, 2009): 135–42.

19. Philip Roth, "Goodbye, Columbus," in *Novels and Stories 1959–1962* (New York: Modern Library, 1995), 73.

20. Sontag, *The Benefactor,* 9.

21. Susan Sontag, interview with Sylvain Bourmeau for *Les Inrockuptibles,* December 15, 2000.

22. The list could go on: William Styron, a Paris expatriate in the 1950s, wrote in the southern tradition and set his novels in Virginia; Irving Shaw, who lived permanently in Cannes, used his French perch to write straightforward plot-driven novels; James Jones, who moved to Paris in the 1960s, used France as a setting for *The Merry Month of May,* but he did it as an American.

23. Rockwell Gary and others, "Interview with Saul Bellow," *TriQuarterly* 60 (1984): 12–37.

24. On Chester, see Field, *The Man Who Would Marry Susan Sontag,* 162.

25. Sontag, *Reborn,* 317.

26. Sontag, *The Benefactor,* 57.

27. Gloria L. Cronin and Ben Siegel, eds., *Conversations with Saul Bellow* (Jackson: University Press of Mississippi, 1995), 217.

28. Naïm Kattan, "Une apologie de l'inaction," *Le Devoir,* November 13, 1965.

29. Annie Brierre, "Un apôtre de l'avant-garde: Susan Sontag," *Les nouvelles littéraires,* October 15, 1966. My translation.

30. Sontag's archives contain a letter that is fascinating for the picture it gives of an experienced expatriate writer passing on her resources to an upcoming writer on an early trip to France—the passing of the baton from one "dark lady" of American letters, as Mary McCarthy was called, to another. McCarthy, from her summer place in Maine, wrote to Sontag c/o the American Express in Paris, on August 11, 1964—a full year before the French translation of *The Benefactor* (*Le bienfaiteur*) appeared—in what looks like a response to a publisher's list of names of people to meet on a publicity tour. She instructs Sontag on the people she needs to know in Paris; explains that she has written to Sonia

Orwell to ask her to introduce Sontag to the Leirises and Marguerite Duras, the Massons (as in André Masson, the painter), the editors of *Œil*, and the essayist Jean-François Revel. From the expatriate world, McCarthy has contacted Stanley and Eileen Geist on Sontag's behalf: "Eileen knows everybody in the Bohemian-American world in Paris. . . . She will surely give a New York style party for you if she's there." The letter ends with a dinner invitation, presumably in Paris, after McCarthy has returned from her Maine summer. (Mary McCarthy to Susan Sontag, August 11, 1964, Susan Sontag Papers, Box 91, Folder 26, Charles E. Young Library, UCLA). The support shown by McCarthy for Sontag's career belies the reports of competition between the two women. It's a very different picture from the one in Frances Kiernan's *Seeing Mary Plain*. Kiernan writes of McCarthy: "But while there was no avoiding Sontag in print or at the home of mutual friends, she saw no reason to get to know her better," and quotes Susan Sontag in an interview: "Mary came into the room like an aircraft carrier" (538).

31. Sontag, *Against Interpretation*, x.

32. Sontag, *Reborn*, 243, 244, 245, 256.

33. Susan Sontag, Journals 1964, Susan Sontag Papers, Box 125, Folder 1, Charles E. Young Library, UCLA.

34. Sontag, Journals 1963–1965, Susan Sontag Papers, Box 124, Folder 11, Charles E. Young Library, UCLA.

35. Roger Grenier, *The Difficulty of Being a Dog*, trans. Alice Kaplan (Chicago: University of Chicago Press, 2000), 28.

36. Florence Malraux to Susan Sontag, re: housekeeping in their apartment, Susan Sontag papers, Box 91, Folder 10, Charles E. Young Library, UCLA.

37. Richard Howard to Susan Sontag, July 7, 1966, Susan Sontag Papers, Box 88, Folder 10, Charles E. Young Library, UCLA. Foucault's *Les mots et les choses* (1966) was translated by Alan Sheridan as *The Order of Things* (New York: Random House, 1970). The French novelist Raymond Queneau assembled Kojève's 1933–39 lectures on Hegel at the Ecole des hautes études.

38. Howard has translated Barthes's *Critical Essays* (1972); *Pleasure of the Text* (1975); *On Racine* (1977); *A Lover's Discourse* (1978); *Eiffel Tower and Other Mythologies* (1979); *New Critical Essays* (1980); *The Empire of Signs* (1982); *Fashion System* (with Matthew Ward 1983); *Michelet* (1987); *The Semiotic Challenge* (1988); *Incidents* (1992); and most of the excerpts in *The Roland Barthes Reader*, edited by Sontag in 1982. Sontag wrote a foreword to Barthes's *Writing Degree Zero* (1968); published *The Roland Barthes Reader* and two essays on Barthes: a eulogy, "Remembering Barthes," reprinted in *Under the Sign of Saturn* (1972), and "Writing Itself: On Roland Barthes," reprinted in *Where the Stress Falls* (2001).

39. Jacques Derrida to Susan Sontag [my translation], January 6, 1966, Susan Sontag Papers, Box 84, Folder 43, Charles E. Young Library, UCL.

40. Jacques Derrida to Susan Sontag [my translation], February 12, 1967, Susan Sontag Papers, Box 84, Folder 43, Charles E. Young Library, UCLA. The articles were absorbed into *De la grammatologie* (1967), which appeared in English only in 1976.

41. Sontag, Journals, 1963–65, Susan Sontag Papers, Box 124, Folder 11, Charles E. Young Library, UCLA.

42. Susan Sontag to Fredric Jameson (draft), September 11, 1976, Susan Sontag Papers, Box 142, Folder 9, Charles E. Young Library, UCLA.

43. *New York Times,* January 12, 1968.

44. Susan Sontag, James Baldwin, Norman Mailer, and LeRoi Jones, Letter to the editor, *New York Times,* May 6, 1968, 40. An open letter in the *New York Review of Books* appeared the same day with a partial list of 85 signatures, including Sontag's (with Baldwin, Mailer, John Marquand, etc.).

45. Steven Shapiro to Susan Sontag, October 9, 1969, Susan Sontag Papers, Box 142, Folder 9, Charles E. Young Library, UCLA.

46. Susan Sontag, *Partisan Review,* Winter 1967, 57, in response to a questionnaire sent out by the editor and reprinted as Susan Sontag, "What's Happening in America," in *Styles of Radical Will* (New York: Farrar, Straus/Picador, 1967): "The white race *is* the cancer of human history: it is the white race and it alone—its ideologies and inventions— which eradicates autonomous civilizations wherever it spreads, which has upset the ecological balance of the planet, which now threatens the very existence of life itself" (203).

47. Communication from Nancy Kates, based on a query to Don Eric Levine. Sontag and Stéphane probably first met 1971, after Sontag's breakup with Carlotta del Pezzo (to whom she dedicated her film *Brother Carl*), although they might have crossed paths at Cannes in 1969.

48. *Les enfants terribles* appears with other Melville films on a list made in 1965 (Sontag, Journals, 1963–65, Susan Sontag Papers, Box 124, Folder 11, Charles E. Young Library, UCLA).

49. In a 1970 notebook, Sontag made a list of technical film production terms in French and English (for example: boom = la perche), and French producers, including Nicole Stéphane (Susan Sontag, Journals, "Film 1970," Susan Sontag Papers, Box 126, Folder 8, Charles E. Young Library, UCLA).

50. See the memoir by Stéphane's sister, Monique de Rothschild, *Si j'ai bonne mémoire* (Saint-Rémy-en-l'Eau: Monelle Hayot, 2001).

51. Sontag's first essay on Walter Benjamin, "The Last Intellectual," appeared in the *New York Review of Books* 25, no. 15 (October 12, 1978) and was reprinted, in revised form, as "Under the Sign of Saturn," in *Under the Sign of Saturn* (New York: Farrar, Straus & Giroux, 1980). In a letter to Scholem on October 16, 1933, Benjamin referred to an invitation from Baronness Golschmidt-Rothschild to live at a house she had reserved for Jewish intellectual refugees (*The Correspondence of Walter Benjamin and Gershom Scholem, 1932–1940,* ed. Rabinbach et al. (Cambridge, MA: Harvard University Press, 1992), 83.

52. In *Swimming in a Sea of Death* (New York: Simon and Schuster, 2008), David Rieff describes his mother's radical chemotherapy in the mid-1970s under the care of Parisian oncologist Lucien Israël, to whom Nicole Stéphane had referred Sontag at a point when her chances for survival seemed nil.

53. Noël Burch, Electronic communication to the author, June 28, 2009.

54. Susan Sontag Papers, Box 53, Folder 9, Charles E.Young Library, UCLA.

55. Susan Sontag to Andrew Wylie, September 30, 1991 (referring to translation problems with the first French edition of *On Photography,* which she had been too ill to correct), Susan Sontag Papers, Box 61, Folder 9. Charles E. Young Library.

56. Susan Sontag to Sophie Bastide-Foltz (regarding a single sentence, and eventually the title of what became *L'amant du volcan,* trans. Sophie Bastide-Foltz [Paris: Christian Bourgois, 1997]), December 16, 1994, Susan Sontag papers, Box 16, Folder 6, Charles E. Young Library. UCLA.

57. Susan Sontag to Philippe Blanchard, July 19, 1987, Susan Sontag Papers, Box 53, Folder 9, Charles E. Young Library, UCLA.

58. Blanchard to Sontag, August 2, 1987, Susan Sontag Papers, Box 53, Folder 9, Charles E. Young Library, UCLA.

59. Susan Sontag, interview with Stefan Jonsson, 1988, in *Conversations with Susan Sontag,* ed. Leland Poague (Jackson: University Press of Mississippi, 1995), 243.

60. "9.11.01" appeared in a reduced version in the "Talk of the Town" column in *The New Yorker* on September 24, 2001; the original version was published posthumously in Susan Sontag, *At the Same Time: Essays and Speeches,* ed. Paolo Dilonardo and Anne Jump (New York: Farrar, Straus, 2007): "Where is the acknowledgement that this was not a 'cowardly' attack on 'civilization' or 'liberty' or 'humanity' or 'the free world' but an attack on the world's self-proclaimed superpower, undertaken as a consequence of specific American alliances and actions?" (105).

61. Sontag's complaint about visual sense is in a diary entry from April 20, 1965: "To see more—(Projects) For instance, colors and spatial relationships, light. My vision is un-refined, insensitive; this is the trouble I'm having with painting." (Susan Sontag, Journals 1963–65, Susan Sontag Papers, Box 124, Folder 11, Charles E. Young Library, UCLA.)

62. Sontag, Journals, 1964. She continues: "That I'm the vehicle, the medium, the instrument of some force beyond myself."

63. Denis Roche to Susan Sontag, June 1, 1980, Susan Sontag Papers, Box 61, Folder 11, Charles E. Young Library, UCLA.

64. Roger W. Straus to Jacqueline Onassis, May 20, 1980, Sontag Papers Box 139, Folder 19, Charles E. Young Library, UCLA.

65. Frédéric de Towarnicki, portrait of Susan Sontag in *Le magazine littéraire,* November 1995: "Figure de proue la plus célèbre de l'intelligentsia nord-americaine, Susan Sontag est venue à Paris pour la sortie de son roman, *L'amant du volcan,* best-seller aux Etats-Unis."

66. Jacqueline Onassis to Susan Sontag, December 16, year unknown, Susan Sontag papers, Box 139, Folder 19, Charles E.Young Library, UCLA.

67. A widely quoted remark, notably by Odile Hellier at the Village Voice Bookstore. See her remembrance of Sontag: www.villagevoicebookshop.com/book_highlights_feb06.html (accessed November 6, 2010).

68. Mendelsohn, "The Collector," in *The New Republic,* April 1, 2009.

69. Susan Sontag, "Vies plurielles: New York/Paris" interview with Chantal Thomas, "A Voix nue: grands entretiens," part two, "New York–Paris," France Culture radio, January 2, 2001, Audio-Visual Archives, Bibliothèque nationale de France.

70. Susan Sontag, interview with Bernard Pivot, host for "Le monde de la photogra-phie," *Apostrophes,* June 8, 1979. Guests: Susan Sontag, Robert Doisneau, Marc Riboud, Helmut Newton, Hans Silvester.

Chapter Five

1. Walton, *Internationalism, National Identities, and Study Abroad*, 151.

2. Angela Y. Davis, foreword to Maryse Condé, *I, Tituba, Black Witch of Salem*, trans. Richard Philcox (Charlottesville: University Press of Virginia, 1992) xi–xiii.

3. Albert Burton Moore, *History of Alabama* (Tuscaloosa: Alabama Book Store, 1951), 81. See his romantic description of the Napoleonic exiles in Philadelphia, their organization of an "Association of French Emigrants for the Cultivation of the Vine and Olive," and their settlements in what would become Marengo county: "The light-hearted French toned-up the spirits of the American farmers with whom they came in contact and introduced new forms of Entertainment, such as the tournament and the round dance. The influence of their social graces upon the manners of their American Neighbors, with whom they intermarried, were long discernible. Marengo, Demopolis, and Linden, these are cherished names in Alabama which perpetuate the Memory of a romantic pioneer experiment."

4. Fania Davis, interview with the author, September 23, 2009.

5. *Freed by the People: The Closing Defense Statement Made in the Angela Davis Case*, brochure printed by the National United Committee to Free Angela Davis, June 1, 1972.

6. Patricia Williams, "On Being the Object of Property," *Signs* 14, no. 11 (1988): 6–7.

7. Fania Davis, interview.

8. Sallye Marguerite Bell Davis, "Reflections of a Life," American Council on Education, http://www.acenet.edu (accessed November 6, 2010).

9. On the red-baiting of the Southern Negro Youth Congress in the 1940s, on its Birmingham leader Louis Burnham and his friendship with Sallye Davis, and on Birmingham in the 1950s and 1960s, see Diane McWhorter, *Carry Me Home: Birmingham, Alabama; The Climactic Battle of the Civil Rights Revolution* (New York: Simon and Schuster, 2001).

10. Angela Davis, *Angela Davis: An Autobiography* (New York: Random House, 1974; rpt. New York: International Publishers, 1989), 90–93. All page references are to the 1989 edition.

11. Yves Bonnefoy, electronic communication to the author, June 14, 2010 (my translation): "She explained to me that in her black school, where there was no French instruction, she improvised a class where she taught herself as she learned."

12. Albert Moore, *History of Alabama*, 1951 edition. For example: "The treatment of slaves differed widely in different cases. It was as varied as the treatment which farm animals received at the hands of their owners. . . Many of the slaves were stubborn and worthless" and "The testimony of men now living; plantation records, diaries, handbooks, planter's instructions, and essays on slavery; and the observations of Northern and foreign travelers—all these point to the fact that leniency and kindness prevailed" (360); "Overseers generally were forbidden to overwork the slaves or to subject them to inhuman treatment" (361);"The Negroes were a fun-making and fun-loving people, and they had many opportunities for merriment" (366); and "The masses of slaves seemed contented and carefree, and were sentimentally attached to their masters and the plantations" (367).

13. Fania Davis, telephone interview with the author, August 28, 2010.

14. Davis, *Angela Davis*, 82–85.

15. Ibid., 83.

16. Bernard Pivot, "Sur le racisme," *Apostrophes*, France 2 Television, May 16, 1975.

17. Davis, *Angela Davis*, 85.

18. Frantz Fanon, *Black Skin, White Masks*, trans. Charles Lam Markmann (New York: Grove Press, 1991), 45.

19. Amy Jaffe, former student at Elisabeth Irwin High School, interview with the author, October 1, 2009; Military records and census records, www.ancestry.com (date accessed). See also Regina Nadelson, *Who Is Angela Davis?* (New York: Wyden, 1972), 59–62, on French at Elisabeth Irwin.

20. Fania Davis, interview.

21. Davis, *Angela Davis*, 86–87.

22. Ibid., 121.

23. Ibid., 120–23.

24. On the status of Muslims in Algeria before 1962, see Patrick Weil, *How to Be French: Nationality in the Making Since 1789* (Durham: Duke University Press, 2008).

25. Pap Ndiaye, *La condition noire: Essai sur une minorité française* (Paris: Gallimard/ Folio actuel, 2008), 1–90. See Kristin Ross, *Fast Cars, Clean Bodies: Decolonization and the Reordering of French Culture* (Cambridge, MA: MIT Press, 1995), on the violent underbelly of modernization.

26. Ndiaye, *La condition noire*, 192.

27. Davis, *Angela Davis*, 122.

28. "Two Muslims killed 9 wounded in Paris," *Paris Herald Tribune*, June 17, 1962.

29. *Paris Herald Tribune*, May 31, 1962.

30. For example, June 25, 1962, *Paris Herald Tribune*, front-page photo of Jacqueline Kennedy on a Duncan Phyfe sofa in the restored Library.

31. *Paris Herald Tribune*, July 3, 1962.

32. See Tyler Stovall, *Paris Noir: African Americans in the City of Light* (New York: Houghton Mifflin, 1996).

33. Beauvoir, reading Gunnar Myrdal on *The American Dilemma*, rejected essential notions of femininity for the idea that one becomes a woman in a cultural situation—in much the way that black Americans were defined by their cultural situation as much as by their race.

34. Sidney Bechet came to France in 1949 and stayed for the rest of his life; he played songs like "Rue d'Antibes" and "Les oignons" with Claude Luter and his orchestra.

35. Quoted by Rebecca Ruquist, "Non, nous ne jouons pas la trompette: Richard Wright in Paris," *Contemporary French and Francophone Studies* (formerly *Sites*) 8, no. 3 (summer 2004): 285–304.

36. Quoted in Tyler Stovall, "The Fire This Time: Black Expatriates and the Algerian War," in "The French Fifties," special issue, ed. Susan Weiner, *Yale French Studies* 98 (2000): 182–200.

37. In a story by Richard Wright called "The Island of Hallucinations," which has never

seen the light of day. See Ruquist, "Non, nous ne jouons pas."

38. William Gardner Smith, *The Stone Face* (New York: Farrar, Straus & Giroux, 1963). See Stovall, "The Fire This Time"; and Kristin Ross, *May 68 and Its Afterlives* (Chicago: University of Chicago Press, 2002).

39. Smith, *The Stone Face*, 208.

40. On Wright, see Stovall, "The Fire This Time"; and Hazel Rowley, *Richard Wright: The Life and Times* (New York: Holt, 2001).

41. James Baldwin, "No Name in the Street" (1972), in *The Price of the Ticket: Collected Nonfiction, 1948–1945* (New York: St. Martin's Press, 1985), 463.

42. See Chester Himes, *My Life of Absurdity: The Autobiography of Chester Himes* (New York: Thunder's Mouth Press, 1995).

43. Davis, *Angela Davis*, 121–22.

44. Ibid.

45. Yves Bonnefoy, electronic communication to the author, June 18, 2010, my translation: "I remember Angela Davis, because of the particularity of her presence at Brandeis (I talked about this with Herbert Marcuse, a friend, whose courses she took with a more intense interest than in any other discipline). Not that she wasn't interested in French literature. I had her as a student in at least one class, two I believe, or perhaps in two different courses. I remember that she found Baudelaire and Rimbaud meaningful, and that she had explained to me that in the black school where she had gone no one was teaching French; she had improvised a class in which she taught others as she was learning. It was impossible not to feel great admiration for her because of her intelligence, her courage, her good humor. She was clearly, at least in this class, the central figure of the little group. We sensed that she would achieve in one way or another some remarkable thing—I imagined in philosophy, seeing the influence of Marcuse. PS I spoke often of Rimbaud, because his poetry, and his life, coincided with the wishes and often with the actions of the young Americans at that moment, involved in the struggle for the extension of civil rights in the south."

46. Milton Hindus, *A Reader's Guide to Marcel Proust* (London: Thames and Hudson, 1962).

47. Davis, *Angela Davis*, 125.

48. Marcel Proust, *In Search of Lost Time*, vol. 6: *Time Regained*, trans. Mayor, Kilmartin, and Enright (New York, Modern Library, 1999), 522.

49. Barbara Zurer Pearson, interview with the author, January 10, 2010.

50. Howard Bloch, interview with the author, July 10, 2009.

51. Christie Stagg to her parents, September 12, 1963. Courtesy Christie Stagg Austin.

52. Vivian Goldberg Auslander, electronic communication to the author, May 17, 2010.

53. Jane Chaplin Jordan, interviews with the author, April 29 and May 27, 2010.

54. *Birmingham World*, April 6, 1963.

55. See *Ebony*, January 1962, on Frontiers International: "the only Negro service organization" on the order of Rotary or Kiwanis. "By 1962 there were 73 chapters." The club continues to exist, with the motto "Advancement through Service."

56. Davis, *Angela Davis*, 127.

57. The NYU Paris program was created in 1969; the Wesleyan Program in Paris began in the late 1960s, with Vassar joining in the late 1990s.

58. The others came from Brandeis, Amherst, Mills, Barnard, Wells, University of Michigan, Northwestern, Simmons, Indiana University, Tufts, Middlebury, Colorado College, New York University, Duke, Stetson, Colby, Harpur (Binghamton), William Smith, Gettysburg, DePauw, Stanford, State University of New York, St. Lawrence, Wooster, UC Berkeley, University of North Carolina at Greensboro, University of New Hampshire, Drew, Bowdoin, and Hood. Information on the 1963–64 program courtesy Hamilton College Archives, and Professor Cheryl Morgan of Hamilton College.

59. Christie Stagg to her parents, October 15, 1963.

60. Davis, *Angela Davis*, 128–31.

61. This is a standard rule for French capitalization, but it's also the kind of minute detail that can be striking for an American student adjusting to the new language.

62. *L'Humanité*, September 16, 1963.

63. Paul Mathias, "Dans le sud, c'est pire que la violence: Nos envoyés spéciaux dans les Etats où une guerre d'Algérie semble commencer," *Paris Match*, no. 755 (September 28, 1963): 42–47.

64. John Simon, interview with the author, March 15, 2010.

65. Information on students and their "tracks," or courses of study, courtesy Hamilton College Archives.

66. Patsy Martin Lightbown, interview with the author, June 28, 2010.

67. Paula Durbin, electronic communication to the author, May 1 and May 3, 2010.

68. Angela Davis, interview with Bernard Pivot (host) on racism, *Apostrophes*, France 2 Television, 1975.

69. I am grateful to Vivian Goldberg Auslander for sending me Piere Curnier's *Pages commentées d'auteurs contemporains* (Paris: Larousse, 1962), with its chapter on Saint-John Perse's *Amers*—one of the texts used in the contemporary literature class.

70. Barbara Zurer to her parents, February 2, 1964.

71. Chaplin Jordan, interviews.

72. Micheline Lamotte, interview with the author, March 7, 2010.

73. The fascist groups later blamed the Croix-de-Feu for the failure of the operation, since de La Rocque refused to give his troops the order to attack.

74. Camille Lamotte, electronic communication to the author, July 24, 2010.

75. Chaplin Jordan, interviews.

76. Jeffrey Mehlman, *Legacies of Anti-Semitism in France* (Minneapolis: University of Minnesota Press, 1983), 16.

77. Sallye Davis, interview in Jean-Daniel Simon's documentary, *L'enchaînement* (1977), courtesy Jean-Daniel Simon.

78. Christie Stagg diary, September 14, 1963.

79. Interview with Christie Stagg Austin, May 4, 2010.

80. Davis, *Angela Davis*, 132, and Christie Stagg to her parents, November 23, 1963.

81. Angela Davis also learned to cross her 7s, and those crossed 7s would be used to identify her handwriting in court.

82. Angela Davis, at a commemoration for Jean Genet, Institut mémoires de l'édition contemporaine, organized by Albert Dichy, May 25–27, 1991; Davis's French speech translated by Eric Benveniste, posted by Justin Desmangles: http://www.sisterezili. blogspot.com/ . . . /tactfulness-of-heart-angela-davis-on.html (accessed May 11, 2011). I'm grateful to Albert Dichy, Mémoires de l'Edition Contemporaine, for checking the text against his original transcript.

Chapter Six

1. Davis, *Angela Davis*, 133–35.

2. Angela Yvonne Davis, "The Novels of Robbe-Grillet: A Study of Method and Meaning," LD571.B66D385, Robert D. Farber University Archive and Special Collections Department, Brandeis University.

3. Alain Robbe-Grillet, *Pour un nouveau roman* (Paris: Editions de Minuit, 1963). Madame de Lafayette's *La Princesse de Clèves* (1678) is considered the first novel in the French tradition.

4. Vivian Goldberg Auslander, electronic communication to the author, May 17, 2010.

5. Davis, "The Novels of Robbe-Grillet," 8.

6. Chaplin Jordan, interviews.

7. Jacqueline Piatier, 1964 interview with Sartre on *Les mots*, *Le Monde*, April 18, 1964; Alain Robbe-Grillet, "Littérature engagée, littérature réactionnaire," *L'Express*, December 20, 1955, 11.

8. Merleau-Ponty, *Phenomenology of Perception* (London, Routledge, 1995), xvi.

9. Olivier Corpet and Emmanuelle Lambert, *Alain Robbe-Grillet, le voyageur du Nouveau Roman: Chronologie illustrée 1922–2002* (Paris: Editions de l'IMEC, 2002), 18. The house in *La jalousie* was modeled on a house in Martinique where Robbe-Grillet lived in 1950, while he was working as a research engineer for the Institut des fruits et agrumes coloniaux (Institute for Colonial Fruits and Citruses).

10. Richard Howard, roundtable presentation, "A Salute to Alain Robbe-Grillet," New York University, October 2, 2009. Howard's translation of the novel was reviewed by the *New York Times* in November 1959.

11. Davis, "The Novels of Robbe-Grillet," 122–23.

12. Onassis, "Introduction," in *Atget's Gardens*.

13. Sontag, "Alain Resnais' *Muriel*."

14. Robbe-Grillet, *For a New Novel*, 41.

15. In evaluating the work of Nazi filmmaker Leni Riefenstahl, for example, Sontag was willing to defend her aesthetic qualities per se in *Against Interpretation*, but by her 1975 *New York Review of Books* essay, "Fascinating Fascism," she had abandoned pure formalism for a critique of fascist aesthetics in Riefenstahl's photographs of the African Nuba tribe.

16. Bonnefoy, electronic communication.

17. Davis, *Angela Davis*, 142–45.

18. Guérin wasn't available in English until 1970. Eventually, the particular prestige and focus on French Studies would wane as texts like Fanon's began to circulate in

English, becoming part of a critical debate around British Commonwealth literature.

19. Cynthia Young, *Soul Power* (Durham: Duke University Press, 2006), 202.

20. Davis, *Angela Davis,* 214.

21. William Divale, in the *Daily Bruin,* July 1, 1969, announced the presence of a communist in the Philosophy Department; Ed Montgomery, in the *San Francisco Examiner,* July 9, 1969, gave her name.

22. Davis, *Angela Davis,* 218.

23. On Lettrists, precursors to the Situationists, see Greil Marcus, *Lipstick Traces: A Secret History of the Twentieth Century* (Cambridge, MA: Harvard University Press, 1990).

24. Yolande du Luart's *Angela Davis: Portrait of a Revolutionary* survives as a single 16 mm. copy, badly in need of restoration, in the holdings of the Library for the Performing Arts, a branch of the New York Public Library.

25. COINTELPRO was the name given by the FBI to operations designed to destroy dissident movements and individuals; tactics ranged from misinformation to murder.

26. August 24, 1970: the story made the rounds from the *Los Angeles Times* to *Newsweek.*

27. Her "Lectures on Liberation" have been reprinted in her new critical edition of Frederick Douglass, *A Narrative of the Life of Frederick Douglass, an American Slave, Written by Himself* (San Francisco: City Lights Publishers, 2009).

28. "Introduction to the 1970 Pamphlet by UCLA Professors," in ibid.

29. See Davis's reminiscences of the event in her 2006 Odéon Speech honoring Genet (see chapter 5, note 82). The *Daily Bruin* covered Genet's UCLA appearance on April 28, 1970. See also Robert Sandarg, "Jean Genet and the Black Panther Party," *Journal of Black Studies* 16, no. 3 (March 1986): 269–82.

30. The idea of prisons as a continuation of slavery and the prison as the new plantation has been a theme of Angela Davis's work since the 1970s.

31. Jackson was represented as a thug and a sociopath by Eric Cummins, *The Rise and Fall of California's Radical Prison Movement* (Palo Alto: Stanford University Press, 1994); as an important theorist of revolution by Brady Heiner, "Foucault and the Black Panthers," *City* 11, no. 3 (December 2007): 313–56.

32. Acquisitions file on *Soledad Brother,* courtesy Pierre Nora. The handwriting is markedly different from Fay Stender's signature, and it is conceivable that the letter was written for her by a French colleague. My translation.

33. "Jean Genet et les Frères de Soledad," *Le Monde,* April 2, 1971.

34. Albert Dichy at the Institut Mémoires de l'Edition Contemporaine shared his understanding of Genet's Panther period. On the Panther period in the context of the writer's whole career, see Edmund White, *Jean Genet* (Paris: Gallimard, 1993).

35. George Jackson, *Soledad Brother* (Chicago: Lawrence Hill Books, 1994), 190, 241. Elsewhere he says that men who read Lenin, Fanon, and Che don't riot; "they mass, they rage, they dig graves" (27).

36. Ibid., 195.

37. "Jonathan Jackson Bright Student: His Principal" in *Afro-American,* August 29, 1970.

38. Mary Timothy, *Jury Woman* (Palo Alto: Glide Publications, Emty Press, 1974), 122.

39. Radio archives from Jean-Daniel Simon, *L'enchaînement*.

40. Archives de la Préfecture de Police, Série G, Etrangers, carton 12, "Angela Davis, membre des panthères noires"; report by Police Judiciaire, August 25, 1970; Fichiers des garnis and Fiche B, Opposition à l'entrée en France, August 28, 1970.

41. Chaplin Jordan, interviews.

42. Simon, interview.

43. Claudine La Haye, "J'ai vu Angela Davis dans sa prison," *L'Express*, November 8–14, 1971, my translation.

44. "Appel pour la création d'un comité de soutien," *L'Humanité*, March 25, 1971.

45. Maxwell Adereth, *The French Communist Party: A Critical History (1920–1984)* (Manchester: Manchester University Press), 304. The party's motto: "Le parti des 75,000 fusillés" referred to the Nazi policy of executing French communist hostages as reprisal for acts of violence by the resistance. The actual number is probably closer to 5,000. According to the French almanac or *Quid?* (Paris: Plon, 1972), 374, the French Communist Party had 459,600 members in the fall of 1970. Statistics on American Communist Party members are harder to come by. According to the 1974 *World Almanac*, ed. George E. Delury (New York: Newspaper Enterprise Association), 764, Gus Hall got 25,595 votes in the 1972 election—though number of votes does not necessarily translate to membership in the party.

46. Genet, *The Declared Enemy: Texts and Interviews* (Stanford: Stanford University Press, 2004) reproduces the texts, especially "Angela et ses frères," from *Le Nouvel Observateur*, August 31, 1970, 19–21.

47. Katharina von Bülow, interview with the author, July 2, 2010.

48. "L'assassinat de George Jackson,"*Intolérable*, no. 3 (Paris: Gallimard, 1971), my translation. The preface is attributed to Jean Genet; the other texts to the Groupe d'Information sur les Prisons.

49. Heiner, "Foucault and the Black Panthers."

50. Letter dated November 19, 1970; published in the *New York Review of Books*, January 7, 1971.

51. James Baldwin on Angela Davis, interviewed by Joe Walker and George Cain 1972, KPFA, #BC0642, Pacifica Radio Archives, North Hollywood, CA.

52. National United Committee to Free Angela Davis, Press release, April 25, 1972, XII.33 microfilm. For a guide to the microfilm, see Ann Fagan Ginger, *The Angela Davis Case Collection* (Berkeley: Meiklejohn Civil Liberties Institute, 1974). Subsequent citations will give pages numbers as they appear in the microfilm transcript. The Meiklejohn microfilm includes material gathered by the defense, such as briefs, memoranda, and research. This supplementary material is unnumbered.

53. "And I think that at this time to point out that the actions of the FBI in apprehending Angela Davis—a rather remarkable story again in the long history of remarkable stories of apprehensions by the FBI—is an indication that once the Federal Government through the FBI moves into an area, this should be warning to those who engage in these

acts that they eventually are going to be apprehended. This is a warning by signing this bill: We are going to give the tools to the men in the Justice Department and the men in the FBI and we shall see to it that those who engage in such terroristic acts are brought to justice." Richard Nixon, Remarks on Signing the Organized Crime Control Act of 1970, October 15, 1970, John T. Woolley and Gerhard Peters, *The American Presidency Project,* http://www.presidency.ucsb.edu/ws/?pid=2720 (accessed November 11, 2010).

54. Bettina Aptheker, interview, May 18, 2010.

55. Jules Borker, interview with the author, June 24, 2010.

56. Borker, interview.

57. The *New York Times* correspondent was later charged with possession—but acquitted.

58. The other books were Edward Hallett Carr, *Studies in Revolution: A Review of Current Literature* (New York: Grosset and Dunlap, 1964); Henry Bienen, *Violence and Social Change: A Review of Current Literature* (Chicago: University of Chicago Press, 1968); Carl Leiden and Karl M. Schmitt, *The Politics of Violence: Revolution in the Modern World* (Upper Saddle River, NJ: Prentice-Hall, 1968).

59. Opening prosecution statement, *The People of the State of California v. Angela Y. Davis* No 52613 (Super. Ct., Santa Clara Cty., Cal., 1972). Microfilm trial transcript, p. 2164: "There were 6 paper back books in the blue briefcase. They were used to conceal the shotgun, the tape and the wire in case anyone looked into the briefcase. The 17 year old young man who had just completed his junior year in high school had three books that were written in French."

60. Dianne Moore, Blair High School, student activities, electronic communication with the author, August 12, 2010.

61. Declared unconstitutional on February 18, 1972, the death penalty was reinstated in 1994.

62. "Opening Defense Statement Presented by Angela Y. Davis," rpt. in *The Angela Y. Davis Reader,* ed. Joy James (London: Blackwell, 1998), 329–46.

63. Ibid., 340–41.

64. Opening prosecution statement, *People v. Davis,* p. 2189.

65. *People v. Davis,* p. 4949.

66. *People v. Davis,* pp. 6459 ff., testimony of Jamala Broadnax.

67. See Mary Timothy, *Jury Woman: By the Foreperson of the Angela Davis Jury* (Palo Alto: Emty Press, 1974), 235–43.

68. Quoted from edited version of an eighteen-page diary-letter from Angela Davis to George Jackson, dated July 8, 1971, referring to a meeting between Angela Davis and George Jackson at San Quentin (offered at Davis's trial as people's exhibit 126a and b). See also Aptheker, *Morning Breaks,* 235.

69. Albert Camus, *The Myth of Sisyphus,* trans. Justin O'Brien (New York: Knopf, 1955). I've revised Justin O'Brien's much-cited translation of the passage: "A man is talking on the telephone behind a glass partition; you cannot hear him, but you see his *incomprehensible dumb show*: you wonder why he is alive."

70. From the eighteen-page diary entry dated July 10, 1971: "Since this whole letter is

more stream of consciousness—," *People v. Davis*, p. 6239.

71. Branton maintained that all the letters showed was "a deep, warm, personal, moving relationship between one human being and another." *People v. Davis*, p. 6287.

72. Memo from Leonard Michaels on Alexander Pope's "Eloise and Abelard," *People v. Davis*, additional defense materials, unnumbered pages.

73. Kathy Kalin, research on love poetry, *People v. Davis*, additional defense materials, unnumbered pages.

74. *People v. Davis*, closing statement, reprinted in *Freed by the People*.

75. *People v. Davis*, p. 4973. Moore refers to the title for the *Recherche* given by Proust's first translator, Scott Montcrieff, *Remembrance of Things Past*.

76. The rue Hamelin, another spoke off the Etoile from Angela Davis's rue Duret. Proust organized a petition of intellectuals in support of Dreyfus. He attended the trial of Zola for criminal libel after publishing his letter to the French president, "J'accuse," in support of Dreyfus. Georg Lukács, in his statement of support for Angela Davis, recalled the Dreyfus trial and compared it to hers. See Davis, *If They Come in the Morning*.

77. Aptheker, 237.

78. *Freed by the People*, 1.

79. Charles L. Sanders, "The Radicalization of Angela Davis," *Ebony* 26, no. 9 (July 1971): 114, 120. Sanders may well have seen a reflection of his own Paris experience in hers.

80. Claudine La Haye, "J'ai vu Angela Davis dans sa prison," *L'Express*, November 8–14, 1971.

81. Edmonde Charles-Roux, "Ce bien cette liberté . . .," *L'Humanité Dimanche*, March 1, 1972, my translation.

82. "Worldwide cry to free Angela grows," in *People's World* (New York: Schomburg Center for Research in Black Culture, n.d.).

83. Petition dated July 1971 and reproduced on www.blanchot.fr (accessed November 10, 2010). Prévert published his prose poem in support of Angela Davis in August 1971; see Jacques Prévert, "Angela Davis," *Choses et autres* (Paris: Gallimard, 1975).

84. University of California at Santa Cruz, Special Collections, Bettina Aptheker papers from the Angela Davis trial, Series 6, Angela Y. Davis Trial, Folder 50: 4–6.

85. Fania Davis, interview with the author, October 3, 1971.

86. Box 168 MO 262, Stanford Special Collections, uncatalogued: card dated November 11, 1970: "Je m'appelle Olivier. J'habite en France, à Paris. J'ai 10 ans. J'espère que vous sortirez bientôt de prison." Letter sent to Angela Davis/Women's House of Detention/6th Avenue New York, NY (forwarded to San Rafael, Jan. 30, 1971). The other letters are also from MO 262, Box 168.

87. Angela Davis, *Angela Davis: Autobiographie*, trans. Cathy Bernheim (Paris: Albin Michel, 1975).

88. France-Inter, May 15, 1975 interview, Audio-Visual Archives, Inathèque, Bibliothèque nationale de France.

89. Pivot, *Apostrophes*.

90. *Témoignages, De la France équinoxiale au Palais du Luxembourg* (Paris: Plon, 1975).

91. Simon was the founder, in the wake of the French events of May 1968, of "La Quinzaine des réalisateurs"—a selection of films outside the Cannes festival competition. La Quinzaine has been crucial in the French film industry for its encouragement of new directors.

92. Gille Deleuze and Félix Guattari, interviewed by Michel-Antoine Burnier in *C'est demain la veille, entretiens* (Paris: le Seuil, 1973), 137–61, translated by David Sweet, as "Capitalism: A very special delirium," in *Chaosophy,* ed. Sylvère Lotringer (New York: Semiotext(e), 1995), 53–73.

93. The episode was also taken up by French playwright Alain Foix, Gertrude Archimède's nephew, who made the encounter between Angela Davis and Gerty Archimède into a play, *Pas de prison pour le vent* (No prison for the wind), 2006.

94. Literary critic Anne Donadey has argued that Daniel Maximin combined the story of Guadeloupe with the story of the Soledad Brothers in order to show a continuity of black experience across national boundaries, uniting all people of African descent displaced by the Atlantic slave trade. He is using the figure of Angela to represent what Paul Gilroy has called the Black Atlantic. See Anne Donadey, "Beyond Departmentalization: Feminist Black Atlantic Reformulations of Outremer in Daniel Maximin's *L'isolé soleil,*" *International Journal of Francophone Studies* 11, nos. 1–2 (June 2008): 49–65.

95. Philip Roth, *American Pastoral* (New York: Vintage, 1998), 160.

96. Yasmina Khadra, an Algerian writer who now directs the Algerian cultural center in Paris, has been announced as the screenwriter on the project.

97. Rachid Bouchareb interviewed in El Watan on October 2, 2009, about several films dealing with the intersection of American and Arab culture. The film project was announced by the Algerian minister of culture in a press release dated November 17, 2010.

Conclusion

1. The school was inaugurated in 2007.

2. Susan Sontag, Journals, 1950, Box 123, Folder 8, Susan Sontag papers, Charles E. Young Library, UCLA.

3. "Optimistique pour Proust, miss you my Love," Sontag telegrammed Stéphane from China during one of her French friend's many negotiations with potential screenwriters. Her word "optimistique" is made-up French—part of the lovers' double language play.

4. Harriet Sohmers Zwerling to the author, January 20, 2011.

5. Davis, *Angela Davis,* 132.

6. Two recent books on Jacqueline Kennedy Onassis's work as an editor give a good sense, if only through lists of the books she published, of the influence of France on her thinking. See chapter 2, note 34.

Acknowledgments

I am grateful to the following people for interviews, for access to documents, and for their correspondence.

For materials on Jacqueline Bouvier Kennedy's Paris, I thank Carl S. Anthony, Johanna Barasz, Jacqueline Duhême, Marjorie Flory, Paul de Ganay, Brenda Gilchrist, Claude du Granrut, Rosamée Henrion, Mary Ann Freedman Hoberman, Mary Ann Peyser Horenstein, Florence Malraux, Michael McBride, Christian Oppetit, Virginia Lyon Paige, Louann Plough, Cordelia Ruffin Richards, Marly Rusoff, Cara Stein, and Martha Rusk Sutphen.

For materials on Susan Sontag's Paris, I thank Noël Burch, John W. Boyer, Jan Goldstein, Daniel Horowitz, Nancy Kates, Sydney Leach, Annette Michelson, Panivong Norindr, David Rieff, Geneviève Sellier, and Harriet Sohmers Zwerling.

For materials on Angela Davis's Paris, I thank Walter Albert, Bettina Aptheker, David Auerbach, Vivian Goldberg Auslander, Christie Stagg Austin, Howard Bloch, Yves Bonnefoy, Jules Borker, Anne-Marie Bourgnon, Katharina von Bülow, Hazel Carby, Fania Davis, Albert Dichy, Paula Durbin, Erica

Mendelson Eisinger, Amy Jaffe, Jane Chaplin Jordan, Barbara Zurer Pearson, Micheline Lamotte, Camille Lamotte, Jean-Pierre Lamotte, Patsy Martin Lightbown, Yolande du Luart, Roland du Luart, Jane Tucker Mitchell, Dianne T. Moore, Cheryl Morgan, Simon Pleasance, Jean-Daniel Simon, John Simon, Alexis Spire, and Patrick Weil.

For access to various collections, I thank the following persons and institutions: Ann Befroy, Miss Porter's School Archives; Bibliothèque historique des postes et des télécommunications, Ivry-sur-Seine; Carrie Cadwell Brown, Alumni Association of Smith College; David Callahan, New York Public Library for the Performing Arts; Alice Château, the Archives of the Sorbonne; Albert Dichy, IMEC Institut mémoires de l'édition contemporaine, Genet Archives; Kathleen Dickson, British Film Institute; Julia Gardner, University of Chicago Special Collections; Françoise Gicquel, Archives of the Paris Préfecture de Police; Luisa Haddad, McHenry Special Collections, University of California, Santa Cruz, Bettina Aptheker papers; L'Inathèque, French radio and television archive at the Bibliothèque nationale de France; Maggie McNeely, Brandeis University Special Collections; Roberto Montoya and Genie Guerard, UCLA, Susan Sontag papers; Antoine Perraud, Jeux d'archives, France Culture radio; Stephen Plotkin, John F. Kennedy Presidential Museum and Library; Daniele Haase-Dubosc, director, Reid Hall, Reid Hall Archives; Professor Cheryl Morgan, Hamilton College in Paris; Pierre Nora, Editions Gallimard; Liza Sacks, Alumni Relations, Elisabeth Irwin School; Paul A. Ryan, Alumni Relations, Hamilton College; Larry Scott and Polly Armstrong, Stanford University Special Collections; Charles Trueheart, Director of the American Library in Paris; and Nanci Young, Smith College Archives and Special Collections.

For research assistance, I thank Gerry Canavan and Marissa Vincenti, Duke University; Elena Goldblatt and Laura Marris, Yale University; Kadzi Mutizwa, New York; and Nathalie Segeral, UCLA. I benefited enormously from Laura Marris's expert work with the final manuscript. At Yale, Agnes Bolton of the French Department provided excellent administrative guidance. For material support, I am grateful for assistance from the Frederick W. Hilles Publication Fund of Yale University. My thanks go as well to the Office of the Provost at Yale, and especially to Emily Bakemeier.

For reading and rereading my manuscript, my deep appreciation goes to Laurel Goldman, Anne Garréta, and Roger Grenier. And for reading and commenting on the manuscript at various phases, for providing critique, encouragement, and expertise, I am grateful to Evelyne Bloch-Dano, Rachel M. Brownstein, Bruno Cabanes, Cathy N. Davidson, Mary Feidt, the members of Laurel Goldman's Tuesday Writing Workshop, Nancy Green, Dolores Hayden, Eddie Lewis, Michèle Longino, Maurice Samuels, Helen Solterer, and Jacqueline Cerquiglini-Toulet. I thank Michèle Longino and Monique Middleton for their invaluable perspective on study abroad, Roberto Dainotto, Melissa Goldman, Stephen Serge, and Terry Vance for their inspiration, and Marly Rusoff and Michael Radulescu at the Rusoff Agency for their support. At the University of Chicago Press, my thanks go to Randy Petilos, Levi T. Stahl, Anita Samen, and Margaret Mahan, and especially to my editor Alan Thomas, whose clear eye keeps me on course.

Acknowledgments

Index

to Onassis and, 73; miscarriage and, 56; as multilingual, 17; nostalgia of, 163; ongoing relationship to France of, 224; orientation to France for, 13–17; papers of, 15, 239n19; parents' divorce and, 11, 238–39n11; Parisian spaces and, 223–24; as phony, 71, 73, 246n53; as photogenic, 32; political judgment of, 57–58; post–JFK assassination interviews and, 72, 232; professors of, 197; pubic suspicions about, 59–60; as Queen Deb, 1; reading habits of, 57–58; rejection of France by, 72–73; road trip with Claude de Renty and, 44–45, 80; schools attended by, 14, 48; secrecy of, 22; separate worlds of, 36; social life of, 27, 35–36, 38–40; social standing of, 24, 48; sources on, 230–32; state dinners and, 167; as student, 227; summer travels of, 43–46; Susan Sontag and, 132, 137–39; translations for JFK by, 110, 251n76; travels with sister and, 55–56; *Vogue* (magazine) and, 49–55, 61, 73–74, 83, 231, 243n9; voice and diction of, 67, 69, 71; White House menus of, 202; White House restoration and, 68–71, 154; writings of, 12–13, 32–33, 37–38, 51–54, 72, 239n14, 243n10; on young women abroad, 5
Bouvier, John Vernou, III ("Black Jack"), 11–12, 57
Bouvier, John Vernou, Jr., 9, 11, 34–35, 54
Bouvier, Michel, 8–9, 65, 69, 245n42
Bouvier, Pierre, 234
Bouvier-Kennedy curse, 10
Bowles, Paul, 99
Boyer, John W., 232
Bradford, Sarah, 231, 241n50
Brandeis University: Alain Robbe-Grillet at, 178; Angela Davis at, 143–44, 150–51, 155, 158–61, 177, 179, 226; humanities program at, 158; study abroad programs and, 260n58
Branton, Leo, Jr., 200, 205–8, 265n71
Brassaï (photographer), 102
Brasserie Balzar, 35, 224
Braun, Wernher von, 21
Breathless (Godard), 5, 98, 163, 250n51
Brecht, Bertolt, 109, 116
Bresson, Robert, 125

Brialy, Jean-Claude, *107*, 108
Britannicus (Racine), 105–7, 228, 251n71
Brodsky, Joseph, 136
Brook, Peter, 132
Brooks, Romaine, 102
Brother Carl (film), 255n47
Browning, Elizabeth Barrett, 206
Browning, Robert, 206
Buchwald, Art, 5
Burch, Noël, 107–8, 134
Burke, Kenneth, 85, 90–91, 248n23
Burnham, Louis, 257n9
Burroughs, William, 97, 99, 118, 157
Butor, Michel, 179

Café de Flore, 95, 102, 109, 140
Café de la Mairie, 86
Café des Beaux-Arts, 99
Café de Tournon, 99, 109, 157, 250n55
Cahiers du cinéma (journal), 117, 211
Caillois, Roger, 127
Callas, Maria, 138
Camargue, La, 15, 77–78
Cameroon, 220
Campbell, Mary, 50, 54–55
Camus, Albert: Angela Davis and, 151, 157, 187, 204; *The Mandarins* (Beauvoir) and, 27; Maria Casarès and, 211; *Myth of Sisyphus* and, 265n69; reaction to, 115; Sartre on, 252n11; Smith College studies and, 40
Cannes film festival, 129–30, 255n47
Capote, Truman, 73, 246n53
Capretz, Pierre, 101
Carr, Edward Hallett, 264n58
Carrière, Jean-Claude, 132
Carve Her Name in Stone (film), 131
Casarès, Maria, 211
Casavini, Pieralessandro, 98–99
Cassini, Igor. *See* Knickerbocker, Cholly (Igor Cassini)
Cassini, Oleg, 60–64, 243n20
Céline, Louis Ferdinand, 158
Central Intelligence Agency (CIA). *See* CIA (Central Intelligence Agency)
Century Club, 77, 247n61
Césaire, Aimé, 153
Chaban-Delmas, Jacques, 21
Champs-Elysées, 218

Index

Index

58; on Jacqueline Kennedy's taste, 70–71; in Paris, 5, 58; themes in writing of, 122

Maintenon, Madame de, 58, 75

Maison de la Radio, 249n37

Malamud, Bernard, 119, 122

Malle, Louis, 111–12, 113

Malraux, André: Charles de Gaulle and, 230–31; cleaning of Paris and, 153; family of, 127; Jacqueline Bouvier and, 18; Jacqueline Kennedy and, 36, 65–68, 167, 224, 227, 244n30, 244n33; love life of, 76; theories of, 52

Malraux, Florence, 127, 134

Mandarins, The (Beauvoir), 27, 104

Manet, Édouard, 66, 244n33

Manhood (Leiris), 127

Man's Fate (Malraux), 52

Mao Zedong, 188, 192

Maran, René, 153

Marchais, Georges, 210

Marc'O, 186

Marcuse, Herbert, 129, 144, 151, 158, 177, 183, 259n45

Marianne (of French Republic), 219

Marquand, John, Jr., 32, 36, 255n44

Marshall Plan, 3, 34, 46

Martin, Patsy. *See* Lightbown, Patsy Martin

Martinique: Angela Davis and, 150, 213, 214, 218; French intellectual life and, 234; immigrants to France from, 152–53, 155, 219; in literature, 261n9; race and, 148, 154; sources on, 234

Marx, Karl, 209

Marxism, race and, 184

Mason, Florence, 152

Masson, André, 253–54n30

Massu, Jacques, 110

Mathews, Harry, 121

Mathias, Paul, 260n63

Matossian, Jean-Pierre, *31*

Matossian, Sonia, *31*

Mauger, Gaston, 101

Maupassant, Guy de, 40

Mauriac, François, 32, 40

Maximin, Daniel, 219–20, 221, 266n94

Maxwell, Elsa, 138

McCain prison (North Carolina), 217

McCarthy, Mary, 6, 253–54n30

McCarthyism, 121, 144, 151, 186, 207

McClain, James, 192

McCullers, Carson, 109, 116

McNair, Denise, 163

Mehlman, Jeffrey, 171

Melville, Jean-Pierre, 130, 131

Memmi, Albert, 183

Memoirs of a Dutiful Daughter (Beauvoir), 104

Mendelsohn, Daniel, 140

Mension-Rigau, Eric, 241n52

Merleau-Ponty, Maurice, 179, 180–81

Merlin (journal), 249n44, 250n55

Mermoz, Jean, 169

Merry Month of May, The (Jones), 253n22

metro, 20, 27, 93, 96, 126, 132

Meyer-Stabley, Bertrand, 241n50

Michaels, Leonard, 205

Michel, Louise, 219

Michelet, Edmond, 23

Michelson, Annette, 107, 116, 233

Miles, Barry, 100

Miles College, 146

Miller, Arthur, 5

Miller, Henry, 70, 98

Miller, Nancy, 253n18

Miro, Joan, 154

Miss Porter's School, 12–13, 225, 230, 239n14

Miterrand, François, 21

modernism, 121

Møhrt, Michel, 122

Molière, 29

Monaco, 99, 157

Mona Lisa (painting), 67, 224, 245n36

Monde, Le (newspaper), 47, 191

Monnerville, Gaston, 66, 153, 215–16, *217*

Monocle Bar, 102

Monroe, James, 69

Montagne, La, 102

Montgomery, Ed, 262n21

Montparnasse, 17, 32, 102, 140, 249n37

Moore, Albert Burton, 257n3

Moore, Howard, 200, 206

Moravia, Alberto, 108

Moreau, Jeanne, 112

Morgan, Cheryl, 234

Morning Breaks, The (Aptheker), 233

Morrissette, Bruce, 178

mots et les choses, Les (Foucault), 127, 254n37

2–3; clothing of, 114; as collector, 128; as critic, 98, 226–27; cultural understanding of, 227; death of, 140; departure from France by, 111–12; dissertation of, 117; divorce of, 113, 252n1; dreams of Europe and, 82–83, 88; dreams of France and, 3–4; eagerness to please and, 125–26, 137–39; early life of, 83–86; education of, 84, 86, 88, 90–92, 99–100, 103–7, 249n32; family life of, 82; on fascism, 261n15; as figurehead of intelligentsia, 138, 256n65; film and, 105, 107–8, 116–17, 129–31, 134, 182, 250n51, 251n72, 255n47, 255n49, 261n15; flight from Paris and, 111, 143; French avant-garde culture and, 116–17; French interviews of, 4–5; French language and, 100–103, 134–36, 249n46, 266–67n3; French legacy of, 228; French studies of, 97; French theater and, 105–6, 109, 228; French Theory and, 136; friends of, 250n50; gathering places of, 157; home country of, 140–41; hygiene of, 81–82; image of, 3, 81–82, 122, 140; interviews with, 235; Jacqueline Kennedy Onassis and, 137–39; life trajectory of, 136–37; lists of writers and, 119; literary tastes and, 136; love life of, 92–93, 104–5, 110, 129–34, 255n47, 266–67n3; Marcel Proust and, 132, 226; marriage of, 87–88, 91–93, 100, 111–12, 248n14, 248n19; Mary McCarthy and, 253–54n30; on material and social world of Paris, 97; modernism and, 121; nightlife and, 102; ongoing relationship to France of, 224; Parisian spaces and, 223–24; Parisian summers and, 126–27; photography and, 137; political work of, 129, 255n44; as public intellectual, 114–15; on racism, 129, 255n46; radicalism of, 225; reading habits of, 83–84, 253n18; Richard Howard collaboration and, 127–28, 181, 254n38; self-evaluation of, 137, 256nn61–62; self-reinvention as European and, 146; sexuality of, 84, 87–88, 91, 100, 102, 113–14, 125; at Sorbonne, 93, 103–4; sources on, 232–33; as student, 227; success of, 125; teachers of, 206; on terrorism, 137, 256n60; translation and, 134–36, 137, 256nn55–56; women intellectuals and, 85; women's movement and, 128–29; writing method of, 84; writings of, 82–85, 89–91, 105, 115, 117–22, 125–26, 128, 248n23, 250n51, 253n17, 255n51; X Factor and, 125–26, 137–39

Sorbonne: Algerian independence movement and, 109; André Malraux's ideas and, 52; Angela Davis at, 166–67, 178, 226, 227; Harriet Sohmers and, 103; lectures at, 41–42; neighborhood of, 95; reforms of 1968 and, 227–28; study abroad programs and, 161, 166; Susan Sontag at, 93, 103–4; "thirty glorious years" and, 2–3

Sorrow and the Pity, The (Ophüls), 168

Soul Power (Young), 233

Souls of Peoples, The (Siegfried), 24

Southern Negro Youth Congress, 146, 151–52, 234, 257n9

Spain, 17, 56, 161–62, 167

Speak, Memory (Nabokov), 101

Spoto, Donald, 241n50

Stagg, Christie, 159–62, 166–68, *169*, 170–71, 173, 194, 234

Starsky and Hutch (television show), 217

Stein, Gertrude, 2, 5, 144

Steinem, Gloria, 73

Stekel, William, 87

Stender, Fay, 189–91, 201, 262n32

Stendhal, 13, 141

Stéphane, Nicole, 129–32, 134, 226, 255n47, 255n49, 255n52, 266–67n3

Stewart, Alexandra, 108

Stewart, Potter, 252n79

Stone Face, The (Smith), 156–57, 165

Stourdzé, Colette, 166–67

Stovall, Tyler, 234

Straus, Roger, 119, 137–38

structuralism, 114–15, 235

Studies in Revolution (Carr), 264n58

study abroad programs, 170–72, 174, 194, 228–30, 237n2

Styles of Radical Will (Sontag), 250n51

Styron, William, 5, 253n22

Sumner, Diana, *162*

Sur Racine (Barthes), 106

Svevo, Italo, 109

Swados, Harvey, 253n18

Index